LITTLE
ENCYCLOPEDIA

OF

Natural Healing

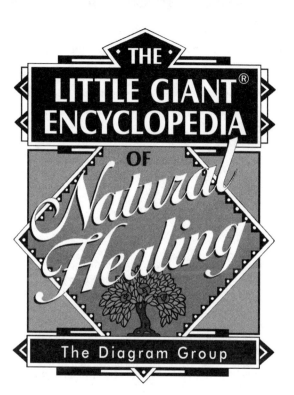

THE
LITTLE GIANT® ENCYCLOPEDIA
OF
Natural Healing

The Diagram Group

Sterling Publishing Co., Inc.
New York

Compiled by Jane Johnson and Maya Pilkington

Library of Congress Cataloging-in-Publication Data

The little giant encyclopedia of natural healing / the
Diagram group.
  p. cm.
  ISBN 0-8069-3948-6
  1. Naturopathy Encyclopedias.   2. Alternative medicine Encyclopedias. I. Diagram Group. II. Title: Natural
healing.
RZ433.L58 1999
615.5'03—dc21
                                                    99–21691
                                                    CIP

10 9 8 7 6 5 4 3 2 1

Published by Sterling Publishing Company, Inc.
387 Park Avenue South, New York, N.Y. 10016
A Diagram Book first created by Diagram Visual Information
Limited of 195 Kentish Town Road, London NW5 2JU, England
© 1999 by Diagram Visual Information Limited
Distributed in Canada by Sterling Publishing
c_b Canadian Manda Group, One Atlantic Avenue, Suite 105
Toronto, Ontario, Canada M6K 3E7
Distributed in Great Britain and Europe by Cassell PLC
Wellington House, 125 Strand, London WC2R 0BB, England
Distributed in Australia by Capricorn Link (Australia) Pty Ltd.
P.O. Box 6651, Baulkham Hills, Business Centre, NSW 2153,
Australia
Manufactured in the United States of America
All rights reserved

Sterling ISBN 0-8069-3948-6

FOREWORD

Have you ever heard about shiatsu or biofeedback or
chakra healing and wondered what they are or what
they involve? Arranged alphabetically, *The Little Giant
Encyclopedia of Natural Healing* provides descriptions
of 92 types of healing, their history, the equipment used
and possible treatment methods. Many have not yet
been fully researched and there is disagreement as to
how certain therapies "work." Despite this, an attempt
has been made to explain the underlying principles
behind each method of healing, and the kinds of
conditions it might be useful to treat.
The Little Giant Encyclopedia of Natural Healing
provides descriptions of alternative medical systems
(such as Ayurvedic medicine, Chinese medicine, and
shamanic healing), touch therapies (such as
aromatherapy, chiropractic, and hydrotherapy), exercise
therapies (such as the Alexander Technique, Do-in and
yoga), nutritional therapies (such as biochemics and
megavitamin therapy), mind-centred therapies (such as
autogenic training and autosuggestion), analytical
therapies (such as aura analysis, iridology and medical
astrology), psycotherapies (such as dream therapy,
psychodrama, and rebirthing), psychic-type therapies
(such as absent healing, and radionics), and non-touch
therapies (such as color therapy and feng shui).
Provided here are descriptions of the well-known
therapies (such as massage, hypnotherapy and
meditation) as well as therapies you may not be familiar
with (such as leeching, cymatics and radiesthesia).

6

CONTENTS

10	Glossary
48	Absent healing
50	Acupuncture
66	Alexander Technique
74	Anthroposophical medicine
78	Aromatherapy
94	Art therapy
96	Aura analysis
106	Auricular therapy
110	Autogenic training
116	Autosuggestion
118	Ayurvedic medicine
130	Bach™ Flower Essences
142	Bates method
146	Behavior therapy
148	Biochemics
154	Bioenergetics therapy
158	Biofeedback
164	Biorhythm diagnosis
168	Breathing therapy
170	Chakra therapy
174	Chinese medicine
188	Chiropractic

192 Christian healing beliefs
198 Clinical ecology
202 Colonic irrigation
204 Color therapy
212 Crystal and gem therapy
220 Cupping
222 Cymatics
226 Dance movement therapy
230 Dietary therapies
234 Do-in
242 Dream therapy
244 Electrotherapy
246 Encircling
250 Encounter therapy
252 Faith healing
260 Feldenkrais method
262 Feng shui
264 Fertility amulets and rituals
268 Flotation therapy
270 Healing amulets
276 Healing shrines
282 Herbal medicine
294 Homeopathy

306 Hydrotherapy
314 Hypnotherapy
320 Ion therapy
322 Iridology
330 Kinesiology
332 Laying on of hands
334 Leeching
338 Macrobiotics
340 Magnetism and mesmerism
348 Manipulative therapies
352 Massage therapy
356 Mazdaznan
358 Medical astrology
362 Meditation
366 Megavitamin therapy
368 Metamorphic technique
370 Moxibustion
372 Music therapy
376 Native American healing
382 Naturopathy
384 Orgone therapy
386 Osteopathy
392 Past lives therapy
394 Pattern therapy
396 Polarity therapy

CONTENTS

400	Primal therapy
402	Psionic medicine
406	Psychic healing
408	Psychodrama
410	Psychosynthesis
412	Psychotherapies
418	Pyramid healing
420	Radiesthesia
424	Radionics
432	Rebirthing
434	Reflexology
442	Reichian therapy
446	Relaxation therapy
450	Rolfing
452	Shamanic healing
456	Shiatsu
470	T'ai-chi ch'uan
474	Therapeutic touch
476	Transactional analysis
478	Visualization therapy
480	Yoga
502	Zone therapy
504	Glossary of medical-related terms
506	Index

GLOSSARY

Absent healing
Also known as distant healing, this is healing at a distance. Sometimes this forms part of *faith healing* (also called spiritual healing).

Acupoints (also called *acupuncture points*, *pressure points* or *tsubos*). Key points on the *meridians* where nerves feel uncomfortable when the flow of energy through the body is blocked.

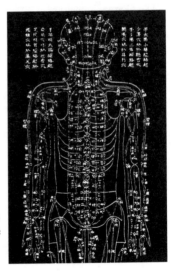

Acupressure (also known as *shiatsu*). A therapy in which pressure is applied to specific points on the body along *acupuncture* meridians, using techniques that include a gentle form of *rolfing*.

Acupuncture
A traditional Chinese method of healing which involves the insertion of fine needles to specific points in the skin.

Acupuncture points (also called *acupoints*, *pressure points*, and *tsubos*).
Key points on the *meridians* where nerves feel uncomfortable when the flow of energy through the body is blocked.

Agni
In *Ayurvedic medicine* this is the digestive fire which converts the five *Bhutas* into *doshas*.

Alexander Technique
A method of retraining the body's movements in order to improve posture, named after its originator, Frederick Matthias Alexander.

Allopathic medicine
Orthodox medicine.

Anthroposophical medicine
A holistic approach to health and illness based on the teachings of Rudolf Steiner, who believed the word *anthroposophy* should be understood to mean awareness of one's humanity.

Anthroposophy
From the Greek "anthropos," meaning man, and "sophia," meaning wisdom, Rudolf Steiner said anthroposophy should mean "awareness" of one's humanity.

Amna
An ancient Japanese system of *massage* that has existed for about 2000 years, in which the hands and feet are rubbed and manipulated.

Applied kinesiology
A type of *kinesiology* which uses muscle testing in relation to all body functions.

Aromatherapy
Using *essential plant oils* to improve physical and mental well-being, often involving *massage*.

Art therapies
A group of therapies including *art therapy, dance movement therapy, drama therapy, music therapy,* and *sound therapy*.

Art therapy
Using the spontaneous creation of art as a means of self-expression in order to improve emotional well-being. Individuals are encouraged by a therapist to express their feelings through collage-making, drawing, modeling, painting, or sculpting.

Asanas
Poses that form part of *yoga*.

Astral body
In *anthroposophical medicine* this is one of four aspects
of man (the other three being the physical body, the
etheric body, and the *ego*) and represents the emotions.

Astrological diagnosis
Also known as *medical astrology*, this is the use of
astrology to aid the diagnosis and treatment of illness.

Aura
An energy field surrounding
the human body which *aura
analysts* describe as a cloud
of light that radiates from a
person, rather like the
phosphorescence of some
sea creatures.

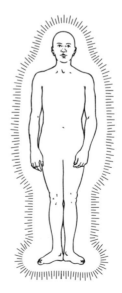

Aura analysis
Analysis of a person's *aura*,
by direct observation or
using a *Kilner screen* or a
Kirlian photograph.

Auricular therapy
Also known as *auriculotherapy*, this is treatment of the
ear to bring about healing in other parts of the body.

Auriculotherapy
Also known as *auricular therapy*, this is treatment of
the ear to bring about healing in other parts of the body.

Autogenic
From the Greek word meaning "coming from within,"
and relating to therapies such as *autogenic training*.

Autogenic training
Developed by a Berlin psychiatrist and neurologist, Dr.
Johannes H. Schultz, this is a method of profound
relaxation training aimed at relieving stress, enabling
the body to heal itself.

Autosuggestion
Also known as *Couéism*, this is a form of self-hypnosis
developed by Emile Coué in 1885 which relies on the
repetition of a positive mantra.

Aversion therapy
A form of *behavior therapy* often used to help treat
people with alcohol or cigarette addictions and which
involves teaching patients to associate an undesirable
habit or behavior (e.g., drinking alcohol) with an
unpleasant experience.

Awareness through movement
Part of the *Feldenkrais method*, this is a series of
exercises taught to groups of pupils and involving slow,
simple movements designed to make people aware of
their habitual patterns of movement.

Ayurveda
From the Sanskrit words "ayur,"
meaning life, and "veda,"
meaning knowledge and
referring to *Ayurvedic medicine*.

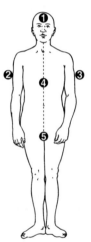

Ayurvedic medicine
A holistic system of traditional
Indian medicine from which
most Western medicine is
derived.

Bach™ Flower Essences/Remedies
Named after their originator, Englishman Dr. Edward
Bach, these are 38 preparations made from wild flowers
and plants, used in a treatment based on *homeopathic*
principles, designed for use at home to treat mental
attitudes.

Balneology
A *hydrotherapy* treatment, this is the therapeutic use of
natural spring waters or mineral waters.

Bates method
A series of exercises designed to
improve eyesight
and developed by
William H. Bates
between 1900 and
1931.

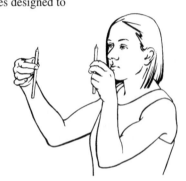

Behavior therapy
Conditioning patients in order to rid them of neurotic
symptoms using a variety of techniques, including
aversion therapy.

Bhutas
In *Ayurvedic medicine* these are the five elements from
which all things are made—air, fire, earth, ether, and
water—and corresponding to a body sense (touch,
sight, smell, sound, taste) and planet (Mercury, Mars,
Jupiter, Saturn, Venus).

Biochemics
Developed in the 1870s by Dr. Wilhelm Heinrich
Schuessler, this is a system of therapy which aims to
restore and maintain the body's natural mineral salts.

Bioenergetics therapy
Helping people to change habitual postures and body
movements in order to unblock the body's energy
(called bioenergy) and improve physical and emotional
health.

Bioenergy
Term used to describe energy within the body as
viewed by *bioenergetic therapists*.

Biofeedback
Also called *neurological feedback*, this is a therapy in
which clients learn to control "involuntary" body
functions (such as heart rate and blood pressure) using
information made available through the use of special
monitoring equipment.

Biorhythm diagnosis
Using three human energy cycles—emotional, physical
and mental, collectively known as biorhythms—to
predict the times of high and low energy.

Breathing therapy
A method used in *relaxation therapy*.

Chakras
Seven centers of intense
energy located down
the spine known as
sahasrara, ajna,
vishudda, anahata,
manipuraka,
swadhisthana, and
muladhara.
According to Hindu
philosophy they are
invigorated through
yoga.

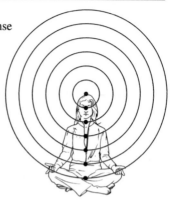

Chakra therapy
The use of gemstones to bring about positive changes
in energy flow within and between *chakras*. A form of
color therapy in which colors are related to *chakras* on
the spine.

Charaka Samhita
An ancient Indian encyclopedia of medicine.

Chi (also known as *ki* and *Qi*).
In Chinese medicine this is the life energy force which
flows around the body via *meridians*, or *energy lines*,
and is the equivalent of the Indian *ojas*.

Chiropractic
From the Greek "cheiro" and "praktikos," meaning
"done by hand," this is a *manipulative therapy* based on

the diagnosis and treatment of mechanical joint
disorders and their effects on the nervous system.

Clinical ecology
The treatment of disorders believed to result from a
person's reaction to his or her environment.

Colonic hydrotherapy
Also called *colonic irrigation*, this is a method of
cleansing the intestines using warm water injected into
the rectum.

Colonic irrigation
Also called *colonic hydrotherapy*, this is a method of
cleansing the intestines using warm water injected into
the rectum.

Color therapy
Using color to bring about healing and sometimes
involving *chakra therapy*.

Combination remedies
Used in *biochemics,* these are remedies which combine
between three and five of the twelve different tissue
salts identified by Dr. Wilhelm Heinrich Schuessler in
the 1870s.

Conception Vessel
One of 14 *meridians* used in Chinese medicine.

Couéism
Also known as *autosuggestion*, this is a form of self-hypnosis developed by Emile Coué in 1885 which relies on the repetition of a positive mantra.

Cranial osteopathy
A technique used by *osteopaths* to gently manipulate the eight bones of the skull.

Cranio-sacral therapy
Manipulation of body tissues in order to bring about a balance in the body's cerebrospinal fluid.

Crystal therapy
The use of naturally occurring crystals for healing purposes.

Cupping
A method of heat stimulation in which small, warm cups, bowls or drums are placed on the skin in order to increase local blood supply.

Cymatics
The use of sound waves to heal.

Dance movement therapy
The psychotherapeutic use of movement to bring about positive changes in a person's emotional, cognitive, and social integration.

Dietary therapies
Therapies which aim to improve health and well-being
by altering the combination of foods regularly eaten by
a person.

Digestive/movement system
In *anthroposophical medicine* this is one of three
systems (the other two being the *nerve/sense system*
and the *rhythmic system*) which together link the
physical, *etheric body*, *astral body*, and *ego*.

Distant healing
Also known as *absent healing*, this is healing at a
distance. Sometimes this forms part of *faith healing*
(also called *spiritual healing*).

Do-in
A form of Chinese self-massage.

Dosha
In *Ayurvedic medicine* the name given to one of three
constitutional types (*vata*, *pitta*, and *kappa*), each
converted from two *Bhutas* (elements) by *agni* and
collectively known as *Tridoshas*.

Dowsing
Traditionally this meant the search for underground
water using a divining rod, but commonly describes the
search for anything hidden, using a divining rod or
pendulum. *Radiesthesia* is a form of medical dowsing.

Dream therapy
Using dreams to help analyze and overcome emotional problems.

ECT
Stands for electroconvulsive therapy, a form of *electrotherapy*.

Effleurage
A gentle technique used in *massage* that involves stroking with the palms of the hands.

Ego
In *anthroposophical medicine* this is one of four aspects of man (the other three being the *astral body*, the physical body, and the *etheric body*) and represents an individual's spiritual core.

Electrotherapy
The use of electricty to treat medical disorders. It may involve *electroconvulsive therapy (ECT)* or the use of a *TENS machine*.

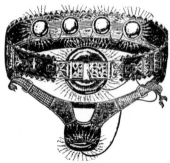

Encircling
The use of circles for healing purposes.

Encounter therapy
A form of group therapy, the aims of which are to help
individuals improve their relationships with others.

Energy lines (also called *meridians*).
Fourteen channels through which the body's energy
flows.

Essential plant oils (also called *essential oils*)
The oils that give plants their distinctive smell, these
are used in *aromatherapy*.

Etheric body
In *anthroposophical medicine* this is one of four aspects
of man (the other three being the *astral body*, the *ego*,
and the physical body) and represents that part of an
individual that opposes the force of gravity, allowing
growth upward, away from the earth.

Eurythmy
Developed by Rudolf Steiner, this is a system of
promoting self-expression through music and may be
used by practitioners of *anthroposophical medicine*.

Faith healing (also called *spiritual healing*).
When the power of a god or spirit serves as a healing
force.

Feldenkrais method
Developed by Moshe Feldenkrais this is a series of
exercises designed to realign the skeleton and make the

body move with minimum effort and maximum
efficiency, improving posture and general health.

Feng shui
The positioning of buildings, rooms, and objects to
achieve harmony with nature.

Fertility amulet
An object made of wood, stone, metal, or other
substance and believed to improve fertility. Often
amulets are inscribed with magical characters and
figures and are expected to invoke the help of great
spirits associated with a culture or religion.

Flotation therapy
Floating in a tank of warm water in order to induce a
state of deep relaxation.

Flower essences
Used in *Bach™ Flower Remedies* (also known as
Bach™ Flower Essences), these are those parts of
plants and flowers thought to contain healing properties.

Frictions
A technique used in *massage* in which pressure is
applied to a small area, often using small circular
movements.

Gate control theory
A theory which states that pain may be relieved by the
application of pressure to certain parts of the body
because the brain receives messages concerning

pressure faster that it receives messages concerning pain. In other words, once a pressure message has reached the brain, the "gateway" for further (i.e., pain) messages is closed.

Gem essence therapy
The use of essences made by immersing gemstones in water and leaving them in the Californian sunshine so that their vibrational qualities percolate the water.

G-Jo
A form of *acupressure* practiced in the West.

Governor Vessel
One of 14 *meridians* used in Chinese medicine.

Hacking
A stimulating technique used in *massage* in which the sides of the hands are used in a chopping motion to invigorate and increase blood flow to an area.

Healing amulet
An object made of wood, stone, metal, or other substance and believed to protect the owner from illness or injury or to dispel illness. Often amulets are inscribed with magical characters and figures and are expected to invoke the help of great spirits associated with a culture or religion.

Healing shrine
A place believed to have healing properties—such as Lourdes.

Herbalism

The use of certain plants for
medicinal purposes, now called
phytotherapy. A herb is usually
defined as a plant whose stem does
not become woody and persistent,
but dies down to ground
level after flowering.

Holistic

In health care, a term used to describe treatments of the
whole person: mind, body, and spirit.

Homeopathy

A system based on the principle of "like curing like,"
which aims to treat the whole person and is the opposite
of *allopathic* medicine in that it does not aim to
suppress the symptoms of illness.

Hydrotherapy

The use of water to heal and involving a variety of
techniques, including *balneology*, *thalassotherapy* and
thermalism.

Hypnosis

Commonly used in *hypnotherapy*, this is an altered
state of consciousness that can be induced by the self or
by another person and during which conscious control
is relaxed, making the contents of the unconscious
more accessible. Hypnosis is from the Greek word
"hypnos," meaning "sleep."

Hypnotherapy
Using *hypnosis* to improve health.

Intradermal needles
Very small, delicate *acupuncture* needles, used for
insertion into points on the head and ears.

Ion therapy
Using ions (charged air particles) to prevent and cure
illness and disease.

Iridology
Examining the eye's iris in order to diagnose conditions
of the body.

Jitsu
Used in treatments such as *shiatsu*, this word describes
an over-activity in the flow of life energy as identified
at *tsubos*.

Kappa
In *Ayurvedic medicine*, this is one of three *doshas* (the
other two being *pitta* and *vata*) and resulting from the
combination of the *Bhutas* earth and water by *agni*.

Ki (also known as *chi* or *Qi*).
In Japanese medicine therapies such as *shiatsu* this is
the life energy force which flows around the body via
meridians, or *energy lines* and is the equivalent of the
Indian *ojas*.

Kinesiology
From the Greek word "kinesis," meaning "movement,"
this was originally a method used by physiotherapists
for testing a person's range of movement and the tone
of his or her muscles but which is today referred to as
applied kinesiology, which uses muscle testing in
relation to all body functions.

Kilner screen
A special type of glass developed by the British
scientist Walter J. Kilner in 1920 and used to observe
the *aura* in *aura analysis*.

Kirlian photography
A method of recording the *aura* of people and plants
onto photographic paper without the use of a camera
and used for *aura analysis*. The technique was
developed in the 1930s by Russian engineers Valentina
and Semyon Kirlian.

Kyo
Used in treatments such as *shiatsu*, this word describes
a depletion in the flow of life energy as identified at
tsubos.

Laying on of hands
A technique used in *spiritual healing* in which the
healing power of a god or spirit is channelled through
the hands of the healer to the patient.

Leeching
Use of blood-sucking animals called leeches for
medical purposes.

Life force energy
Alternative name for the *etheric body*

Originators	Name of life force
Ancient Chinese	Vital energy
Ancient Chinese	Ch'i energy
Ancient Hindu	Prana
Cabalists	Serpent wisdom
Polynesian Huna	Mana
Paracelsus	Munis or Mimia
van Helmot	Magnale magnum
The alchemists	Ether
Mesmer	Animal magnetism
Reichenbach	Odic force
Keely	Motor force
Blonlot	N-Rays
Radiesthetists	Etheric force
L.E. Eeman	'X' force
Soviet scientists	Bioplasmic energy
Czech scientists	Psychotronic energy
Wilhelm Reich	Orgone energy
Wilhelm Reich	Vegetative streamings
Contemporary medicine	Psychosomatic phenomena

Macrobiotics
A term used by Japanese philosopher George Ohsawa
to describe a dietary system first devised by a Japanese
doctor, Sagen Ishizuka.

Magnetic Field Therapy
The modern use of
magnets for healing
purposes.

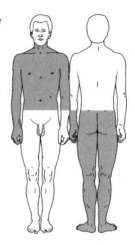

Manipulative therapies
A group of therapies in which practitioners use their
hands to bring about positive changes in a person's
physique and which include the *Alexander Technique*,
bone setting, *chiropractic*, the *Feldenkrais method*,
kinesiology, the *laying on of hands*, *massage*,
osteopathy, *polarity therapy*, *reflexology*, *rolfing*,
therapeutic touch, and traction.

Mantra

A letter, word, sound, or phrase which may be used in *meditation* and repeated continually as you breathe in or out. The best known mantra is "Om."

Marma massage

A form of *massage* in which the therapist attempts to press marmas (107 points which in *Ayurvedic medicine* correspond to organs in the body).

Massage

From the Greek word "massein," meaning "to knead," this is a *manipulative therapy* designed to relax, stimulate, and invigorate the body by kneading, stroking, and pressing the soft tissues of the body.

Mazdaznan

A practice of healing based on the philosophy of two great prophets and of the Ahura Mazda, the Creative Intelligence of ancient Middle Eastern thought.

Medical astrology

Also known as *astrological diagnosis*, this is the use of astrology to aid the diagnosis and treatment of illness.

Meditation

Training one's attention or awareness to bring mental processes under voluntary control, of which there are various types including *transcendental meditation*.

Megavitamin therapy
Also once termed *orthomolecular medicine*, this is the
use of large doses of vitamins to improve physical and
mental health.

Meridians (also called
energy lines).
Fourteen channels
through which the
body's energy flows.

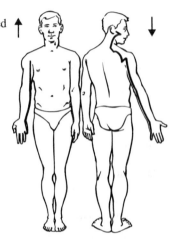

Mesmerism
Name given to a type of therapy developed by Franz
Mesmer who believed he had the ability to harness the
magnetic forces of the planets and whom some believe
to be the originator of hypnotism.

Metamorphic technique
Also called *prenatal therapy*, this is the manipulation of
the feet, hands, and head to help people come to terms
with long-term problems, perhaps stemming from the
nine months spent in the womb.

Miasmas
Emanations from leftover vestiges of previously acute
conditions, such as childhood measles, or by toxins
from current conditions, such as influenza or a period
of worry or grief.

Miraculous healing
A type of *faith healing* in which cures appear to be
miraculous. Examples of the healing power of Jesus are
often described as miracles.

Mother tincture
Used in *Bach™ Flower Remedies* (also known as
Bach™ Flower Essences) this is a preparation of spring
water in which *flower essences* have been impregnated,
together with a few drops of brandy.

Moxa
The dried leaves of Chinese wormwood used in
moxibustion.

Moxibustion
A method of heat stimulation in which burning *moxa* is
placed on or near the skin, or to the top of *acupuncture*
needles.

Music therapy
A means of promoting self-expression through
improvised music-making with the aim of facilitating
positive changes in behavior and emotional well-being.

Native American healing
The healing concepts and
rituals of North American
Indian tribes.

Naturopathy
A system which aims to treat the underlying cause of
illness by encouraging the body to cure itself.

Nerve/sense system
In *anthroposophical medicine*, this is one of three
systems (the other two being the *digestive/movement
system* and the *rhythmic system*) which together link the
physical, *etheric body*, *astral body,* and *ego*.

Neurofeedback
Also called *biofeedback*, this is a therapy in which
clients learn to control "involuntary" body functions
(such as heart rate and blood pressure) using
information made available through the use of special
monitoring equipment.

Ojas
In *Ayurvedic medicine* this is the life energy force
which flows around the body and is the equivalent of
the Chinese *Qi* (or *chi*) and Japanese *ki*.

Orgone therapy
Part of *Reichian therapy*
designed to restore the
body's energy.

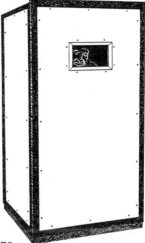

Orthomolecular medicine
Now called *megavitamin therapy*, this is the use of
large doses of vitamins to improve physical and mental
health.

Orthomolecular psychiatry
The use of large doses of vitamins to improve mental
health.

Oriental massage
Non-Western *massage* such as *reiki*, *tuina*, and thai
massage.

Osteopathy
From the Greek words "osteo," meaning "bone," and
"pathos," meaning "disease," this is a therapy aimed at
restoring proper movement and functioning of the body
by manipulating the musculoskeletal system.

Panchakarma
In *Ayurvedic medicine* this is a type of cleansing
involving enemas, induced vomiting, nasal inhalation,
and purging.

Past lives therapy
A therapy based on the belief in reincarnation and that
by addressing troublesome events in former lives
clients may be helped to resolve problems in the
present.

Pattern therapy
Using certain shapes, proportions, and positions to
positively influence well-being, as in *pyramid healing*.

Pétrissage
A technique used in *massage* in which fleshy areas of
the body are kneaded in order to stretch and relax tight
muscles.

Phytotherapy
From the Greek "phyton" meaning "plant" and
"therapeuein" meaning "to take care of, to heal," this is
the term used to describe medical *herbalism*.

Pitta
In *Ayurvedic medicine* this is one of three *doshas* (the other two being *kappa* and *vata*) and resulting from the combination of the *Bhutas* fire and water by *agni*.

Polarity therapy
Use of diet, self-help techniques, and manipulation to re-balance the body's vital energy flow.

Pranayama
Breathing exercises that form part of *yoga*.

Prenatal therapy
Also called *metamorphic technique*, this is the manipulation of the feet, hands, and head to help people come to terms with long-term problems, perhaps stemming from the nine months spent in the womb.

Press needles
Acupuncture needles designed to stay in the skin for several days. They can be pressed or manipulated by the patient as required.

Pressure points (also called *acupoints, acupuncture points*, or *tsubos*).
Key points on the *meridians* where nerves feel uncomfortable when the flow of energy through the body is blocked.

Primal therapy
A means of helping people to come to terms with negative experiences of childhood.

Prismatic needles
Acupuncture needles about $2\frac{1}{2}$ inches long , used in the treatment of acute diseases.

Psionic medicine
A system of medicine that combines orthodox medicine with *radiesthesia* in order to tackle the original causes of disease, avoiding the use of synthetic chemicals.

Psychic healing
The use of psychic powers for healing purposes such as
in *radiesthesia*, *radionics*, and *psychic surgery*.

Psychic surgery
A form of *psychic healing* particularly popular in Brazil
and the Philippines in which healers claim to be able to
perform surgical operations using no anesthetic or
instruments and causing no pain.

Psychodrama
A therapy which aims to help individuals release their
emotions by acting out real-life situations.

Psychosynthesis
A form of self-development in which people are
helped to discover the true aspects of their identities
and to take control over all aspects of their
personalities.

Psychotherapies
Therapies which use psychological rather than surgical
or ordinary medical means to treat people suffering
from emotional or mental problems and which include
behavior therapy, *co-counselling*, *encounter groups*,
family therapy, *gestalt therapy*, *primal therapy*,
rebirthing, and *transactional analysis*.

Pyramid healing
A type of *pattern therapy* in which pyramidal structures
are used for healing purposes.

Qi (also known as *chi* or *ki*)
In *Chinese medicine* this is the life energy force which
flows around the body via *meridians*, or *energy lines,*
and is the equivalent of the Indian *ojas.*

Radiesthesia
From the French word meaning "dowsing," radiesthesia
is a form of medical *dowsing* and is used as a
diagnostic technique in *psionic medicine* and *radionics.*

Radionics
Treatment used to bring about positive changes in a
person's energy field and often involving *radiesthesia.*

Rebirthing
A therapy in which clients are asked to reenact their
own births.

Reflexology
Developed from *zone therapy*, this
is a method of bringing about
relaxation, balance, and
healing through the
stimulation of
specific points on
the feet, or the
hands.

Reflex point
Nerve endings commonly stimulated during *reflexology*
treatments.

Reichian therapy
Movements designed to systematically release physical
tension and repressed emotions, developed by
psychiatrist Wilhelm Reich and incorporating *orgone
therapy*.

Reiki
As a type of *oriental massage* this is a form of *touch
therapy* in which therapists sense which parts of a
person's body are emitting weak energy by laying their
hands close to or on the sites.

Relaxation therapy
Term used to describe a variety of techniques used to
induce relaxation.

Rhythmic system
In *anthroposophical medicine* this is one of three
systems (the other two being the *digestive/movement
system* and the *nerve/sense system*) which together link
the physical, *etheric body*, *astral body,* and *ego*.

Rolfing
Also called *structural integration*, this is a form of deep
massage designed to correct posture, developed by Ida
Rolf.

Samhita
An ancient encyclopedia of Indian medicine written at
the University of Banaras and forming part of the basis
for *Ayurvedic medicine*.

Sclerology
Analysis of the sclera (white of the eye) which is
usually part of an *iridology* assessment.

Seven-star needle
A hammer 4–6 inches long, the head of which contains
seven (or sometimes five) standard slim acupuncture
needles. It is used in *acupuncture* for gently hammering
over the skin surface.

Shamanic healing
Healing carried out by a
primitive and tribal doctor
known as a shaman,
from the Tunguso-
Manchurian word,
"saman," meaning "he
who knows."

Shen Tao
A form of *acupressure* where a practitioner uses light
finger pressure to tap subtle energy patterns.

Shiatsu
Also known as *acupressure*, *shiatsu* is Japanese for
"finger pressure," and describes a therapy in which
pressure is applied to specific points on the body along
acupuncture meridians, using techniques that include a
gentle form of *rolfing*.

Spiritual healing
Also called *faith healing*, this is when the power of a
god or spirit serves as a healing force.

Sports massage
A form of *massage* commonly used for the treatment of
sports people and sporting injuries.

Structural integration
Also called *rolfing*, this is a form of deep *massage*
designed to correct posture, developed by Ida Rolf.

Swedish massage
A popular form of Western *massage* originally called
Swedish Movement Treatment and developed by
Swedish gymnast Per Henrik Ling and combining
therapeutic massage with exercises for muscles and
joints.

Swedish Movement Treatment
A popular form of Western *massage* more commonly
known as *Swedish massage*.

T'ai-chi ch'uan
A non-violent martial
art in which exercises
are used to stabilize
the forces of *Yin* and
Yang and improve
overall well-being by
easing the internal
flow of life energy
known as *chi*.

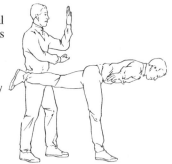

TENS machine
A device used in electrotherapy for a variety of
purposes including pain control and (in beauty clinics)
as a slimmiing aid. TENS stands for Transcutaneous
Electrical Nerve Stimulation.

Thalassotherapy
From the Greek word, "Thalassa," meaning "sea," this
is the tonic effect of time spent in the sea or in
seawater.

Therapeutic touch
Healers (rather than therapists) use their hands to bring
about healing, by placing them directly on a patient's
body or a small distance away from it. Contrary to the
practices of *faith healing* and the *laying on of hands*,
therapeutic touch therapists do not necessarily believe
they are channelling the power of a god or a spirit.

Thermalism
In health care this is the use of the pressure of moving water of various temperatures to massage the muscles and stimulate the circulation.

Tissue salts
Salts which occur naturally in the body, twelve of which were identified by Dr. Wilhelm Heinrich Schuessler in the 1870s and used as part of a therapy known as *biochemics*.

Transactional analysis
Concerned with the transactions between individuals, this form of therapy analyzes how we communicate and aims to help people realize and express their needs more clearly.

Transcendental meditation
A form of *meditation* in which a *mantra* is used.

Tridoshas
In *Ayurvedic medicine* the collective name for the three constitutional types (*vata*, *pitta*, and *kappa*).

Triple burner
Also called the *triple heater*, this is one of 14 *meridians* used in Chinese medicine and controls the endocrine gland.

Triple heater
Also called the *triple burner*, this is one of 14
meridians used in Chinese medicine and controls the
endocrine gland.

Tsubos (also called *acupoints, acupuncture points*, or
pressure points).
A Japanese word for key points on the *meridians* where
nerves feel uncomfortable when the flow of energy
through the body is blocked.

Tuina
Used in China alongside *acupuncture* and *herbal
medicine*, this is a form of intense, deep *massage* used
to balance energy flow.

Vata
In *Ayurvedic medicine* this is one of three *doshas* (the
other two being *pitta* and *kappa*) and resulting from the
combination of the *Bhutas* air and ether by *agni*.

Vedas
A collection of ancient Hindu scriptures originating
between 800 and 600 B.C., one of which is the
Ayurveda.

Visualization therapy
The use of mental images to improve overall health and
well-being.

Yang

A word originating from the Old Chinese and meaning "heaven, the force of expansion." *Yang* is the opposite of *Yin*.

Yin

A word originating from the Old Chinese and meaning "earth, the force of contraction." *Yin* is the opposite of *Yang*.

Yoga

From the Sanskrit word for "union," or "oneness," *yoga* is a system of attaining spiritual, mental and, physical well-being and of which there are many types, including bakti, hatha, jnana, karma, and raja. *Yoga* involves *asanas* and *pranayama*.

Zone therapy

Developed by American surgeon Dr. William Fitzgerald, this is an early Western form of reflexology in which healing can be brought about by massaging certain zones in the foot.

ABSENT HEALING

Definition
Healing at a distance. Sometimes this forms part of
faith healing (also called spiritual healing) in which the
power of a god or spirit serves as a healing force.
How does it work?
No one knows how absent healing works. Some
practitioners believe that once they have projected their
thoughts to both the patient and to the spirit world, they
have opened a channel through which healing forces
may flow. Others believe that healing forces may be
transmitted without divine intervention.
Believing that you will get well from an illness may in
itself affect the outcome of the illness, as doctors have
discovered who give patients placebo medicines.
History
For thousands of years prayers have been used as a
means of accessing the healing power of a god or spirit
(see FAITH HEALING) and they are today still used
for this purpose.

WHAT CONDITIONS IS IT USED FOR?
Absent healing is often sought when all other forms
of treatment have failed. Practitioners offer
treatment for any physical, mental, or spiritual
distress, especially for:

- Babies and young children
- Animals
- Those who are very ill
- Those who are unconscious
- Those with mental disorders

Treatment methods

Different healers use different techniques. Healers do not examine patients or diagnose illness. Neither do they claim to be able to effect instant cures. Some may ask for a patient to sit quietly at a certain time each day while the healer (who is not present) reads out a list of patients requiring help. The healer may then meditate for a while in an attempt to project a healing force. Some healers believe that it is not necessary for a patient to take part, although patients may be more receptive if they are feeling relaxed and positive about the healing.

HEALERS
Some healers believe they are successors to the early Christians and carry a divine healing force, (see the LAYING ON OF HANDS section). They use prayer and meditation to channel their divine healing powers in order to bring about a positive change in a person's life force. Others believe that the dead can communicate with the living and do so in order to help us. Such people believe they are a medium through which a spirit (usually that of a doctor or someone who was a healer in his or her lifetime) provides them with information they need to heal, even going so far as to guide their movements. For example, famous British healer Harry Edwards believed that Louis Pasteur was one of his healing guides. Other healers believe that illness is caused by a deficit or imbalance in the energies in and around the human body and that they are somehow able to re-balance these energies to bring about healing.

ACUPUNCTURE

Definition

Acupuncture is a traditional Chinese method of healing which involves the stimulation of acupuncture points on the skin using fine needles.

Types

Acupuncture points may be stimulated in a variety of ways. Therapists usually insert and manipulate fine needles, but may also use SHIATSU (finger pressure), MOXIBUSTION (stimulation using burning moxa), CUPPING (to increase blood flow to an area), and electrical devices.

How does it work?

Acupuncturists believe that disease is caused by a disturbance in Qi, the flow of life energy around the body, and that the stimulation of acupoints affects Qi, re-balancing a person's physical, emotional, and spiritual well-being. This may bring about relief from the pain caused by certain symptoms.

It is known that certain techniques used in acupuncture can excite, inhibit, or induce responses, affecting heart beat, blood count, blood flow, or hormone secretion, and may result in the reduction of congestion or inflammation. Needling certain points on the body has been shown to increase the number of white blood cells and intensify phagocytosis. Acupuncture therefore strengthens the resistance to diseases and stimulates the natural healing processes of the body. The stimulation of some points inhibits pain and can produce temporary anesthesia.

**Chinese diagram
of acupuncture
points and
meridians.** For a
fuller description of
meridians see
pages 57–65.

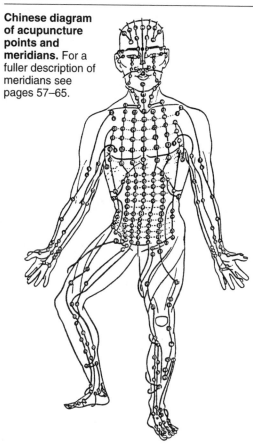

WHAT CONDITIONS IS IT USED FOR?

The World Health Organization has stated that
acupuncture may be used to treat:

Type of disorder	Examples	
Addictions	Alcohol Drugs	Nicotine
Bone/joint/ muscular	Back, neck, and shoulder pain	
Circulatory	Anemia Angina pectoris	Arteriosclerosis Hypertension
Emotional/ psychological	Anxiety Depression	
Gastrointestinal	Anorexia Constipation Diarrhea	Indigestion Food allergy Peptic ulcer
Gynecological	Infertility Menstrual problems	
Neurological	Sciatica Neuralgia	
Respiratory	Allergies Asthma Bronchitis	Emphysema Sinusitis
Urogenital	Stress incontinence Urinary tract infection	

History

The origins of acupuncture may lie in ancient stories about soldiers who had recovered from arrow wounds and unaccountably recovered from chronic illnesses. During the Shang Dynasty (1783–1122 B.C.), it was realized that massage with sharpened pieces of stone relieved painful areas of the body. Soon needles were being manipulated at certain points on the body, and new points of relief were discovered.

The earliest needles were made from bone, horn, and bamboo. Later, iron, bronze, gold, and silver became popular. The first record of successful treatment by needling described how Pien Chuch, who lived from 407 to 310 B.C., cured a very sick prince. Then, at about 300 B.C., *The Yellow Emperor's Classic of Internal Medicine* was written. It was the first Chinese medical book and in it 132 points suitable for needling are described.

Although the general use of acupuncture declined during the mid-seventeenth century, it continued to be practiced by rural communities and re-emerged after the establishment of the People's Republic in 1949.

Today acupuncture is used extensively around the world.

Equipment

Therapists often palpate an area to determine the exact location of an acupuncture point although some use an electronic device called an acusometer.

Stimulation of acupuncture points is usually achieved using fine needles made from stainless steel, although other devices may be used, including heated moxa, mechanical vibrator, and magnetic oscillator.

ACUPUNCTURE NEEDLES

a A standard needle varies in length from $1/2$ inch to 3 inches.

b Prismatic needles are about $2^1/2$ inches long and used in the treatment of acute diseases.

c A seven-star needle is a hammer 4–6 inches long. The head of the hammer has seven (or sometimes five) standard slim needles. This is used for gently tapping over the skin surface and is especially useful for the treatment of skin diseases and children.

d Interdermal needles are very small and delicate. These are used for insertion into points on the head and ears.

e Press needles are designed to stay in the skin for several days and can be pressed or manipulated by the patient as required. They are used for chronic conditions and are extremely effective when a person needs to resist the temptation to smoke, for example, since the sufferer can apply extra stimulation at the exact moment temptation strikes.

Although there is much disagreement among professionals and between traditions as to the effectiveness of a needle, it has been suggested that effectiveness depends on:

- The size of the needle bore.
- The depth to which the needle penetrates.
- The sharpness of the needle.
- The amount the needle is moved about.
- The length of time the needle is left in place.
- The frequency of treatment.

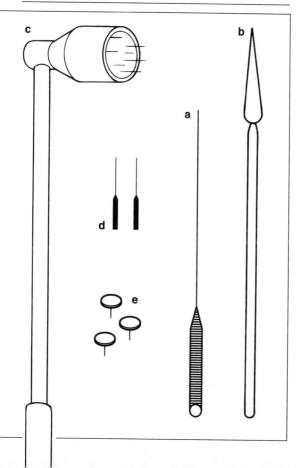

NEEDLING

The depth to which needles are inserted may vary and is measured in terms of fens. A fen is one tenth of an ACI or Anatomical Chinese Inch (slightly less than 1/10th of an ordinary inch). The insertion may be as little as 1 fen (e.g. in the head), or as much as 30 fen (e.g. in the buttocks). Prismatic needles are never inserted more than 1 fen.

There are around fifty different ways for needles to be inserted. Three angles of insertion using standard needles are:

a Perpendicular
b Angle of 45 degrees
c Sliding just under the skin surface

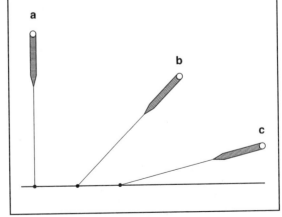

Treatment methods

After taking case notes and examining your pulse, the therapist identifies those acupuncture points to be used and inserts acupuncture needles accordingly. Of the 500 or so recognized acupuncture points on the body, around 100 are commonly used. As the needles are very fine, there is usually no pain, although some people experience a dull ache or slight tingling.

Acupuncture points may be further stimulated during treatment by the vibrating or heating of inserted needles, by moxibustion, lasers, or by electron-acupuncture.

The importance of meridians

Meridians carry the vital life energy, Qi, which can be accessed at certain points. As the line of a meridian has a lowered electrical impedance (a property of nerves) it was once speculated that they are nerve pathways, although it has now been shown that this is not the case. There are twelve main meridians, each one controlling a specific organ. Just as all phenomena in Eastern medicine are categorized Yin or Yang, so too are the meridians. Yin meridians run upward from the toes; yang meridians run downward from the head to the toes.

Two of the organs listed in Eastern medicine are not recognized in Western medicine: the triple burner (which controls heat and water) and the xin bas (sometimes known as the pericardium).

There are two meridians placed centrally on the body, one down the front and one down the back. These are the conception vessel (Yin) which begins near the anus and flows centrally up the front of the body to the mouth, and the governor vessel (Yang) which begins near the anus and flows centrally up the back, over the head to the mouth.

Meridian	Yin	Yang	Element
Heart	*		Fire
Small intestine		x	Fire
Bladder		x	Water
Kidney	*		Water
Pericardium	*		Fire
Triple burner		x	Fire
Gall bladder		x	Wood
Liver	*		Wood
Lungs	*		Metal
Large intestine		x	Metal
Stomach		x	Earth
Spleen	*		Earth

THE TWELVE MERIDIANS

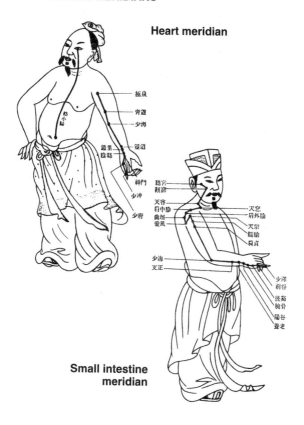

Heart meridian

Small intestine meridian

THE TWELVE MERIDIANS (continued)

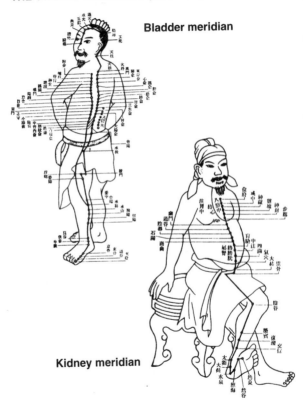

Bladder meridian

Kidney meridian

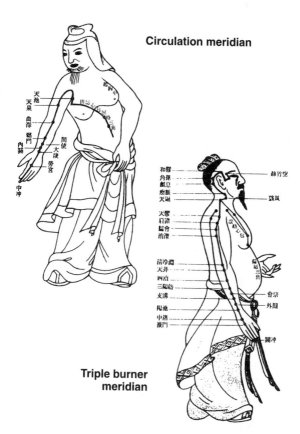

Circulation meridian

Triple burner meridian

THE TWELVE MERIDIANS (continued)

Gall bladder meridian

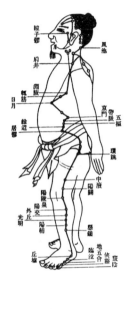

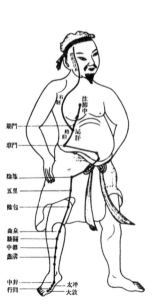

Liver meridian

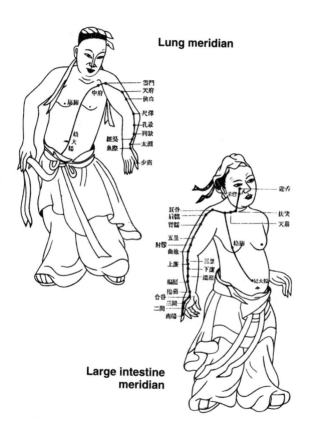

Lung meridian

雲門
天府
俠白
尺澤
孔最
列缺
太淵
經渠
魚際
少商

中府
·屬肺

絡大腸

**Large intestine
meridian**

迎香
扶突
天鼎

巨骨
肩髃
臂臑
五里
肘髎
曲池
上廉
下廉
溫溜
偏歷
陽谿
合谷
三間
二間
商陽
三里

不恒

絡肺

屬大腸

THE TWELVE MERIDIANS (continued)

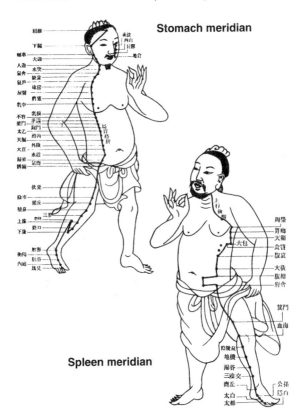

Stomach meridian

Spleen meridian

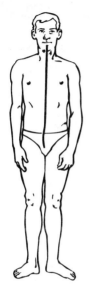

Conception vessel meridian

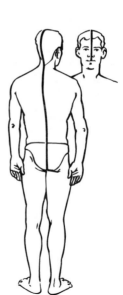

Governor vessel meridian

ALEXANDER TECHNIQUE

Definition
A method of retraining the body's movements in order
to improve posture.

Equipment
None necessary.

How does it work?
Since all bones of the skeleton are held together by
cartilage and ligaments at the end-points of each
muscle, it follows that any chronic misuse of muscles
will eventually distort the skeleton, and this in turn will
affect the nervous system, the circulatory system, and
other organs of the body. Improving the way we use our
bodies will therefore lead to improvements in
breathing, circulation, and digestion.

History
The technique was developed by Australian reciter of
poetry and humorous pieces, Frederick Matthias
Alexander, who began to lose his voice on stage and
was forced to turn to self-help treatment after the
medical profession failed to improve his condition.
Performing in front of a mirror, Alexander noticed that
his posture changed when he began to speak, he shrank
in height and had difficulty breathing; he pulled his
head back and tightened his throat. He noticed too that
even the thought of projecting his voice resulted in a
tightening of his vocal chords, reinforcing his belief in
the mind-body relationship.
By careful observation and experiment Alexander cured
his problem and concluded that for any activity to be

performed efficiently there must be a balanced relationship between the head, neck, and spine. Alexander agreed with the founders of osteopathy and chiropractic that it was important to integrate the spinal column, and argued that vertebrae may be misaligned as a result of misuse. Such misuse was the result of bad habits developing in the way we talk, sit, and walk, for example.

Alexander began teaching his technique to others in Australia and New Zealand in 1894, arguing that bad postural habits need to be quite deliberately broken and replaced with new, better habits for improvements to take place. In 1904 Alexander moved to London, England, and it was not until 1930 that several prominent physicians and philosophers endorsed his technique, after which his popularity soared. He published *The Use of Self* in 1932 and his technique became popular throughout the Western world.

WHAT CONDITIONS IS IT USED FOR?
Teachers of the Alexander Technique claim that conditions which respond well to treatment include:

- Anxiety
- Asthma
- Colitis
- Depression
- Exhaustion
- Headaches
- High blood pressure
- Irritable bowel syndrome
- Lower back pain
- Migraine
- Muscular-skeletal disorders
- Osteoarthritis
- Peptic ulcers
- Respiratory disorders
- Rheumatoid arthritis
- Sciatica
- Whiplash

Alexander taught pupils to imagine that a hook on the head was gently pulling the spine upward, into the correct alignment.

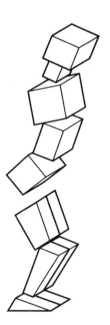
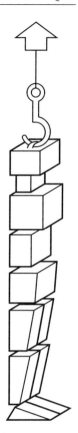

Treatment methods

As a "pupil" you will be taught by a "teacher" how to change harmful postures and will be shown how to regain the habit of using muscles with minimum effort and maximum efficiency. The teacher may ask what kind of work you do and will observe how you use your body. By gently laying hands on you, the teacher persuades your muscles to relax, enabling the limbs to re-align themselves. Over a series of lessons you will be taught how to correct your posture yourself, during everyday activities including standing, walking, sitting, and working at a desk. Diagrams on the next four pages show spinal curvature when standing and sitting in different ways, and highlights differences between good and bad postures.

SEVEN PRINCIPLES UNDERLYING THE TECHNIQUE

1 It is important to be aware of your body and how it functions if you want to make changes in order to improve a condition.

2 Muscles begin to move the second you *think* about moving.

3 The posture you maintain may not be correct and you may be damaging yourself without knowing it.

4 Habits are usually learned and can therefore be changed.

5 The body is interconnected so that what happens to one part affects the whole body.

6 You have the ability to exert conscious control over your habits.

7 Success depends on concentrating on the process of change.

Standing

Standing with a slouched posture (**a**) results in
excessive curvature of the vertebrae in the neck and
lower back. Standing erect corrects these imbalances.

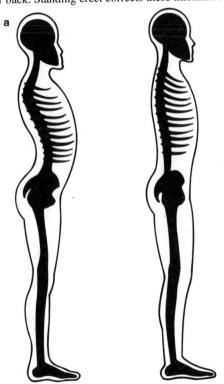

Sitting

Craning the neck back to sit down results in excessive curvature of the lower spine (**b**). Keeping the head poised without craning results in much less severe spinal curvature.

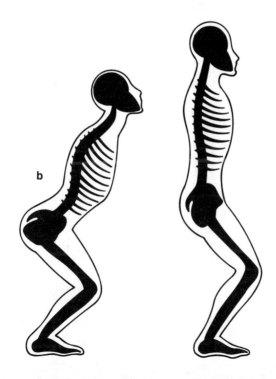

POSTURE

Bad posture	**Good posture**
a Tired outlook	Positive outlook
b Stiff neck	Supple neck
c Rounded shoulder	Capable shoulders
d Restricted breathing	Full breathing
e Lower back pain	Pain-free back
f Tight pelvic area	Swinging pelvic area
g Easily pushed off balance	Can keep balance

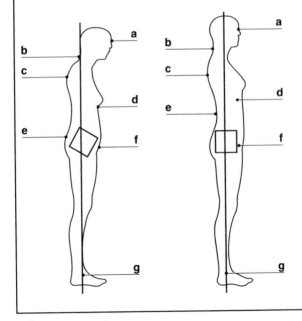

Comparing postures

A Carrying a heavy shoulder bag can distort the body sideways.

B The best way to carry a bag is backsack style.

C High heeled shoes throw the pelvis forward and the spine develops a curvature.

D Flat shoes or bare feet help to keep postural balance.

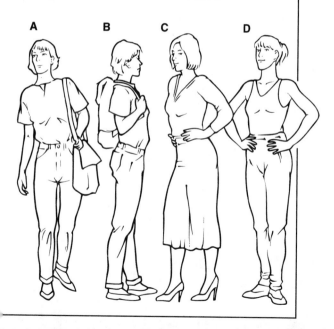

A   B   C   D

ANTHROPOSOPHICAL MEDICINE

Definition

A holistic approach to health and illness based on the teachings of Rudolf Steiner, who believed the word "anthropology" should be understood to mean "awareness" of one's humanity.

History

Austrian scientist and philosopher Rudolf Steiner founded the first anthroposophical clinic in Arlesham, Switzerland and, with the Dutch physician Dr. Ita Wegman, produced *Fundamentals of Therapy*. Steiner

ASPECTS OF MAN ACCORDING TO STEINER		
Aspect	**Description**	**Greek element**
Physical	The body's tangible components	Earth
Etheric body	This opposes the force of gravity, allowing individuals to grow upward, away from the earth.	Water
Astral body	Emotions	Air
Ego	An individual's spiritual core.	Fire

believed that there were three aspects to man (see table, *below left*) in addition to his physical component: an etheric body, an astral body, and the ego. These corresponded to the Greek elements, earth, water, air, and fire, and are connected to each other by way of three body systems: the digestive/movement system, the nerve/sense system, and the rhythmic system (see table, *below*).

ANTHROPOSOPHICAL MEDICINE'S THREE BODY SYSTEMS		
System	**Dominated by**	**Controls**
Digestive/ movement	Physical and etheric bodies	Extraction Glandular system Restoration and rebuilding The body during the night
Nerve/sense	Ego and astral bodies	Conscious processes: thought, perception, self-awareness The body during the day
Rhythmic	Formed by the alternation of the other two systems	Circulation Breathing

Health and illness: two opposing forces

Anthroposophical doctors believe that the body has
bodily activities that alternate between two poles: a
warm pole representing movement and a cool pole
representing rest. For example, at the warm pole,
metabolic cells are active and ready to regenerate; at
the cool pole, brain and nerve cells are constantly
dying. Tension between different types of activity is
inevitable and continuous. Practitioners divide illnesses
into two main groups: inflammatory (or feverish), and
degenerative (or hardening) (see table, *right*).

Good health

Good health signifies a temporary balance between the
two opposing states, but cannot continue indefinitely.

Illness

Anthroposophical practitioners believe that illness is
not just a physical condition, but that it is particularly
meaningful with respect to reincarnation, either to past
lives or future lives. Practitioners also believe that the
process of illness allows individuals to become more
whole.

The function of the doctor

Individuals need to take responsibility for their own
development and can only do this if they become aware
of the opposing processes, constantly at work in
themselves. It is not the job of anthroposophical doctors
to eliminate illness from the body, but to guide it in the
most beneficial way. This is achieved by using
remedies that aid the disease process in its resolution
rather than by destroying the process altogether, and
allows doctors to view abnormalities in a positive way.

ANTHROPOSOPHICAL CLASSIFICATION OF ILLNESS

Type	Arising from	Relevant conditions
Inflammatory: conditions common in childhood	The digestive/ movement system becoming too strong	All fevers Chickenpox Measles
Degenerative: conditions common in older people	The hardening/ contracting influence of the astral body and ego on the nerve/sense system	Arterial hardening Cancer Immune-deficiency diseases

Treatment methods

Anthroposophical practitioners may use a variety of therapies: aromatherapy, art therapy, herbalism, homeopathy, hydrotherapy, massage, and speech therapy, as well as conventional drugs and surgery. Some practitioners teach eurythmy, a system of promoting self-expression through music. (For more information see MUSIC THERAPY.)

AROMATHERAPY

Definition
Using essential plant oils to improve physical and emotional well-being, and often involving massage.

TYPES OF AROMATHERAPY
Although the use of essential oils is basically the same, there are two main branches of aromatherapy, categorized according to the circumstances in which oils are used:

Type	Uses
Aesthetic/ beauty therapy	Oils are used by beauty therapists to help conditions such as stretch marks and acne, and to relax clients.
Complementary medicine	Oils and massage are used in holistic treatments for a variety of physical and emotional disorders. They are also used in conjunciton with orthodox medicine and in the treatment of seriously ill patients, such as those with cancer.

Equipment
There are over 400 different types of essential oils. Those used by aromatherapists are different from the plant essences used by herbalists—aromatherapy oils are concentrated, used in very small quantities, and diluted with vegetable oil.

ESSENTIAL OILS

What are they?

Essential oils are aromatic volatile substances present as tiny droplets within the flowers, leaves, fruit, seeds, and bark of plants. They vary within plants themselves—orange oil distilled from the rind of a fruit has different properties from the oil distilled from the flowers, for example.

How are they obtained?

Essential oils are usually expensive to buy because it takes a great deal of plant material to produce them and their exact properties cannot be reproduced synthetically. It takes, for example, two thousand pounds of rose petals to produce one pound of essential rose oil by the process of enfleurage. True essential oils are obtained by steam distillation or, in the case of citrus oils, by expression.

Other methods of obtaining oils include:
- The use of solvents
- Enfleurage
- Maceration
- Carbon dioxide extraction

How does it work?

It is not clear exactly how essential oils work, although there are several theories, three of which are mentioned here:

1 Essential oils are complex and contain substances known as esters, alcohols, aldehydes, ketones, and terpenes. During massage, the tiny molecular structures of these oils are readily absorbed through the skin (perhaps through sweat pores and hair follicles) and enter the bloodstream. Once in the blood they may affect the functioning of different organs.

2 Aromatic substances are inhaled and act on the olfactory system and the part of the brain known as the limbic system. The limbic system is connected with mood control, strong emotions, and instinctive behavior. It is believed that, through its impact on the limbic system, aromatherapy stimulates the release of hormones and neurochemicals in the body, bringing about changes in emotion and feelings of relaxation or well-being.

3 Certain oils have been shown to fight bacteria and are therefore used as antibiotics.

History

Essential oils were in common use in many ancient civilizations. For example, five thousand years ago the ancient Egyptians were devoted to the use of aromatic oils for medical and cosmetic purposes and used oils such as clove, eucalyptus and lavender to treat skin disorders. When Tutankhamen's tomb was opened in 1922 it contained many scent pots, including large amounts of the very expensive frankincense and myrrh.

Avicenna, an 11th-century Persian philosopher and
physician, refined the distillation process that was
currently being used to obtain essential oils, and in
doing so was able to produce much purer substances.
Knowledge about how to use essential oils was
probably introduced to Europe by the Romans,
although the general use of herbs for medicinal
purposes was already widespread at this time.

In 1597 German physician Hieronymus Braunschweig
published a tome which listed 25 essential oils and their
uses, although the term "aromatherapy" was not used
until the beginning of the twentieth century when it was
coined by French chemist René Maurice Gattefossé.
After pouring some lavender oil over his badly burned
hand Gattefossé was surprised how quickly it healed. In
1928 he published the first book on aromatherapy.

In 1938 M. Goddissart, another Frenchman, working in
Los Angeles, was treating wounds, skin cancers, and
gangrene with essential oils and getting good results.
A third Frenchman, the army surgeon Dr. Jean Valnet,
used the essences to heal wounds and reduce scarring
during World War II and published his work in 1964.
Aromatherapy was re-introduced into Britain and
popularized by Robert Tisserand in 1969.

What conditions is it used for?

Aromatherapists claim to be able to treat a huge variety
of conditions. These are listed on the following pages.

COMMON AILMENTS AND USEFUL OILS

Ailment	Essential oils	
Acne	Bergamot Juniper Lavender	Niaouli Petit Grain

Arthritis	Black pepper
	Camomile
	  (Roman)
	Juniper
		Lavender
		Lemon
		Marjoram
		  (sweet)

Asthma	Benzoin Camomile (Roman) Eucalyptus Lavender	Lemon Niaouli Pine Thyme (sweet)
Bites	Lavender Tea tree	
Boils	Camomile (Roman) Lavender	Lemon Tea Tree Thyme (sweet)
Breathing (difficult)	Cypress Eucalyptus	Mandarin
Bronchitis	Black pepper Cajuput Eucalyptus Frankincense Lavender Lemon	Marjoram (Spanish) Niaouli Peppermint Pine Tea Tree

Ailment	Essential oils	
Burns	Benzoin Camomile (German)	Lavender Niaouli
Colds	Black pepper Cypress Eucalyptus Lemon Juniper	Marjoram (Spanish) Peppermint Pine Thyme (sweet)
Constipation	Basil Black pepper Camomile (Roman) Coriander Fennel	Ginger Mandarin Marjoram Orange (bitter) Rosemary
Cough	Benzoin Black pepper Cardamom Cypress	Eucalyptus Frankincense Juniper Peppermint
Cramp (intestinal)	Basil Camomile (Roman)	
Cystitis	Basil Eucalyptus Fennel Juniper Lavender	Niaouli Sandalwood Tea Tree Thyme (red and sweet)

COMMON AILMENTS AND USEFUL OILS (continued)

Ailment	Essential oils	
Depression	Basil	Melissa (true)
	Bergamot	Neroli
	Camomile	Patchouli
	(Maroc)	Pine
	Geranium	Rose
	Jasmine	Sandalwood
	Petit Grain	Ylang-ylang
	Lavender	
Diarrhea	Black Pepper	Lavender
	Camomile	Lemon
	(Roman)	Myrrh
	Geranium	Orange
	Ginger	Peppermint
	Juniper	Sandlewood
Eczema	Basil	Geranium
	Benzoin	Juniper
	Bergamot	Lavender
	Camomile	Myrrh
	(German)	Rose Water
	Frankincense	Sandalwood
Earache	Camomile	
	(Roman)	
	Lavender	
Fainting	Basil	Lavender
	Black pepper	Peppermint
	Camomile	Rosemary
	(Roman)	

Ailment	Essential oils	
Fever	Black Pepper Camomile (Roman) Eucalyptus	Lavender Lemon Tea Tree
Flatulence	Bergamot Black Pepper Cardamom Camomile (Roman) Coriander Fennel Ginger	Lavender Marjoram (sweet) Myrrh Orange (bitter) Peppermint Rosemary Thyme (sweet)
Hay fever	Camomile (Roman) Cypress	Marjoram
Headaches	Camomile (Roman) Lavender Lemon	Marjoram (sweet) Peppermint
Hemorrhoids	Cypress Niaouli	
Hepatitis	Basil Eucalyptus Juniper Lemon	Petit Grain Rosemary Thyme

COMMON AILMENTS AND USEFUL OILS (continued)

Ailment	Essential oils	
Hiccups	Tarragon	
High blood pressure	Juniper Lavender Lemon	Marjoram (sweet) Ylang-ylang
Indigestion	Basil Bergamot Black Pepper Cardamom Caraway Camomile (Roman) Coriander Fennel Frankincense	Ginger Lavender Lemon Marjoram (sweet) Orange (bitter) Peppermint Rosemary
Influenza	Black Pepper Camomile (Roman) Coriander Cypress Eucalyptus Lavender Lemon	Niaouli Peppermint Pine Rosemary Tea Tree Thyme (sweet)

Ailment	Essential oils	
Insomnia	Camomile (Roman) Lavender Marjoram (sweet) Neroli	Orange (bitter/sweet) Rose Water Sandalwood Tea Tree Ylang-ylang
Laryngitis	Black Pepper Cajaput Eucalyptus	Lemon Sandalwood Tea Tree
Menstrual problems	Camomile (Roman) Clary Geranium Juniper	Lavender Melissa (true) Rose Water Thyme (sweet)
Mental fatigue	Basil Cajaput Cardamom Juniper Berry	Peppermint Rosemary Rosewood Thyme (sweet)
Migraine	Aniseed Basil Camomile (German) Eucalyptus Lavender Lemon	Marjoram (sweet) Melissa (true) Peppermint Rosemary

COMMON AILMENTS AND USEFUL OILS (continued)

Ailment	Essential oils	
Mouth ulcers	Basil Geranium Myrrh	Niaouli Ravelsau Tea Tree
Nausea	Black Pepper Ginger Lavender Lemon	Melissa (true) Peppermint Rose Sandalwood
Nervous tension	Basil Benzoin Bergamot Camomile (Roman) Clary Geranium Jasmine Lavender	Marjoram (sweet) Melissa (true) Neroli Patchouli Petit Grain Rose Sandalwood Ylang-ylang
Rheumatism	Basil Black Pepper Camomile (Roman) Eucalyptus Juniper Lavender Lavondin	Niaouli Petit Grain Pine Rosemary Savory Thyme (sweet)

Ailment	Essential oils	
Sciatica	Camomile (Roman) Eucalyptus Ginger Lavondin	Marjoram (sweet) Peppermint Pine Sandalwood
Shock	Camomile (Roman) Melissa (true)	Neroli Peppermint Ylang-ylang
Sinusitis	Cajeput Eucalyptus Lavender Lemon Marjoram (Sp. & sweet)	Niaouli Peppermint Pine Thyme (sweet) Rosemary Tea Tree
Skin (dermatitis)	Benzoin Cajeput Camomile (Roman) Geranium Juniper Berry	Lavender Patchouli Rose Water Tea Tree Thyme (sweet)
Skin (dry)	Camomile (German/ Roman) Geranium Jasmine Lavender Neroli	Petit Grain Rose Water Sandalwood Ylang-ylang

COMMON AILMENTS AND USEFUL OILS (continued)

Ailment	Essential oils	
Skin (oily)	Bergamot Cypress Frankincense Geranium Juniper Lavender	Lemon Orange Sandalwood Ylang-ylang
Skin (mature)	Benzoin Camomile (German) Frankincense Lavender	Myrrh Orange blossom Rose Water
Skin (sensitive)	Camomile (German) Jasmine Neroli	Rose Water Rosewood
Sore throat	Eucalyptus Lavender Lemon Niaouli	Peppermint Thyme (sweet)
Stomach ulcers	Black Pepper Camomile (Roman) Coriander	Ginger Lemon Sandalwood
Toothache	Cajeput Camomile (Roman)	Lavender Pine

Ailment	Essential oils	
Varicose veins	Cypress	Niaouli
	Juniper	Patchouli
	Lemon	Sandalwood
	Neroli	Tea Tree
Warts	Lemon	
	Tea Tree	
Wrinkles	Frankincense	
	Neroli	
	Rose Water	

Treatment method

Treatment usually begins with the aromatherapist taking a case history—asking questions about your health, lifestyle, diet, and sleeping habits, for example. They may also assess your posture and appearance. The therapist then decides which essential oils are appropriate for you, and these are blended together with a carrier oil and are often applied in the form of a massage. The therapist may recommend a blend for you to use at home.

Ways in which essential oils may be used are shown in the box, *below*.

APPLICATION

Essential oils may be used in a variety of ways.

1 Diluted in a base oil, oils may be rubbed into the skin during massage.
2 A few drops of oil may be added to a bath.
3 Oils may be inhaled, (to help clear nasal congestion, for example).
4 Oils may be applied to a cloth and used as a compress.
5 Some oils may be used in an oil burner (shown here). The ceramic bowl (**a**) is filled with water, and a few drops of oil added. A small candle (**b**) heats the mixture from below.

Warning:
Essential oils can be obtained by the public for use at
home and are safe to use in most circumstances
provided the instructions are followed. However,
essential oils should be avoided in pregnancy. Some
oils may irritate sensitive skin; certain oils may react to
sunlight causing skin damage. It is therefore important
to always read oil labels or instructions carefully and to
consult only qualified therapists.

ART THERAPY

Definition
Using the spontaneous creation of art—collage-making, drawing, modeling, painting, or sculpting—as a means of self-expression in order to improve emotional well-being.

Types
Art therapy may be carried out on a one-to-one basis or in a small group of usually no more than eight people.

Equipment
Almost any kind of art material can be used, and commonly includes the use of paper, cardboard, newspaper, crayons, charcoal, clay, and paint.

How does it work?
Art therapy has many advantages:
1 The process of creating artwork is itself therapeutic. A client may use the therapy to safely express anger, for example, and this may in turn reduce feelings of tension or hostility.
2 Pictures or models can be interpreted by clients. By exploring the meaning of what they have created, therapists may help clients to learn about themselves.
3 Pictures or models may be interpreted by therapists and may aid diagnosis. Emotions suppressed by people with mental disturbances may be released during art therapy and the results can be examined by therapists to help monitor a patient's condition.
4 Encouraging patients to examine their own work facilitates an improved relationship between the therapist and the patient.

WHAT CONDITIONS IS IT USED FOR?
- Alcohol addiction
- Anxiety
- Depression
- Drug addiction
- Eating disorders
- Those who have difficulty expressing feelings
- People with mental illness, including psychosis
- People having experienced loss or bereavement
- People with low self-esteem

History

Art therapy was first practiced in England in the 1940s as a result of the work of artist Adrian Hill and psychotherapist Irene Champernowne. Hill used his art as a means of passing time creatively when he was in hospital with tuberculosis and encouraged other patients to start drawing and painting also. In addition to taking their minds off recovery, painting and drawing appeared to help patients to express their anxieties and the scenes they had witnessed in battle during World War II. Irene Champernowne studied psychotherapy under Carl Gustav Jung and became interested in the way Jung encouraged patients to use art to express their unconscious feelings. The center she helped set up in 1942 employed artists, dancers, and musicians alongside medical experts.

Treatment methods

Art therapy draws upon a variety of disciplines. There is no universally agreed procedure for art therapy, although all patients are encouraged to work spontaneously.

AURA ANALYSIS

Definition

Analysis of a person's aura, an energy field surrounding the human body which analysts describe as a cloud of light that radiates from a person, rather like the phosphorescence of some sea creatures.

Equipment

Auras can be seen directly by psychics; otherwise a Kilner screen or Kirlian photograph is necessary. A Kilner screen is a special type of glass developed by the British scientist Walter J. Kilner in 1920. Modern therapists may use a pair of cobalt-tinted glasses. Strictly speaking, Kirlian photography is not photography but a process invented in the 1930s by Russian engineers Valentina and Semyon Kirlian. In 1939 Davidovich Kirlian invented a machine which generated high frequency electrical oscillations that enabled him to record the bioluminescence of living things onto photographic paper, for which no camera is required. This process is known as electrophotography.

How does it work?

Those who can see the aura say that it changes color, size, and the rate at which it pulsates depending on an individual's mood, emotional balance, and overall physical condition. Examining the color of the aura enables therapists to assess the condition of an individual and suggest appropriate treatment.

What conditions is it used for?

Like spiritual healers, those who use aura analysis for healing do not accept that any condition is incurable.

History

Many ancient works of art show figures surrounded by area or lines of light, such as the halo depicted in Western religious art.

Christ healing a leper in this illustration by Karl Thymann.

In 1901 and 1902 C.W. Leadbeater published *Thought Forms* and *Man Visible and Invisible* respectively. He proposed that the aura comprised three ovoids of light, each a different "body"—astral, mental, and causal. In the 1930s Valentina and Semyon Kirlian discovered that it was possible to capture images of the auras from the leaves of plants. They put a leaf from a healthy plant and a leaf from a diseased plant between photographic plates and high-voltage, high-frequency electrical charges. The resulting photographs revealed a vivid aura around the healthy leaf but a weak aura around the leaf from the diseased plant.

Healthy leaf image made using Kirlian photography

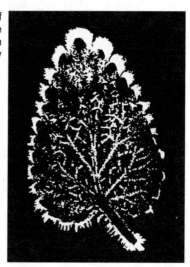

In addition to the aura "photographs," Kirlian and his wife also devised optical equipment that enabled them to observe the auras of their own hands in motion. What they saw was a display of moving, colored light; sometimes there were sparks and brief flashes, at other times a soft, steady glow. The colors ranged from pale blue to rose pink and there were dim cloudy areas too. In 1972, The American Academy of Parapsychology and Medicine held a symposium entitled *The Dimensions of Healing*. In the transcript of that symposium, Dr. Thelma Moss of the Neuropsychiatric Institute of UVCLA presented a paper on photographic

Image of diseased leaf made using Kirlian photography

evidence of healing energy on plants and people.
In particular, she outlined research on the transfer of
energy from a person to a plant as an example of the
healing effect. Her team discovered that leaves became
healthy and gave off healthy auras when handled by
people who themselves had a healthy aura at the time of
handling the leaf. These people were said to have the
"green thumb" effect on the leaves. Their thumb aura
was glowing blue or pink and showed the thumb print.
The thumb aura of people who were ill or generally
debilitated was a yellowish-brown color, consisted of

Kirlian prints of a thumb aura before and after
treatment

sharply-pointed sparks, and the thumb print was invisible. When these people handled the leaves, they failed to thrive and the leaf aura became disturbed. The team searched for explanations and checked their work many times, always with the same results. They took photographic records of patients on admission to hospital and after their recovery from illness. The aura evidence was consistent: there was clearly a healthy aura and a sick aura.

Treatment methods

Therapists who use this form of analysis may start by observing your aura, noting its size, shape, color (see tables on the next few pages) and vibrational pattern. In rare cases the therapist may touch the aura.

A healthy aura is generally bright, large, and glows blue; the aura of a sick person is small, dull, and may appear yellowish.

Once the assessment has been made the therapist may channel universal spiritual energy to "feed" extra color to the aura. This is achieved by touching your aura or visualizing the transition of energy.

It is likely that you will be required to take an active part in the healing process. It may be suggested that you strengthen your aura through techniques such as COLOR THERAPY or SOUND THERAPY.

COLOR OF THE AURA

Color	Relates to	Physical associations
Black	Damage to the aura	Anesthesia Illness Negative emotions Negative thoughts Stress
Blue	Idealism Inspiration Integrity	Breathing Ears Nose Speech Throat Thyroid gland
Gray	Damage to the aura	Anesthesia Illness Negative emotions Negative thoughts Stress
Green	Healing Nature Regeneration	Circulatory system Heart Thymus gland
Indigo	Moral values Transcendence of the non-physical world	Lymphatic system Pituitary gland

Color	Relates to	Physical associations
Orange	Energy Health	Adrenal glands Sexual function Spleen
Red	Energy Passion Strength Vigor	Excretion Nerve endings Sex glands
Violet	Insight Love Spiritual enlightenment	Nervous system Pineal body
White	Ideals Perfection Truth	
Yellow	Intelligence	Childbirth Digestive system Pancreas

ANALYZING COLORS OF THE AURA

The amount and strength of a color indicates one or
more of the following personality traits/emotions:

Color	Personality trait/emotion
Black	● Negative emotions ● Negative thoughts
Blue, pale	● The potential for learning
Gray	● Negative emotions ● Negative thoughts
Green	● Adaptability ● Liveliness ● A versatile mind
Indigo	● Intuition ● Seeking spiritual truth
Indigo, excessive	● Benevolence ● Calmness ● Irritability
Orange	● Consideration ● Disillusionment ● Fear ● Illusion ● Strong personality

Color	Personality trait/emotion
Orange, excessive	● Ambition ● Selfishness
Red, dark	● Anger ● Sensuality
Red, light	● Nervousness ● Tension
Red, excessive	● Materialism ● Selfishness ● Willfulness
White	● This balances the effect of gray or black in the aura
Yellow	● Frustration ● Intelligence ● Optimism ● Worry
Yellow, golden	● Insight ● Spiritually developed
Yellow, pale	● Indecisiveness ● Weakness

AURICULAR THERAPY

Definition
Also known as auriculotherapy, this is treatment of the ear to bring about healing in other parts of the body.

History
The use of needling had been widely used in ancient China, Egypt, Greece, and India and was standard medical practice in the Mediterranean countries four centuries before the birth of Christ. However, it was not until during the 1950s that it began to gain popularity in the West when Dr. Paul Nogier of Lyons, France, published books showing that acupuncture points on the ear reflected different parts of the body. Dr Nogier

---

WHAT CONDITIONS IS IT USED FOR?
Practitioners claim auricular therapy is valuable for the treatment of a variety of conditions including:

- Anxiety
- Arthritis
- Asthma
- Back pain
- Colitis
- Depression
- Hay fever
- Headaches
- Hiatus hernia
- Indigestion
- Insomnia
- Menstrual pain
- Migraine
- ME
- Nervous disorders
- Obesity
- Pain in childbirth
- Pain in dentistry
- Sciatica
- Shingles
- Sinusitis
- Tendonitis
- Tennis elbow
- Urinary problems

also noticed that when he joined up these points on a diagram, they formed the shape of an upside down baby, leading him to conclude that the ear reflected the entire body.

Equipment

Tiny acupuncture needles may be used or press needles (which look like drawing pins). Press needles are left in place for several days and are used by the patient to stimulate acupressure points, for patients who are heavy smokers, for example.

How does it work?

No one really knows how auricular therapy works. The ear is believed to have more than 200 acupuncture points which relate to other parts of the body and therapists believe that stimulating the nerve endings at appropriate points in the ear results in a "healing wave" being sent along the nerve to a part of the body that requires treatment.

Treatment methods

After taking a detailed case history the therapist assesses the state of the patient's ear and diagnoses acupuncture points. The therapist may insert tiny acupuncture needles, use a pen-shaped electrode to stimulate the points, or may use a laser (for children). Pain in the hip, for example, would be treated by stimulating that point on the ear which corresponds with the hip.

ACUPUNCTURE POINTS ON THE EAR

Some selected points which affect different areas of the body (*shown below*):

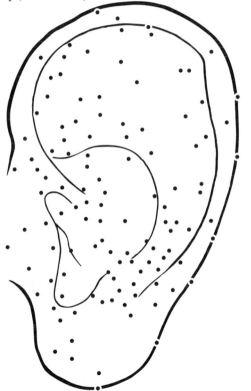

Parts of the body that can be affected by auricular acupuncture

Abdomen
Adrenal gland
Ankle
Anus
Appendix
Brain stem
Bronchus
Buttocks
Cardiac orifice
Cervical
 vertebrae
Cheek area
Clavicle
Diaphragm
Duodenum
Elbow
Esophagus
External ear
External genital
 organs
External nose
Eye
Finger
Forehead
Gallbladder
Heart
Heart point
Heel
Hip joint

Kidney
Knee
Large intestine
Liver
Lower jaw
Lower section
 of rectum
Lumbar
 vertebrae
Lung
Mandible
Maxilla
Mouth
Neck
Ovary
Pancreas
Parotid gland
Pelvic cavity
Sacral
 vertebrae
Sciatic nerve
Shoulder
Small intestine
Spleen
Stomach
Temple
Thoracic
 vertebrae
Thorax

Thyroid gland
Toes
Tongue
Tonsils
Upper jaw
Ureter
Urethra
Urinary bladder
Uterus
Wrist

AUTOGENIC TRAINING

Definition
A method of using profound relaxation in such a way that it relieves stress and enables the mind or body to heal. Autogenic training is not based on any cultural or religious philosophies.

Equipment
Equipment is not required.

WHAT CONDITIONS IS IT USED FOR?
Autogenic training is valuable for the treatment of a variety of conditions including:

- AIDS
- Allergies
- Anxiety
- Arthritis
- Asthma
- Backache
- Bladder disorders
- Bowel problems
- Bronchitis
- Chest pains
- Circulation disturbances
- Colitis
- Depression
- Eczema
- Examination nerves
- Fatigue
- Gynecological problems
- Headaches
- High blood pressure
- Indigestion
- Insomnia
- Migraine
- Muscular pain
- Negativity
- Nervous sweating
- Obesity
- Pain
- Palpitations
- Panic attacks
- Phobias
- Skin problems
- Speech disorders
- Tiredness
- Writer's cramp

How does it work?

Autogenic relaxation techniques are now known to affect involuntary conditions (such as heart rate and blood pressure) which form part of the body's response to stress. A prolonged state of stress can be harmful—it is believed to increase blood pressure and lower the immunological response, for example—and should therefore be avoided. By "switching off" the body's stress response autogenic training allows individuals to achieve a state that is conducive to healing.

History

Autogenic training was developed in the 1920s by the Berlin psychiatrist and neurologist, Dr. Johannes H. Schultz. Schultz was a student of Oskar Vogt, a Berlin neuropathologist who observed that under hypnosis his patients tended to lose some of the psychosomatic disorders that had been troubling them. Drawing on these observations, Schultz began to develop techniques designed to help people achieve deep mental and psychological relaxation at will.

Schultz was joined in his research and development of autogenic training by Dr. Wolfgang Luthe, and five textbooks resulted from their collaboration.

Treatment methods

The procedure for autogenic training requires a self-induced state of relaxation and is quite straightforward. However, the physical and emotional effects can be profound. It is therefore essential for anyone interested in exploring this type of therapy to attend a course of sessions run by a qualified therapist.

Treatment involves learning a series of mental exercises

taught to individuals or small groups over a period of eight to ten weeks. Participants learn to focus their attention inward for a few minutes and practice three or four times a day. There are three postures recommended for practicing the exercises. Exercises consist of thought repetition of standard phrases, while using passive concentration on the relevant part of the body. Autogenic training encourages the release of

THE THREE AUTOGENIC POSITIONS
a The armchair position
b The sitting position

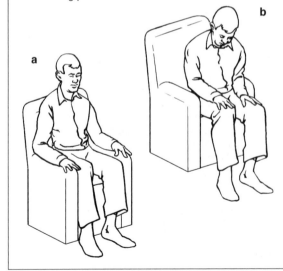

negative effects of old stress, which can show as
fleeting memories of old injuries and illnesses, etc. As
well as this, sensations relating to deep relaxation are
common: floating, warmth, sense of calm within.
Advanced techniques are also available for the
treatment of specific disorders and deep-rooted
anxieties.

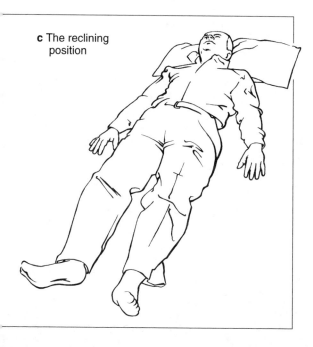

c The reclining
   position

SIX STANDARD EXERCISES

Autogenic training involves six standard exercises.
Autogenic exercises are related to the body in its
relaxed state. Each new stage focuses on a different
area. The response is entirely spontaneous — the

Areas of focus

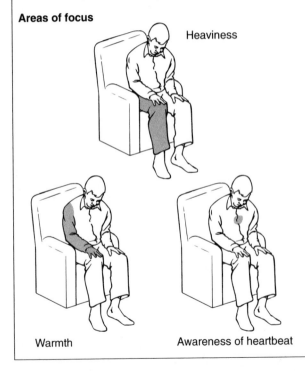

Heaviness

Warmth

Awareness of heartbeat

person adopts an attitude of passivity which allows the system to react without interference. It is not required that a "result" emerges, e.g., a heavy arm, or warm leg.

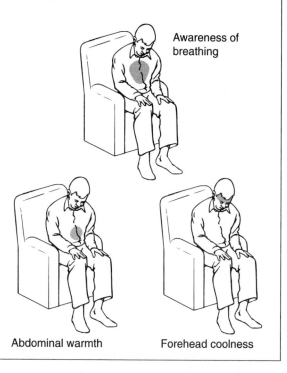

Awareness of breathing

Abdominal warmth

Forehead coolness

AUTOSUGGESTION

Definition
Also known as Couéism, this is a form of self-hypnosis.

History
Autosuggestion was developed in 1885 by Frenchman Emile Coué, who became interested in the power of the mind to heal when one of his patients was cured of a long-standing disorder by a newly-available treatment which turned out to be little more than colored water. Traveling to Nancy in the 1880s, Coué observed the work of Dr. A. A. Liebault as he treated patients using hypnotism, after which he decided that hypnotism worked not because of *hetero*-suggestion, but as the result of *auto*-suggestion. Coué argued that it was not human *will power* that enabled individuals to overcome illness, but the power of their imaginations.

Unfortunately, during the 1920s when many people began to adopt autosuggestion as a means of self-help, they repeated Coué's mantra (such as "every day, in every way, I'm getting better and better") in the hope that it would help them will themselves better. This was precisely the opposite of what Coué was trying to achieve.

Doctors criticized Couéism—they were able to accept that people might use their will to help themselves recover, or to delay the progress of illness, but they could not accept that the same was true of the human imagination.

Today the power of imagination as a healing force has been demonstrated and Couéism has been established as a viable therapy for certain individuals.

How does it work?

Therapists say that autosuggestion works by allowing the imagination to stimulate performance. If we imagine ourselves better, so the theory goes, we are likely to get better. This is achieved through the repetition of positive statements (such as "every day, in every way, I'm getting better and better").

Treatment methods

Autosuggestion is incorporated into many therapies, including autogenic training and visualization therapy. Coué advocated educating the imagination through:

1 Yoga, and the search for concentration.

2 The use of a mantra.

One of his disciples, Charles Baudouin, suggested that patients sit quietly for a few minutes in the mornings and evenings repeating their mantra until it has become a habit.

WHAT CONDITIONS IS IT USED FOR?
- Addictions
- Allergy
- Anxiety
- Asthma
- Pain
- Phobias
- Psychosomatic illness
- Tension

AYURVEDIC MEDICINE

Definition

A holistic system of traditional Indian medicine from which most Western medicine is derived.

The Veda are a collection of ancient Hindu scriptures originating between 800 and 600 B.C., one of which is the Ayurveda, the science of life.

Types

There are many branches of Ayurveda but one universally attractive characteristic is the gentle, meditative ritual of many of the treatments. The philosophical concepts of the physical medicine of Ayurveda are intertwined with religion and ritual and may vary in different geographical areas.

There are eight branches of Ayurvedic medicine:

- Aphrodisiac
- ENT
- General medicine
- Geriatrics
- Pediatrics
- Spirituality
- Surgery
- Toxicology

History

According to one of several legends, 50 sages (known as the Rishis) met one day 3000 years ago on the slopes of the Himalayas to discuss how disease could be eradicated from the world. After meditating together the Rishis acquired the divine knowledge of what became the Ayurvedic system of medicine.

The first school to teach Ayurvedic medicine was at the University of Banaras in about 500 B.C., where the Charaka Samhita was written, an encyclopedia of medicine regarded as sacred.

The Ayurvedic medical system was later augmented by the teachings of Buddha and was practiced by increasing numbers of Buddhist monks.

Western medical practices became popularized during British rule in India and many believed Ayurveda to be outdated. Ayurveda was almost completely unknown in the West, until the Maharishi Mahesh Yogi came to Europe and America in the 1960s, introducing a modernized version of this ancient art. In the 1970s an increasing interest in Eastern philosophies developed in the West and in many of the practices inherent to Ayurvedic medicine (such as massage, herbal therapy and detoxification).

In 1980 the National Congress of India decided that it was important for Ayurvedic and Western medicine to enjoy equal status and they have continued to do so.

ANCIENT CAUSES OF ILL HEALTH

In primitive times all ill-health was thought to be due to imbalances, the causes of which were thought to include:

- An ancestral spirit, for mischief or revenge
- A demon of the supernatural world
- The evil eye or evil mouth (or a person)
- The gods, to punish wrong-doings
- Sorcery practiced by an enemy
- Inauspicious planetary influences
- Personal bad karma

WHAT CONDITIONS IS IT USED FOR?
Ayurvedic practitioners claim that everyone can
benefit from Ayurvedic treatments, and that it can be
used to treat a whole range of conditions including:

- Acne
- Arthritis
- Asthma
- Diabetes
- Eczema
- Fatigue
- Gout
- Impotence
- Indigestion
- Infertility
- Irritable bowel
  syndrome
- Menstrual problems
- Migraine
- Premature ejaculation
- Psoriasis
- Rheumatism
- Stress
- Tension
- Tuberculosis
- Ulcers

How does it work?

Over the centuries, Ayurveda has been changed and
modernized, yet the essential philosophy and basic
approach to treatment survives.

Ayurveda is based on the philosophy that health is a
natural state and ill-health only occurs when the
balanced flow of intelligence from mind to body is
interrupted. Ayurveda is therefore designed not to
alleviate or cure illness but to achieve a state of health
through a variety of techniques.

Ayurveda aims to balance the life force known as
"ojas" (equivalent to the Chinese Qi and Japanese ki).
It is impossible to describe the entire Ayurvedic system
in a comprehensive manner in just a few pages. Some
of the key elements are as follows:

THE BODY IN AYURVEDIC MEDICINE

Humans are composed of five elements called Bhutas:
air, fire, earth, ether, and water. Each Bhuta corresponds
to one of the five senses and to a planet.

THE FIVE BHUTAS

Bhuta	Description	Equivalent to	Planet
Air (1)	Light	Touch	Mercury
Fire (2)	Hot; gives color	Sight	Mars
Earth (3)	Heavy; moist	Smell	Jupiter
Ether (4)	All around	Sound	Saturn
Water (5)	Flowing, wet	Taste	Venus

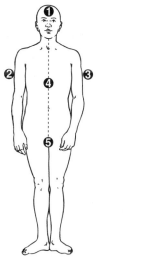

THE THREE DOSHAS

The five basic elements are converted by agni, the digestive fire, into three humors, or doshas and these influence our health and temperament. Doshas are bodily energies, collectively known as Tridoshas (see table, *below*). Vata is usually portrayed blue pitta is portrayed red, and kappa is yellow. Each dosha is related to certain parts of the body.

Elements	Dosha (humor)	Body parts
Earth + water =	kappa (phlegm)	Bronchi Lungs Nostrils Sinuses Throat
Fire + water =	pitta (digestive juices)	Duodenum Gall bladder Liver Pancreas Spleen Stomach
Air + ether =	vata (wind)	Large intestines Small intestines

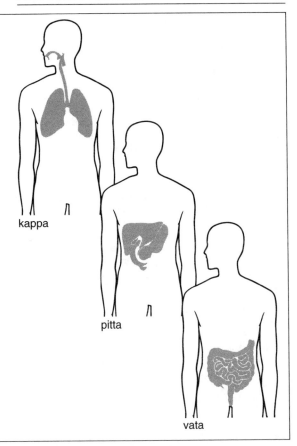

kappa

pitta

vata

TYPICAL VATA CHARACTERISTICS

Physical
- Pulse (the "snake") of 80–100 beats per minute; described as fast, narrow, cool and irregular
- Rapid metabolism
- Thin body
- Does not gain weight readily
- Thin hair
- Thin eyelashes
- Small eyes
- Dry skin
- High, thin, cracked tone of voice
- Erratic memory
- High sex drive

Personality
- Active
- Bites nails
- Changeable
- Creative
- Decisive
- Insomniac
- Quick
- Restless
- Unreliable
- Worries
- May have clairvoyant or psychic abilities
- Able to earn money quickly
- Has difficulty sustaining relationships
- Spiritual

Health problems
- Anxiety
- Depression
- Heart problems
- Irritable bowel syndrome
- Migraine
- Nervous system disorders
- Tension

TYPICAL PITTA CHARACTERISTICS

Physical
- Pulse (the "frog" is erratic at 70–80 beats per minute
- Strong metabolism
- Smooth skin
- Thin hair, prone to baldness; goes gray early
- Good appetite
- Small green, brown, or gray eyes
- Not prone to rapid weight gain
- Moderate sex drive

Personality
- Ambitious
- A leader
- Creative
- Decisive
- Highly intelligent
- Open to new ideas
- Stable

Health problems
- Digestive problems
- Gall bladder problems
- Headaches
- Liver complaints
- Skin complaints
- Ulcers

TYPICAL KAPPA CHARACTERISTICS

Physical
- Pulse (the "swan") is 60–70 beats per minute and described as slow, steady, soft, broad, regular, and warm
- Heavy bones
- Lethargic
- Often overweight
- Gains weight easily
- Thick, oily skin
- Big eyes
- Lustrous hair
- Strong nails
- Strong-smelling body odor
- Copes well with hard physical work
- Sleeps well
- Low sex drive

Personality
- Calm
- Clinging and greedy in personal relationships
- Conserves energy, strength, and money
- Finds fidelity easy
- Forgiving
- Good in business
- More materialistic than spiritual
- Ponderous
- Resistant to change
- Romantic
- Slow to absorb information
- Slow to anger
- Tolerant
- Wealthy

Health problems
- Asthma
- Bronchitis
- Circulatory disorders
- Diabetes
- Eczema
- Heart disease
- Hypertension
- Sinusitis

We are all usually made up of a combination of doshas, with one being dominant.

The body is also made up of seven tissues, or Dhatus: rasa, rakta, mansa, medas, ashti, majja, and sukra, imbalances which lead to illness.

THE SEVEN DHATUS

Dhatu	Represents	Dhatu	Represents
Rasa	Food juice	Ashti	Bones
Rakta	Blood	Majja	Marrow
Mansa	Flesh	Sukra	Semen
Medas	Fat		

DISEASE
Causes of disease

In Ayurvedic medicine disease may be caused by external factors, imbalances in the doshas, or mental imbalance.

Causes of disease include:
EXTERNAL FACTORS
       Acts of God
       Evil spirits
       Fire and accidents
       Harmful gases (environmental pollution)
       Planetary influences
       Poisons and toxins

IMBALANCES IN THE DOSHAS
(vata, pitta and kappa)

MENTAL IMBALANCE

There are also different categories of illness: accidental, mental, natural, and physical.

TYPES OF ILLNESS

Accidental	• Bites • Blows • Cuts	• Stings • Physical accidents
Mental	Arising from: • Anger • Fear • Hatred • Laziness	• Misery • Pride
Natural	• The result of aging	
Physical	• Blockages • Inflammations • Tissue degeneration • Tumors	

Treatment methods

Ayurvedic treatment begins with a complete assessment, using a variety of techniques and taking into account a larger number of factors than Western medicine.

AYURVEDIC ANALYSIS INCLUDES:

- A thorough medical check-up using Western diagnostic methods
- Ayurvedic pulse-taking questioning
- Analysis of your character (i.e. vata, pitta, or kappa)
- Analysis of your mood
- An appreciation of the weather and season

Types of treatment

Treatments usually fall into three categories:

- Dietary regimes
- Medicinal remedies (herbal and vegetable drugs).
- Practical aids (e.g. baths, breathing exercises, enemas, massage, meditation, yoga)

You may be prescribed one of many different Ayurvedic programs. A typical Panchakarma program, for example, consists of a series of procedures. First there is a week's cleansing, at home, known as the Virechana treatment. This involves taking increasing amounts of ghee (clarified butter) for four days, to loosen impurities lodged in the digestive tract. A day is spent resting before taking a dose of castor oil, which clears out the dislodged impurities.

Then, in five days spent at an Ayurvedic clinic, treatments may include: Abhyanga, a complete body massage done by two people in silence and using warm herbal oils; Netra Tarpan, a very delicate treatment of the eyes using cool liquid ghee; Swedana, a very gentle herbalized steam bath; Shirodhara, in which a warm, soothing flow of fine aromatic oil is poured onto the forehead; Pizzichilli, known as the royal treatment, because in the past it was only available to kings and queens, a lengthy massage on a specially constructed table, during which warm, herbalized oils are applied to all parts of the body; and Basti, a painless enema treatment to clean out all impurities dislodged by the other treatments.

BACH™ FLOWER ESSENCES

Definition

Named after their originator, English physician Dr. Edward Bach, these are 38 preparations made from wild flowers and plants, used in a system of treatment based on homeopathic principles, and designed for home use.

Types

There are 38 different different "essences" (known in

THE 38 BACH™ FLOWER ESSENCES

Essence (Plant)	Latin name
1 Agrimony	*Agrimonia eupatoria*
2 Aspen	*Populus tremula*
3 Beech	*Fagus sylvatica*
4 Centaury	*Centaurium umbellatum*
5 Cerato	*Ceratostigma willmottianum*
6 Cherry Plum	*Prunus cerasifera*
7 Chestnut Bud	*Aesculus hippocastanum*
8 Chicory	*Cichorium intybus*
9 Clematis	*Clematis vitalba*
10 Crab Apple	*Malus pumila*
11 Elm	*Ulmus procera*
12 Gentian	*Gentiana amarella*
13 Gorse	*Ulex europaeus*
14 Heather	*Calluna vulgaris*
15 Holly	*Ilex aquifolium*
16 Honeysuckle	*Lonicera caprifolium*
17 Hornbeam	*Carpinus betulus*
18 Impatiens	*Impatiens glandulifera*
19 Larch	*Larix decidua*

UK as "remedies"), each named after a different wild
flower or plant. In addition to these, Rescue Remedy is
designed "to comfort and reassure," and is a
combination of Cherry Plum, Clematis, Impatiens,
Rock Rose and Star of Bethlehem.
Equipment
None needed. Bach™ Flower Essences are usually
available in health food stores and come ready made in
bottles fitted with pippettes so a few drops can be
diluted in spring water.

Essence (Plant)	Latin name
20 Mimulus	*Mimulus guttatus*
21 Mustard	*Sinapis arvensis*
22 Oak	*Quercus robur*
23 Olive	*Olea europaea*
24 Pine	*Pinus sylvestris*
25 Red Chestnut	*Aesculus carnea*
26 Rock Rose	*Helianthemum nummularium*
27 Rock Water	Natural spring water
28 Scleranthus	*Scleranthus anuus*
29 Star of Bethlehem	*Ornithogalum umbellatum*
30 Sweet Chestnut	*Castanea sativa*
31 Vervain	*Verbena officinalis*
32 Vine	*Vitis vinifera*
33 Walnut	*Juglans regia*
34 Water Violet	*Hottonia palustris*
35 White Chestnut	*Aesculus hippocastanum*
36 Wild Oat	*Bromus ramosus*
37 Wild Rose	*Rosa canina*
38 Willow	*Salix vitellina*

History

Trained in orthodox medicine, Dr. Bach was a bacteriologist at the University College Hospital in London in 1915 when he first came across the practice of homeopathy. After working at the London Homeopathic Hospital he ran a private practice combining orthodox medicine and homeopathy, then in 1930 retired to Wales to study flowering herbs and trees. Bach began selecting plants that he intuitively judged had a curative effect on the seven main mental attitudes that he observed to be synchronous with illness (see box, *below*). In common with homeopathic doctors, he treated the person not the disease.

From his observations of people, Bach concluded that mental attitudes, such as fear, anxiety, mistrust or possessiveness, provide excellent environments for the invasion of illness. When the patient's outlook became

---

WHAT CONDITIONS IS IT USED FOR?

Believed to be safe for babies, children, and animals, users say the flower remedies can be taken by anyone. Treatments are used to help counter the effects of a particular mental attitude.

According to Dr. Bach, the seven main mental attitudes are:

1 Fear
2 Uncertainty and indecision
3 Loneliness
4 Insufficient interest in present circumstances
5 Over-sensitivity to ideas and influences
6 Despondency or despair
7 Over-care for the welfare of others

more positive—through the use of the flower remedies—the illness would leave, because it could no longer survive.

Even Bach recognized that damage already done by an illness might not be reversible, but he was sure that much sickness should be avoided by changing mental attitudes. Thus his remedies were also used to prevent disease and to reduce the effects of unavoidable conditions.

Dr. Bach published details of the first flower remedies in 1933, calling them the Twelve Healers. Before he died in 1936 he had made a collection of 38 remedies.

How does it work?

Some users argue that Bach™ Flower Essences leave a unique pattern in the water which then affects the body. However, nobody knows how they work because, when analyzed, the preparations are shown to contain only spring water and alcohol. It has been suggested that current scientific methods are not yet sophisticated enough to measure the healing properties of these essences.

> *"Disease is in essence the result of conflict between soul and mind—so long as our souls and personalities are in harmony all is joy and peace, happiness and health. It is when our personalities are led astray from the path laid down by the soul, either by our own worldly desires or by the persuasion of others, that a conflict arises."*
>
> Dr. Edward Bach

HOW THE REMEDIES (OR ESSENCES) ARE MADE

Dr. Bach originally collected warm, morning dew from the flowers or fruit of plants but because of the laborious nature of this method of collection, others are now used:

1 Flowers are placed in a glass bowl of pure spring water and stood in the sun for three hours. Or, parts of the plant are boiled in spring water for half an hour.
2 The water from either

TREATMENT METHODS
Bach™ Flower Essences are designed for use at home, in conjunction with orthodox medical treatment.
1 First identify your mental and emotional state.
2 Select the most appropriate essence, using the information provided on the next six pages. You can choose up to seven essences at the same time.
3 Once you have selected the appropriate essence or essences, add two drops to each

method is then mixed 50/50 with brandy to preserve it. This is known as mother tincture.

3 The mother tincture preparation is further diluted with brandy to form a basic stock bottle. It is these basic stock bottles that are available in some health food stores.

from a basic stock bottle (**a**) to a 30ml (1 oz) dropper bottle nearly full of spring water (**b**).

4 From the prepared treatment bottle, take four drops at least four times a day, either straight on the tongue or in a little water.

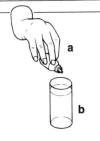

ESSENCES AND CONDITIONS THEY MAY BE USED TO TREAT

Essence	Condition
Agrimony	Mental torment behind a brave face
Aspen	Fears and worries of unknown origin
Beech	Intolerance
Centaury	Subservience
	Being weak-willed
Cerato	Needing advice and confirmation from others
Cherry Plum	Fear of the mind giving way
Chestnut Bud	Failure to learn from past mistakes
Chicory	Being selfishly possessive
Clematis	Dreaminess
	Lack of interest in the present
Crab Apple	Self-hatred
	Feeling unclean
Elm	Overwhelmed by responsibility
Gentian	Despondency
	Discouragement
Gorse	Hopelessness and despair
Heather	Self-centered
	Self-concern
Holly	Envy
	Hatred
	Jealousy
Honeysuckle	Living in the past
Hornbeam	"Monday morning" feeling

Essence	Condition
Impatiens	Impatience
Larch	Lack of confidence
Mimulus	Fear of known things
Mustard	Gloominess without origin
Oak	Exhausted but struggling on
Olive	Lack of energy
Pine	Guilt
	Self-reproach
Red Chestnut	Fear or over-concern for others
Rock Rose	Terror
Rock Water	Self-denial
	Self-repression
Scleranthus	Indecision
Star of Bethlehem	Aftereffects of shock
Sweet Chestnut	Extreme mental anguish
Vervain	Over-enthusiasm
Vine	Dominance
Walnut	Protection from change and outside influences
Water Violet	Aloofness
	Pride
White Chestnut	Mental arguments
	Unwanted thoughts
Wild Oat	Uncertainty as to the correct path in life
Wild Rose	Apathy
	Resignation
Willow	Resentment

CONDITIONS AND SUITABLE ESSENCES

Condition	Suitable essence
FEAR	
Fears and worries of unknown origin	Aspen
Fear of known things	Mimulus
Fear of the mind giving way	Cherry Plum
Fear or over-concern for others	Red Chestnut
Terror	Rock Rose
UNCERTAINTY AND INDECISION	
Despondency	Gentian
Discouragement	Gentian
Hopelessness and despair	Gorse
Indecision	Scleranthus
Monday morning feeling	Hornbeam
Needing advice and confirmation from others	Cerato
Uncertainty as to correct path in life	Wild Oat

Condition	Suitable essence
LONELINESS	
Aloofness	Water Violet
Impatience	Impatiens
Pride	Water Violet
Self-centered	Heather
Self-concern	Heather
INSUFFICIENT INTEREST IN PRESENT CIRCUMSTANCES	
Apathy	Wild Rose
Dreaminess	Clematis
Gloominess without origin	Mustard
Failure to learn from past mistakes	Chestnut Bud
Lacking energy	Olive
Lack of interest in present	Clematis
Living in the past	Honeysuckle
Mental arguments	White Chestnut
Resignation	Wild Rose
Unwanted thoughts	White Chestnut

CONDITIONS AND SUITABLE ESSENCES (continued)

Condition	Suitable essence
OVER-SENSITIVITY TO IDEAS AND INFLUENCES	
Envy	Holly
Hatred	Holly
Jealousy	Holly
Mental torment behind a brave face	Agrimony
Protection from change and outside influences	Walnut
Subservience	Centaury
Weak-willed	Centaury
DESPONDENCY OR DESPAIR	
Aftereffects of shock	Star of Bethlehem
Exhausted by struggling on	Oak
Guilt	Pine
Extreme mental anguish	Sweet Chestnut
Lack of confidence	Larch
Overwhelmed by responsibility	Elm

Condition	Suitable essence
DESPONDENCY OR DESPAIR	
Resentment	Willow
Self-hatred	Crab Apple
Self-reproach	Pine
Sense of uncleanliness	Crab Apple
OVER-CARE FOR THE WELFARE OF OTHERS	
Domineering	Vine
Inflexible	Vine, Rose Water, Vervain
Intolerance	Beech
Over-enthusiasm	Vervain
Selfishly possessive	Chicory
Self-denial	Rock Water
Self-repression	Rock Water

BATES METHOD

Definition
A re-educational practice designed to improve eyesight,
developed by Dr. William H. Bates.

History
Dr. William H. Bates was a prominent New York eye
specialist who taught in the Post Graduate Medical
School when the current theory was that vision defects
were genetically determined and were therefore
irreversible. Having examined thousands of eyes, Bates
disagreed with this view and argued that eyesight could
be improved by the method of re-education which he
developed, between 1900 and 1931.

How does it work?
Bates argued that poor vision was caused by strain and
would be improved by relaxation.

What conditions is it used for? The Bates method is
suitable for a variety of eye problems (see box, *below*).

Treatment methods
There are several basic exercises which form part of the
Bates method (see box, *right*).

CONDITIONS HELPED BY THE BATES METHOD

Condition	Description
Myopia	Difficulty with distant vision
Hypermetropia	Difficulty with near and far vision
Astigmatism	Distorted vision
Strabismus	Squinting
Presbyopia	Near-sight difficulties in old age

BATES TREATMENT METHODS

Method	Description
Blinking	This clarifies vision. The normal eye blinks frequently and gently, so the habit of blinking is encouraged.
Sunning	Two or three minutes spent lying in the sun with eyes closed and head slowly moving from side to side. never look directly at he sun, nor lie with head still. After, spend some time palming.
Palming (**a**)	Placing the palms over the closed eyes to exclude all light, without pressure, or an eye-mask can be used. This rests and relaxes the eyes.

a

continued

BATES TREATMENT METHODS (continued)

Method	Description
Swinging (**a**)	To counteract staring, which puts enormous strain on the eyes. Swinging the whole body by partly rotating from side to side is the most effective. The aim is to allow the eyes to remain still and the focus to relax and sweep across the scene without stopping and staring.
Splashing (**b**)	Splash the eyes with water at least twenty times in the mornings and evenings.

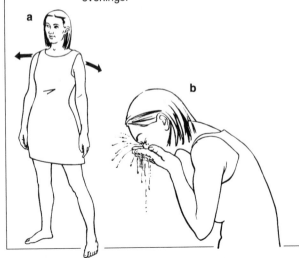

Method	Description
Imagination	Bates encouraged all his patients to practice using their imagination and their memory, since impairment of either adds imperfections to the visual image.
Near and far focusing (**c**)	Hold two pencils or similar objects at a certain distance from your face. Focus on one pencil and then blink before focusing on the other pencil. This helps to rest the eyes.
Shifting (**d**)	When looking at an object try to avoid staring at it. Instead, shift your gaze constantly from one side of the object to the other. The smaller the shift, the better.

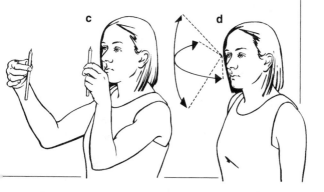

BEHAVIOR THERAPY

Definition
Conditioning patients in order to rid them of neurotic
symptoms.

History
Russian scientist Ivan Pavlov trained dogs to salivate at
the sound of a bell, a process he called conditioning.
Later, American J.B. Watson developed similar ideas
which became known as behaviorism. American
psychologist B. F. Skinner developed the theory of
reinforcement in which rewards were used to increase
the likelihood of a behavior being repeated.

Types
There are many different forms of behavior therapy,
including aversion therapy (often used with patients
addicted to alcohol or cigarettes) during which patients
are taught to associate an undesirable habit or behavior
with an unpleasant experience.

How does it work?
Behavior therapists use rewards and punishments to
help people overcome unreasonable fears, harmful or

WHAT CONDITIONS IS IT USED FOR?

- Alcoholism
- Bedwetting
- Fears
- Obsessive compulsive
  behavior
- Phobias
- Problems with social
  adjustment (exposure,
  theft, violence)
- Smoking

antisocial behavior. They argue that bad behavior is often learned as a child and that it can be unlearned. Therapists say that aversion therapy works because patients start to link unpleasant experiences with undesirable behavior and this eventually leads them to limit the extent to which they engage in undesirable behavior. For example, alcoholics may be given a drug which makes them sick when they drink alcohol. After a while, they associate drinking alcohol with being sick—even when the drug has been withdrawn—and are therefore less likely to drink alcohol.

Treatment methods

After discussing your condition with a therapist you will begin a course in behavior retraining. There are many different techniques, for example:

- **Aversion therap**y may be used if you have an addiction to cigarettes or alcohol.
- **Flooding** (also called forced exposure). A form of shock treatment in which patients are confronted with their worst fear. They are naturally terrified but the fear gradually subsides and patients learn that they are not going to come to any harm.
- **Systematic desensitization** is often used for the treatment of phobias and fears. Patients imagine an increasingly frightening situation while remaining in a calm, relaxed state. The therapist then encourages patients to experience the real situation (for example, being in a room with a spider), while helping patients to remain relaxed. Eventually, patients learn to remain relaxed while confronting the source of their fear.

BIOCHEMICS

Definition
A system of therapy which aims to restore and maintain the body's natural mineral salts.

Types
There are an accepted 12 tissue salts and 18 combination salts. Experts argue that there are a further 30 essential salts used in the body, or even more.

The 12 tissue salts are used in HOMEOPATHY but in a different way from biochemics.

Equipment
Other than the salts, no equipment is required.

How does it work?
Tissue salts exist in the body and are essential to its well-being. Biochemics believes that lack of a particular salt results in specific symptoms. Once the deficiency has been determined, it can be remedied by taking the appropriate salt or combination of salts.

What conditions is it used for?
Combination salts may be used to treat specific disorders (see table, *right*), or individual salts may be used (see tables on the next four pages).

History
The use of tissue salts was devised in the 1870s by German doctor and chemist Dr. Wilhelm Heinrich Schuessler. Schuessler believed that every disease state could be attacked by the appropriate use of tissue salt and began investigating which salt was essential to the maintenance of which life process.

Treatment methods

Biochemic tissue salts are available to the public and may be taken at home provided instructions are followed carefully.

COMBINATION BIOCHEMIC TISSUE SALTS

Labelled A to S, these are a combination of between three and five salts which are together thought to be beneficial for specific ailments.

Combination	Used for
A	Neuralgia, neuritis, sciatica
B	Convalescence, debility, nervous exhaustion
C	Acidity, dyspepsia, heartburn
D	Minor skin ailments
E	Colic, flatulence, indigestion
F	Headache, migraine
G	Backache, lumbago, piles
H	Hay fever
I	Fibrositis, muscular pain
J	Chest, colds, coughs
K	Brittle nails, hair loss
L	Varicose veins
M	Rheumatic conditions
N	Menstrual pain
P	Aching feet and legs
Q	Catarrh, sinus problems
R	Infants' teething pains
S	Biliousness, stomach upsets

TWELVE TISSUE SALTS

Tissue salt	Common name
1 CALC.FLUOR.	Calcium fluoride
2 CALC.PHOS.	Calcium phosphate
3 CALC.SULF.	Calcium sulfate
4 FERR.PHOS.	Iron phosphate
5 KALI.MUR.	Potassium chloride
6 KALI.PHOS.	Potassium phosphate

Function	Uses	
Maintains elasticity of tissues	Bad circulation Cold sores Piles Stretch marks	Tooth enamel Varicose veins
Essential for the formation of bones, teeth, and gastric juices	Chilblains Indigestion Teething	
Purifies the blood	Acne Catarrh Pimples	Sores Wounds
Essential for oxygenation of the blood	Colds Congestion Coughs Fevers	Rheumatism Skin inflammations
Keeps the blood in good condition	Asthma Bronchitis Catarrh Chickenpox	Colds Coughs Measles Tonsillitis
A nutrient essential to nerves	Depression Headaches Indigestion Sleep loss	Stress Worry

TWELVE TISSUE SALTS (continued)

Tissue salt	Common name
7 KALI.SULF.	Potassium sulfate
8 MAG.PHOS.	Magnesium phosphate
9 NAT.MUR.	Sodium chloride
10 NAT.PHOS.	Sodium phosphate
11 NAT.SULF.	Sodium sulfate
12 SILICA	Silicic oxide

Function	Uses	
Oxygenates tissue cells	Catarrh Loss of hair Poor nails Skin complaints	Stuffiness
The nerve stabilizer	Cramp Hiccups Menstrual pains Neuralgia	Sciatica Spasms

Distributor of water	Constipation
	Drowsiness
	Muscular
	  weakness
		Loss of taste
		  or smell
		Tears

Acid neutralizer	Blood acidity Fibrositis Gastric problems Heartburn	Lumbago Rheumatism

Eliminator of excess water	Biliousness
	Colic
	Digestive
	  problems
		Headache
		Influenza
		Liver
		  problems

Conditioner, cleanser and stimulator	Body odor Boils Brittle nails	Dull hair Sties

BIOENERGETICS THERAPY

Definition
Helping people to change habitual postures and body movements in order to unblock the body's energy and improve physical and emotional health.

History
The concept of an energy form that permeates both the body and mind is central to many Eastern therapies (such as acupuncture and yoga). Sigmund Freud developed the concept of the libido, or psychic energy, and one of his colleagues, Wilhelm Reich, later renamed this "orgone." Reich believed orgone to be sexual energy (see ORGONE THERAPY) and argued that the repression of emotions and sexual instincts could result in rigid patterns of behavior (character armor) and the tightening of certain muscles (body armor), both of which were caused by blockages to the body's energy. Reich believed ill-health would result if energy blockages were allowed to remain untreated.

WHAT CONDITIONS IS IT USED FOR?

Bioenergetics is used as a means of personal growth rather than as a form of therapy designed to treat specific ailments. It may therefore be useful for:
- People who want to have "more energy."
- People who suffer from a poor self-image.
- People who wish to increase general body awareness.

One of Reich's pupils, American Dr. Alexander Lowen
rejected the theory of orgone but accepted that there
was a fundamental form of energy in the human body.
He called this "bioenergy," and developed the theory of
bioenergetics in the 1960s which is now used by many
psychotherapists. Lowen emphasized three areas of
importance: breathing, grounding, and character
structure (see box, *below*).

Norwegian therapist Gerda Boyesen developed the
School of Biodynamic Psychology in which body
armor is broken down using special massage
techniques.

LOWEN'S AREAS OF IMPORTANCE	
Breathing	By analyzing a person's breathing pattern it is possible to identify defensive blockages deriving from muscular tension. Strong emotions often result in unnatural breathing patterns such as hyperventilation.
Grounding	It is important for people to become aware of their dependency on others. How we stand (or "ground") reveals our emotional security.
Character structure	There are five basic character types, each with a muscular pattern which provides insight into our emotional behavior (see box on next page). Most of us demonstrate aspects of each, rather than one particular type.

LOWEN'S FIVE CHARACTER TYPES

Masochistic   Muscular pattern reveals tension
               resulting from blocked feelings of
               rights and needs.

Oral   Muscular pattern reveals a fear of
               abandonment or isolation.

Psychopathic   Muscular pattern reveals holding up
               against the fear of failure.

Rigid   Muscular pattern reveals a holding
               back against emotions.

Schizoid   Muscular pattern reveals that the
               body is being held together out of
               fear of it falling to pieces.

How does it work?

Bioenergetics therapists believe that there is a form of
energy (sometimes referred to as *Qi*, the life force,
prana, etc,) interacting between body and mind. In
response to psychological problems we develop
"character armoring," habitual postures and body
movements resulting in muscular tension and the
suppression of emotions. By learning to "unblock" this
armoring, therapists believe the body is able to function
more naturally and emotions are released.

Treatment methods

Different techniques are used to help people become
aware of their habitual body patterns. For example,
therapists place a patient's breathing under stress,

perhaps by using breathing' stool (**a**) or bioenergetics back stretching (**b**) in order to help the patient become aware of his or her breathing pattern.

Exercises may be used to help people explore different ways of using their feet and to explore how they might ground themselves differently.

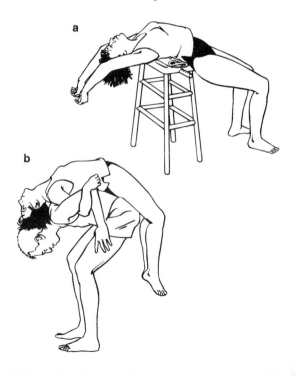

BIOFEEDBACK

Definition

Learning to control "involuntary" body functions (such as heart rate and blood pressure) using information made available by special monitoring equipment. Biofeedback is relevant to techniques used in RELAXATION THERAPIES and MEDITATION.

Equipment

A variety of equipment is used and includes:

- A hand-held temperature meter.
- Electrodes. These may be attached to the palms of the hands to record electrical activity on the surface of the skin.
- An electroencephalogram (EEG) which records brain-wave frequencies.
- An electromyograph (EMG) which measures muscle tension.
- The "mind mirror." This shows what is happening on both sides of the brain.

Other equipment is used to measure changes in blood pressure and in visceral responses (such as acid secretion in the digestive system).

Instruments record bodily changes in a variety of ways. For example:

- as the movement of a needle on a chart
- as a pattern of electrical "waves"
- as changes in color
- as clicking noises
- as flashes of light
- as images of brain activity

WHAT CONDITIONS IS IT USED FOR?
- Addiction to eating, drinking, and smoking
- Anxiety
- Epilepsy
- Headaches
- Heart irregularities
- High blood pressure
- Insomnia
- Stammering

How does it work?

It was thought until quite recently that certain bodily functions (such as temperature, blood pressure, and heart rate) were involuntary and were regulated by the autonomic nervous system. It was believed that temporary changes in these systems may be brought about by fluctuations in emotional states, for example, but that it was not possible to voluntarily alter one's blood pressure. Biofeedback has shown that these functions can be brought under voluntary control and that people can learn how to do this. In order to effectively control certain bodily responses it is important to be aware of what those responses are doing, and that is why monitoring equipment is used. Using the information received from the equipment, individuals can make changes in the bodily functions being monitored. For example, tension increases perspiration, and this in turn affects the electrical conductivity of skin, which can be monitored. By trying to reduce the signal received from the skin sensors (whether in the form of a needle on a chart or a sound or flashing light), individuals learn to reduce the electrical conductivity of the skin and in doing so reduce muscle tension.

Another method used to bring about bodily changes is to record a person's brain-wave patterns and to try and alter these patterns. Because different patterns are associated with different physiological conditions, changing the brain-wave pattern results in physiological changes. For example, beta waves are associated with arousal, alpha waves are associated with feelings of relaxation and well-being, and delta waves are associated with deep sleep or meditative states.

History
About a century ago, research into hypnosis revealed that emotional changes were accompanied by physiological reactions. French neurologist Charles Féré showed that variations in mood were accompanied

---

DETECTING BRAIN WAVES
1 Electrical signals ripple across the brain as millions of brain cells fire repeatedly.
2 Electrodes at intervals along the head reveal a set of electrical brain-wave traces.

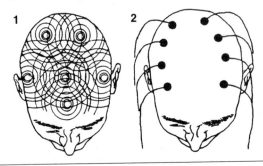

by changes in the electrical resistance of the skin. In the
1930s, German scientist Hans Berger reported that by
attaching electrodes to the scalp it was possible to
record electrical signals of different wavelengths.
Neuropsychiatrist Joe Kamiya later proposed that if
physical states were related to brain-wave activity,
perhaps it was possible to alter the physical state by
learning how to achieve a particular wavelength. In his
experiments, Kamiya showed that it was possible for
people to shift from one wavelength to another.
In India in 1970, television cameras filmed a man
surviving for more than five hours in a sealed box
where an ordinary person would have suffocated in that
time. Forty-six-year-old Ramanand Yogi was a Hindu

3 One trace may combine waves of several
frequencies.

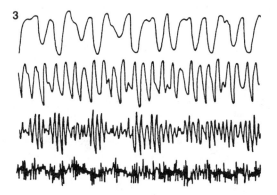

who practiced yoga. Instruments monitoring Yogi's breathing in the box showed that he had little more than half the calculated minimum amount of oxygen required to keep him alive — yet further evidence that individuals were able to voluntarily control "involuntary" bodily functions.

In his experiments with rats, Professor Neal Miller at the Rockefeller University, New York, showed that these animals could learn how to control what were thought to be involuntary bodily functions.

Elmer and Alyce Green of the Menninger Foundation combined AUTOGENIC TRAINING with Kamiya's technique of biofeedback and demonstrated how people, too, could learn to alter functions (such as raising the temperature of their fingertips), especially where they were provided with information about what these functions were doing.

Harvard professor Herbert Benson showed that patients with high blood pressure could learn to reduce it.

Many other researchers have since added information regarding biofeedback and we now know that people can learn to control certain bodily functions given the right training.

Treatment methods

A course in biofeedback training is usually taught to individuals on a one-to-one basis or to small groups. Using a selection of the equipment mentioned earlier, clients are taught how to distinguish between being passive and being truly relaxed, and by observing the information provided by the monitoring devices, learn how to bring about bodily changes.

The man shown here is attempting to alter the way his body normally works by concentrating on the readings given by various instruments measuring brain waves, blood pressure, etc.

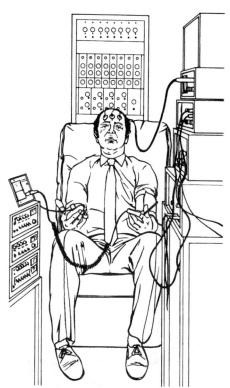

BIORHYTHM DIAGNOSIS

Definition
Using three human energy cycles—physical, emotional, and intellectual, collectively known as biorhythm—to predict the times of high and low energy.

History
Dr. H. Swoboda and Dr. W. Fliess in Vienna and Berlin respectively, developed the theory of biorhythm.

How does it work?
Beginning at birth, our emotional, physical, and mental activities follow cycles of slightly different length. These can be printed out on a graph and indicate days of high and low energy and times when we are most vulnerable, say, to accidents. Using an on-going biorhythm chart, problems can be avoided by taking advantage of high-energy periods and resting during low-energy periods.

Biorhythm charts do not determine what will happen; they only indicate your probable disposition and can be useful when planning ahead.

The cycles
The creation and discharge of energy by living things is a fundamental of biological theory. Early this century three human energy cycles were observed, lasting 23, 28, and 33 days. These were named the physical, emotional, and intellectual cycles and are known collectively as biorhythm.

A biorhythm cycle can be shown graphically as a wavy line called a sine curve. Starting from the baseline on the day of birth, the wave represents the energy available for physical, emotional or intellectual activities. In the first part of the cycle, available energy rises to a peak; then it falls below the baseline to a trough. As energy is replenished it rises again to the baseline to complete the cycle.

Positive and negative periods

A positive period occurs when the cycle is above the baseline; this is favorable for inspiration and high energy activities. The negative energy period occurs when the cycle is below the baseline; this time is favorable for slower and more pedantic activities.

A triple critical day occurs when all three cycles cross, even if they are not in the same phase. On these days, which happen once a year, prudence is the best policy when planning demanding activities.

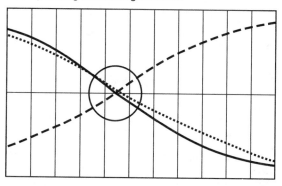

SECTIONS FROM A BIORHYTHM CHART

1 Physical cycle
Length 23 days
Peak day   6th
Trough day   17th
Critical days   11th, 23rd

Affects a broad range of physical factors such as
fitness, coordination, speed, adaptability, resistance
to disease, healing, and all basic body functions.

2 Emotional cycle
Length 28 days
Peak day   7th
Trough day   21st
Critical days   14th, 28th

Affects emotional factors such as perceptions,
attitudes, prejudices, sensitivity, moods, and general
mental health.

3 Intellectual cycle
Length 33 days
Peak day   8th
Trough day   24th
Critical days   16th, 33rd

Affects intellectual abilities such as memory,
alertness, learning, generation of ideas, and the
analytical function of the mind.

Physical cycle: 23 days

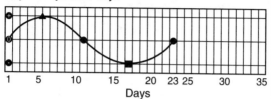

Days

Emotional cycle: 28 days

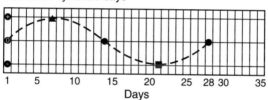

Days

Intellectual cycle: 33 days

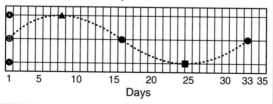

Days

BREATHING THERAPY

This section deals with a method of breathing designed
to improve health and well-being. Such methods are
often used as part of relaxation therapy.

How we breathe

Lungs are operated by a muscular sheet called a
diaphragm and by muscles that move the ribs in and
out. To breathe in, the ribs move up and out and this
expands the chest cavity, drawing air into the lungs.
When we feel stressed or anxious, many of us breathe
quickly, taking small, shallow breaths in and out
through the mouth. The diaphragm is not pulled all the
way down and air is drawn into the top of the lungs
only (**1**). What we should be doing, say advocates of
breathing therapy, is taking slow, deep breaths, in and
out through the nose, pulling the diaphragm down and
fully inflating the lungs with oxygen (**2**).

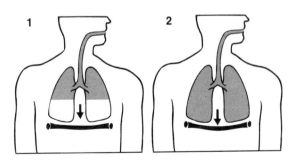

How does it work?

Advocates claim that correct breathing helps to keep body tissues healthy, charges the body with energy, and results in sharpened mental ability. Many of the benefits of correct breathing are shown in the box (*below*).

BENEFITS OF PROPER BREATHING

- Breathing through the nose (instead of the mouth) filters the air, helping to trap foreign particles. It also warms and moistens the air before it reaches the lungs.
- Proper breathing necessitates the use not only of the diaphragm, but of many muscles of the chest and back. Shallow breaths use these muscles less, which are consequently weakened.
- Deep breathing has a massaging effect on internal organs such as the bladder, intestines, stomach, and kidneys as the diaphragm is pulled all the way down.
- Deep breathing forces air into the bottom of the lungs where blood supplies are oxygenated. Shallow breathing allows air to be drawn into the top of the lungs where less blood is oxygenated.
- Breathing quiets the sympathetic nervous system, relieving stress.
- Some people believe that different parts of the brain are stimulated when you breathe through each nostril separately: breathing through the left nostril is thought to enhance passive experiences; breathing through the right nostril helps the brain respond to active situations.

CHAKRA THERAPY

Definition
The use of gemstones to bring about positive changes
in energy flow within and between chakras (energy
centers inherent to yogic philosophy).

History
The philosophies inherent to yoga were published in
India beginning in 3000 B.C. The use of gemstones to
"heal" chakras is a more modern invention.

Chakra	Indian name	Associated endocrine gland	Associated colors
Crown (1)	Sahasrara	Pituitary	White Violet
Brow (2)	Ajna	Pineal	Indigo Violet
Throat (3)	Vishudda	Thyroid	Blue
Heart (4)	Anahata	Thymus	Green Yellow
Solar plexus (5)	Manipuraka	Adrenal	Yellow Green
Spleen (6)	Swadhisthana	Pancreas	Orange
Base (7)	Muladhara	Gonads	Red

How does it work?

According to Hindu philosophy, the cosmos consists of seven ascending planes, each of which has a focus in the body (known as a chakra). Each chakra is believed to be associated with a different endocrine gland and a different color (see table, *below left*). Some people believe that trauma of any kind can block the flow of energy in chakras and that gemstones can be used to re-balance energy flows by placing them on chakra points.

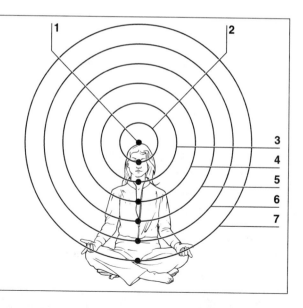

Treatment methods

These vary between practitioners. Some place
gemstones directly onto the chakra, others circle the
chakra with the stone they believe to be most

Chakra	Indian name	Suggested gemstone
1 Crown	Sahasrara	Clear quartz
2 Brow	Ajna	Amethyst
3 Throat	Vishudda	Aquamarine
4 Heart	Anahata	Citrine
5 Solar plexus	Manipuraka	Aventurine
6 Spleen	Swadhisthana	Carnelian
7 Base	Muladhara	Garnet

appropriate for healing purposes. Listed here are the suggestions of *one* practitioner for the kinds of gemstones suitable for each of the chakras.

Used to treat	
Intestinal problems Stomach problems	
Headaches Injuries	Insomnia Tension
Coughs Eyesight problems Fluid retention	Thymus function
Eliminates toxins	
Improves complexion Improves muscle tissue Lowers cholesterol	Stimulates metabolism
Improves blood quality Improves food assimilation Improves appetite	
Encourages hormonal balance Speeds the healing of wounds Stabilizes circulation	

CHINESE MEDICINE

Some of the therapies and methods described in this book are oriental in nature and may be practiced by therapists whose fundamental philosophies are the same. Although it is impossible to adequately explain the entire philosophy and processes of Chinese medicine in just a few pages, this section provides the reader with some basic information as to the underlying principles followed by practitioners of therapies such as acupuncture, auricular therapy, Chinese herbal medicine, and shiatsu.

A Chinese view of the the body

Chinese medical practitioners categorize all phenomena according to whether they are Yin or Yang, represented by this black and white symbol. The symbol indicates that situations are always changing and the small dots show that there is some Yin within Yang, and some Yang within Yin. Yin and Yang are qualities of energy that control a person's health, and ill-health is therefore the result of an energy imbalance.

THE QUALITIES OF YIN AND YANG

Yin qualities include:
- Cold
- Passivity
- Stillness
- Darkness
- Internal
- Downward
- Decrease
- Inwardness

Yang qualities include:
- Heat
- Aggression
- Movement
- Light
- External
- Upward
- Increase
- Outwardness

In addition to Yin and Yang, the human body is governed by five elements: wood, metal, water, fire, and earth.

Element	Contribution	Direction
Fire	Activity; warmth	Upward
Earth	Nourishment; stability	Center
Metal	Clarity and elimination	
Water	Moistens; softens	Downward
Wood	Flexibility; growth	

The interactions between the natural forces (Yin and Yang and all five elements) create a vital life energy known as Qi (also spelled ki in Japanese). Qi is closely related to the Indian *prana*, the Greek *pneuma* and the Latin *spiritus vitalis*. Qi flows around the body via meridians, or energy lines.

The Chinese approach to illness

Practitioners of Chinese medicine are primarily concerned with the whole person, rather than with a particular part of the body, symptom, or disease. Health is maintained when Qi is balanced, whereas illness results when it is imbalanced. In order to re-establish harmony, practitioners need to assess the nature of the imbalance by deciding whether there is too much of a Yin or a Yang quality, or of one of the five elements. This is achieved by clinical examination.

Importance of meridians

Meridians carry the vital life energy, Qi. As the line of a meridian has a lowered electrical impedance (a property of nerves) it was once speculated that they were nerve pathways, although this is now known to be false.

There are twelve main meridians, each one controlling a specific organ. Just as all phenomena are categorized Yin or Yang, so too are the meridians. Yin meridians run upward from the toes; yang meridians run downward from the head to the toes.

Two of the organs listed in traditional Chinese medicine are not recognized in Western medicine: the san jias (or triple burner, which controls heat and water) and the xin bas (sometimes known as the pericardium).

There are two meridians placed centrally on the body,
one down the front and one down the back. These are
the conception vessel (Yin) which begins near the anus
and flows centrally up the front of the body to the
mouth, and the governor vessel (Yang) which begins
near the anus and flows centrally up the back, over the
head to the mouth.

Meridian	Yin	Yang	Element
Heart	*		Fire
Small intestine		x	Fire
Bladder		x	Water
Kidney	*		Water
Pericardium	*		Fire
Triple burner		x	Fire
Gall bladder		x	Wood
Liver	*		Wood
Lungs	*		Metal
Large intestine		x	Metal
Stomach		x	Earth
Spleen	*		Earth

THE TWELVE MERIDIANS

Heart meridian

Small intestine meridian

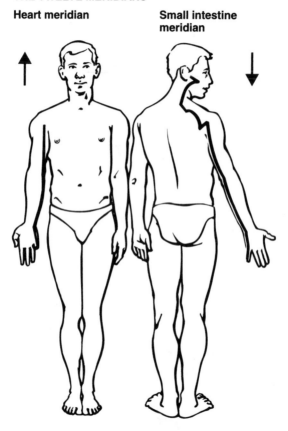

Bladder meridian **Kidney meridian**

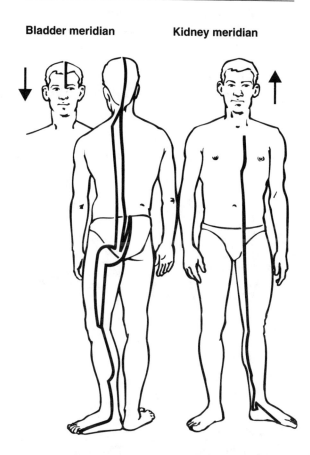

THE TWELVE MERIDIANS (continued)

Pericardium meridian   **Triple warmer meridian**

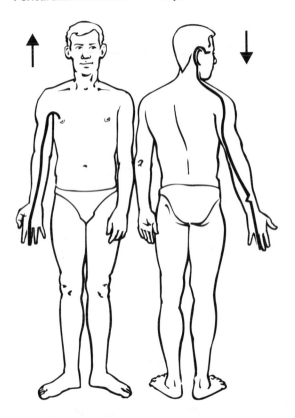

Gall bladder meridian   **Liver meridian**

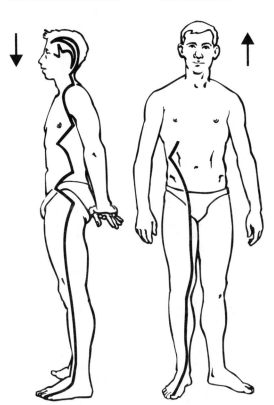

THE TWELVE MERIDIANS (continued)

Lung meridian

Large intestine meridian

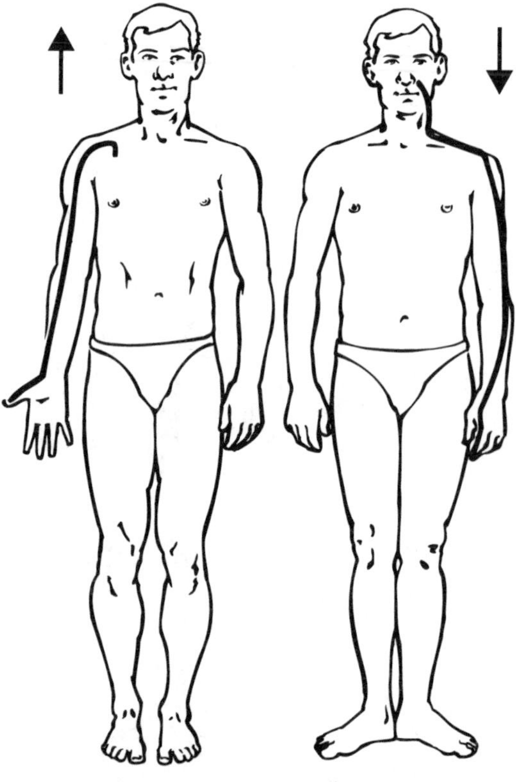

Stomach meridian

Spleen meridian

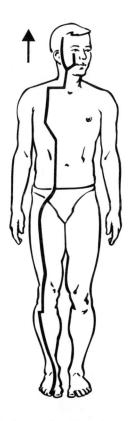
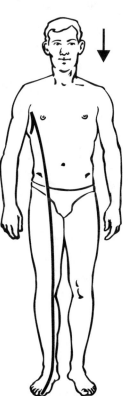

THE TWELVE MERIDIANS (continued)

Conception vessel meridian

Governor vessel meridian

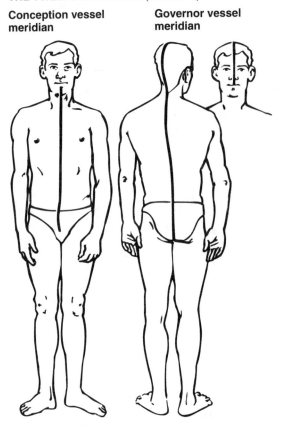

Body organs

Traditional Chinese medicine does not describe internal organs in the same way as Western anatomists. Instead of referring to them as physiological structures, the body's organs are divided into groups of six Fu (or Yang) and six Zang (or Yin) organs, according to their nature and function. Each of these represents one of the five elements and works with another, complementary organ. For example, the liver complements the gall bladder. The energy which connects organs flows to them via the channel of meridians, both horizontally and vertically through the body.

Accessing Qi

Because interior and exterior aspects of the body are related, internal imbalances can be treated by working on the external part of the body. Along each of the meridians there are certain points where Qi may be accessed and manipulated. These points are known as acupressure points (as used by acupressure/shiatsu practitioners), acupuncture points (as used in acupuncture), or tsubos (as used in shiatsu). Acupuncture points along a meridian are numbered according to the direction of energy flow, and manipulation of different points is believed to result in changes in Qi, the consequence of which is relief from symptoms of particular conditions. Different meridians have different numbers of points. For example, the bladder meridian has 67 points; the heart meridian has nine.

THE YIN AND YANG OF DISEASE

About AD 200, Dr. Zhang Zhongjing wrote in his
treatise —*Shan Han Lun* — on disease caused by
cold, that the process of an illness advances in six
stages.

1 Greater Yang The beginning of any illness. There is
a strong superficial pulse, some pain, chills, fever,
coughs, headache, or stiffness. The patient can cure
himself by wrapping up to induce sweating. There may
be a rapid cure or a change toward a deeper, Yin state.

2 Lesser Yang The normal route if care is taken and
the illness is mild. There may be sickness,
constipation, and a yellow tongue, but fever will reduce
and normal balance will be regained.

3 Bright Yang If care is not taken and the general
health is not good anyway, the first stage may move
directly into this severe Yang stage: strong deep pulse,
pain in stomach, constipation, hard abdomen, vomiting,
dizziness, bitter taste in mouth, thirst, fast heartbeat,

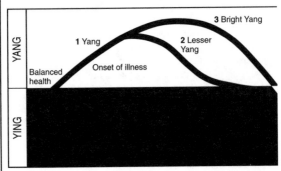

loss of appetite. If the treatment is correct, the disease will change for the better. If not, it will quickly change into a Yin disease.

4 Greater Yin The first stage of any Yin disease and the fourth stage of an illness. The stomach is soft and aches; there is no appetite; constipation may change to diarrhea; there may be vomiting; feet become cold; the deep pulse becomes weak. Proper treatment here will return the patient to normal.

5 Lesser Yin The heart weakens. The patient cannot sit up. Earlier symptoms continue; all pulses weaken. Weight loss. People with a Yang constitution may die suddenly; people with a Yin constitution may get better or may deteriorate over months or years.

6 Terminal Yin This is the most serious stage when all the organs deteriorate. Appetite is gone and the head may be hot while the feet are cold. There is usually loss of fluid.

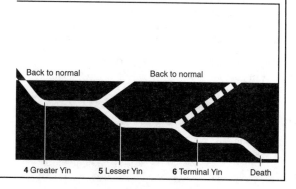

Back to normal   Back to normal

4 Greater Yin   **5** Lesser Yin   **6** Terminal Yin   Death

CHIROPRACTIC

Definition
A manipulative therapy based on the diagnosis and treatment of mechanical joint disorders and their effects on the nervous system and similar to OSTEOPATHY.

Types
There are two types of chiropractic: a straightforward form and one that involves swift movements developed by John McTimoney and Hugh Corley, known as McTimoney or McTimoney-Corley chiropractic.

Equipment
Chiropractics frequently use x-rays but the therapy itself requires no special equipment.

How does it work?
Nerves spread out from the spinal chord to feed different parts of the body and in doing so must pass through parts of the vertebrae (see box, *right*). Chiropractors assert that slight deviations (called subluxations) of bony parts (especially in the vertebrae) may impair nerve transmission and that this may result

---

WHAT CONDITIONS IS IT USED FOR?

- Arm pain
- Asthma
- Back pain
- Constipation
- Irritable bowel syndrome
- Joint problems
- Migraine
- Neck pain
- Painful menstruation
- Postural problems associated with pregnancy
- Shoulder pain
- Sports injuries
- Tension headaches

---

in health problems. Abnormalities in muscles and joints may result from everyday activities (such as carrying children or heavy shopping, driving for long distances, or sitting at a desk for long periods of time), mental and physical stress, accidents, and postural imbalances. Chiropractors believe that pain and disability result

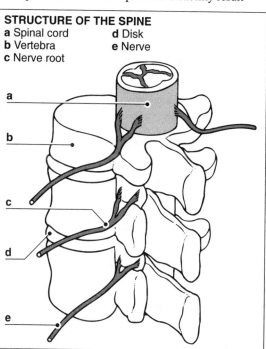

STRUCTURE OF THE SPINE
a Spinal cord d Disk
b Vertebra e Nerve
c Nerve root

from pinched nerves (whereas osteopaths originally believed pain and disability result from pinched blood vessels) and that by using manipulative techniques they are able to correct imbalances alleviating nerve impingement, thereby improving a person's health.

History

Descriptions of chiropractic techniques can be found in Ancient Egyptian manuscripts and the ancient Assyrian, Babylonians, Chinese, and Hindus also used manipulative therapies. Greek physician Hippocrates noted that vertebrae of the spine may become misaligned, producing serious complications. Modern chiropractic was founded in 1895 by a Canadian, Dr. David Daniel Palmer of Iowa who, after curing a janitor, Harvey Lillard, of back pain and deafness by massaging and manipulating the vertebrae in his neck, gave up mesmerism and magnetic healing to investigate anatomy and physiology.

Treatment methods

The chiropractor begins by taking a detailed case history; there is a physical examination, often involving x-rays and blood and urine tests. Once a diagnosis has been reached the chiropractor may decide to manipulate you by pressing on skin, muscles, and connective tissue to stretch muscles, and using thrusting movements. Clients may also be given advice on diet and recommended to try other therapies such as massage, heat treatments, or yoga.

Some people feel sleepy, sore, or stiff after treatment but this is usually short-term, lasting no more than 24 hours.

When standing (**1**) the lower spine has a natural hollow but when sitting (**2**) becomes more straight, placing undue stress on just a few disks. Modern chairs are designed to help the spine retain its correct curvature.

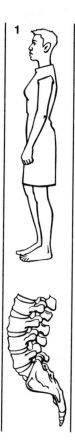

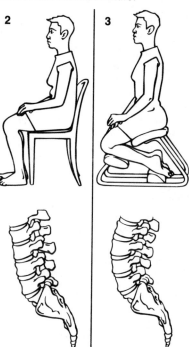

CHRISTIAN HEALING BELIEFS

Definition

Healing beliefs held by people of the Christian religion.
(See also the section on HEALING SHRINES.)

History

Religion and healing have always had a close
relationship and the miracle of healing has often
enhanced the power of religious beliefs. Believers have
turned to their prophets, saints, and icons when praying
for relief from disease and disability.

What may be called a superstitious act by some usually
has its source in stories about the life of Jesus Christ.
The use of the cross as a symbol for healing, or healing
by touching something used by a saint, both have their
origins in these stories. The cross on which Christ was
crucified is a holy symbol used to ward off evil and
being healed by touching a holy article originates from
the story of the woman who was healed when she
touched the hem of Christ's garment.

How does it work?

The way of the believer is healing by no other means
than the power of God, which can act either directly or
through the medium of a special place or person, such
as a shrine or holy well, a church or at the hand of a
saint or his remains. There are few records of what
actual effect these practices had, but it is clear that
many people fervently believed in their efficacy. The
fear of disease would be extreme in those early times
when there was little hope for cure by any other means.

HEALING BY MAKING CROSSES

There are many stories about crossing used as a cure in folk medicine in England up to the 19th century.

Crossing one finger from each hand for general protection from disease is still practiced today as are adjacent crossed fingers for good luck.

Examples of the use of crosses for healing:

- Making a cross on rising bread protected it from being bewitched.
- Using saliva to cross a sleeping foot would awaken it.
- Making a cross on the tongue, the head, and the chest was believed to cure fever.
- Making a cross on the forehead with balsam, and on every limb with petroleum would cure a man who is out of his wits.

Crosses cure whooping cough

According to folklore, the mark of a cross on the neck of a donkey was left there by Christ as he rode into Jerusalem on Palm Sunday. A child suffering from whooping cough should be tied to a donkey with the cross in its fur and taken to a crossroad and walked up and down each road until the child is cured.

Healing from ablutions

Another medical cure for whooping cough was to drink the ablution, i.e. the water and wine with which the chalice is cleansed after the priest has taken communion. A common practice was to wash out the mouth of a baptized child with holy water, to prevent the child from suffering toothache. Holy water was also used to wash the eyes of anyone who had seen a ghost, to prevent repetition of the unnerving event.

A person suffering from severe fevers or possession was advised to drink a mixture of herbs, garlic, holy water, and ale from the church bell, while mass was said over it seven times.

Healing by touching holy artifacts

Wearing a heart made from church metal was a very common form of protection against disease. For example, a cure for sore breasts was to be found by going to a church at midnight, taking a little lead from every diamond-shaped window and making a heart to be worn in a bag hung round the neck.

In about 316 St. Blaise, the Bishop of St. Sebaste, is said to have brought back to life a boy who was choked by a fishbone. Ever since then, St. Blaise has been asked to cure sore throats, thorn pricks, and all forms of choking and suffocation. A reliquary in gold and precious stones was made in Germany in the 11th century, said to contain the arm of St. Blaise, and is touched by pilgrims.

The Roman tribune, Quirinus, claimed that his daughter was cured of a disease of the throat after she kissed the chains that had held St. Peter.

St. Apollonia, who was martyred in Alexandria under
Emperor Philip, had her teeth beaten out for her
Christian beliefs. According to legend, she was
standing at the gate of heaven and it was decreed that
she should never again have pain in her teeth. Hence,
St. Apollonia is often asked to heal toothache.

St Guthlac's belt was said to cure headaches and the
knife, shirt, and boots of St. Thomas à Becket in
Canterbury Cathedral, England, were touched to aid
childbirth.

Votives for healing

Votives are offerings made to affirm a vow and were
given while asking for healing. Two common European
medieval votives were coins and candles.

A penny, which was a thin silver disk, would be bent in
the name of a saint as prayers were said for the patient
on a sickbed. The bent coin would be held above the
patient and specifically over the sick part of the body
whenever possible. The same coin would be used over
and over again when prayers were said for that patient.
The coin would later go to the saint's church, and was
no doubt some recompense for the loss of lead from the
windows.

Candles were, and still are, lit to aid prayer. From at
least the 6th century, in cases of severe sickness, the
patient would be measured with a thread. The thread
would then be covered in wax and the candle taken for
burning to a shrine or church. Measurement was an
automatic response to illness or accident. A medieval
text tells of a girl who fell into a well near Canterbury,
Kent in England. When she had been pulled out of the

water, her first words were, "Measure me to St. Thomas." This meant measure her length in string, make a candle with it, and take it to Canterbury to ask St. Thomas à Becket to guard her from any sickness that might result from her fall. In many churches today, every candle is a prayer.

Wells and holy water

Springs and wells associated with saints have always been places where the sick have sought to be cured. There was a curious connection between the head and the well in Great Britain, in particular in Scotland. The early Celtic dwellers of Scotland were head-hunters at one time in their development. Later the head became associated with the soul and was of such importance that even after death the head was often kept. Legends tell of heads that ate feasts and gave advice.

The places where decapitated heads rested were often regarded as holy places and, according to legend, many springs appeared where such heads had fallen. The water from those springs was believed to be holy water that could cure the sick. Quite often a skull would be placed in or near the well so the water could be drunk from it using the skull. Measles, whooping cough, and epilepsy were the most common diseases for which a cure was sought.

Coventina's Well

One of the best known holy wells in Great Britain is Coventina's Well, which is near Hadrian's Wall in Northumberland, close to the border between Scotland and England. In the 1870s three bronze heads and a real

human skull were found in the well, together with huge
quantities of brooches, coins, and broken pottery,
thrown in as votives of gifts for prayers answered, or to
ensure a prayer for healing would more likely be
answered. There are the remains of several Celtic altars
nearby, dedicated to the Celtic goddess, Coventina.

Well of the Heads

There are several sites known as Tobar bab Ceann
(Well of the Heads) in the islands and on the mainland
of Scotland.

One of these wells is quite close to the modern road
that runs between Inverness and Fort William at
Glengarry. It was made by an obelisk topped with
carvings of seven heads. In common with many "Wells
of the Heads" it was believed that drinking some water
from this well before sunrise on the first Sunday in May
would protect the drinker from all harm for a full year.

Holy water amulets

A less pleasant but religiously more potent use of water
for healing was the practice of washing the remains of
saints' clothing, possessions, and even the dead body,
and retaining the water in a phial around the neck to
protect the wearer.

The severely sick would drink some of the water, which
was often stored locked up in churches, since the
supply of such water was limited.

CLINICAL ECOLOGY

Definition
The treatment of disorders believed to result from a
person's reaction to his or her environment.

History
In America in the 1920s there was great interest in the
kinds of adverse reactions people might have to foods.
Wheat and dairy products, for example, were known to
affect some people. Similar interest developed in
Britain in the 1970s and many people now accept that
sensitivity (rather than allergy) to environmental factors
may cause illness.

How does it work?
Clinical ecologists believe that people are sensitive to
chemicals in the environment, such as in dust,
household cleaners, weedkillers, pesticides, fungicides,
gasoline fumes, and substances used in food

WHAT CONDITIONS IS IT USED FOR?
Clinical ecologists believe that the following
conditions may be caused by a person's reaction to
the environment:

- Asthma
- Bladder problems
- Bloating
- Depression
- Digestive problems
- Dizziness
- Eczema
- Fatigue
- Headaches
- Hyperactivity
- Insomnia
- Night sweats
- Palpitations
- Psoriasis
- Stomach upsets
- Rheumatoid arthritis

MECHANISMS GIVING RISE TO ABNORMAL REACTIONS:
- Irritation to the lining of the stomach or intestine. This occurs especially when the lining is unsound and may be triggered by substances such as wheat or spiced foods.
- Enzyme deficiency. Patients who are enzyme deficient may have difficulty coping with particular foods. For example, people with insufficient lactose have difficulty coping with milk.
- For some people, a psychological reaction to a certain food may trigger an abnormal immune response.
- For some people, taking antibiotics may kill friendly bacteria in the bowel as well as the harmful bacteria. Lack of friendly bacteria may cause sensitivity to some foods.

preparation and preservation. Symptoms are alleviated when offending chemicals are identified and eliminated from the diet or environment where possible.

Treatment methods

The therapist will attempt to identify those foods or chemicals to which you are sensitive. This is achieved using eight different techniques (see box, *next page*). Once danger foods and chemicals have been identified, they should be avoided. In some cases, avoidance of many foods would lead to nutritional deficiency and patients have to be desensitized to the offending items. In order to do this the therapist will work out what level of food or chemical the patient is able to tolerate, so that this may be incorporated into the diet.

TECHNIQUES USED BY CLINICAL ECOLOGISTS

Auricular cardiac reflex
Suspect foods or chemicals are placed within the
patient's electrical field. Changes occur in the
patient's pulse if a substance is introduced to which
he or she is particularly susceptible.

Cytotoxic testing
Concentrated forms of suspect substances are
added to a sample of a patient's blood, the white
blood cells of which change markedly if the patient is
susceptible to the substance.

Electrical testing
A low-voltage electrical current is applied to the
patient (usually by means of an electrode placed on
an acupuncture point such as the tip of the toe). A
suspect substance is then placed in a glass bottle
which is incorporated into the electric circuit. The
reading over the patient's acupuncture point
changes if the patient is susceptible to the
substance contained in the bottle.

Elimination diet
A patient is given only fluids for about five days
which puts him or her in a hypersensitive state.
Suspect items of food are gradually introduced into
the diet, one at a time, to which the patient quickly
has a strong reaction if it is a food to which he or
she is particularly sensitive.

Kinesiology
A suspect food is placed under a patient's tongue or in the hand. If it is a substance to which the patient is susceptible, changes occur in his or her muscles.

Intradermal testing
A patient has small amounts of diluted substances injected under the skin. Symptoms occur within three hours if the substance is one to which the patient is particularly sensitive.

Sublingual drop testing
A patient is given nothing but fluid for five days, after which a drop of solution containing the suspect food is placed under the tongue. Symptoms develop within minutes if this is a substance to which the patient is particularly sensitive.

Radio-allergic solvent test
A sample of blood is analyzed to discover how much IgE (a blood protein) has been produced as an allergic reaction to a particular food. Results from this test do not reveal whether a person is sensitive, intolerant, or allergic to a substance.

COLONIC IRRIGATION

Definition
Also called colonic hydrotherapy, this is a method of cleansing the intestines using warm water injected into the rectum.

History
Purging the body through the use of enemas has been practiced for hundred of years. It was used in Ancient Egypt and Ancient China, and in London in the early twentieth century people could have their colons cleansed in "colon laundries."

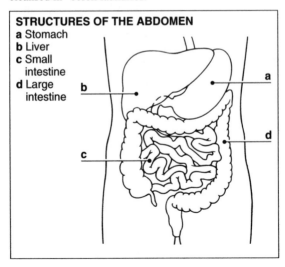

STRUCTURES OF THE ABDOMEN
a Stomach
b Liver
c Small intestine
d Large intestine

WHAT CONDITIONS IS IT USED FOR?
Advocates claim colonic irrigation:
- Alleviates depression
- Alleviates symptoms of myalgic encephalomyelitis (ME)
- Alleviates irritable bowel syndrome symptoms.
- Helps with weight reduction.

How does it work?
Too much dairy produce and processed foods may clog the intestines with impacted waste matter and micro-organisms that may lead to problems such as acne, eczema, constipation, and fibroids. Colonic irrigation is believed to cleanse the bowel of toxins, helping to restore health.

Treatment methods
Patients lie on their sides with their knees bent while a lubricated speculum is inserted into the rectum and water gently pumped into the intestine via a sterile tube. The therapist may massage the abdomen to stimulate the release of waste matter.

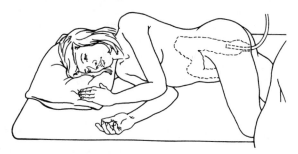

COLOR THERAPY

Definition
The use of color to bring about positive changes in health.

Types
Although color is used in many ways (e.g., by psychologists who may use it to assess personality or by image consultants offering advice about personal grooming), color *therapy* generally refers to the use of color as a healing aid.

Equipment
Color therapists may project color from special lamps, use stained glass filters, or may show clients bottles of colored liquid, colored fabrics, cards, or crystals.

How does it work?
Color therapists believe that our bodies absorb the electromagnetic waves emitted by different colors, and that we emit these colors ourselves in the form of an aura. Exposing part or all of the body to certain colors, therapists assert, will change the molecular structure of cells, thereby alleviating the effects of disease.

Different physical conditions are believed to respond to different colors. Some therapists work via the chakras, seven centers of intense energy down the spine. Each chakra is said to respond to a different color, which corresponds to the body function served by the chakra (see table pages 206–207).

It is known that our non-visual systems are also sensitive to color. This means that even blind people can be treated by color therapists as the skin is believed to be sensitive to different colors.

What conditions is it used for?

Color therapists treat any disorder but stress that their methods should be used in conjunction with traditional medical treatments. In psychological terms, the most fundamental effect of color is on the emotions, which underly a great deal of illness.

History

The use of color and light for healing purposes has ancient origins. The sun-cult of heliotherapy was practiced by the Incas in South America, and the Ancient Greeks spent much time sunbathing and airbathing. The Egyptians thought gemstones were concentrated color and used them in powder form for the treatment of the sick. In India and China the importance of color has been held in high esteem for centuries.

Colored lotions, unguents, and medicines were recommended by philosopher Aurelius Celsius in the 1st century, and by the 10th century the magical properties of color were common knowledge, although not everyone agreed about those properties. Avicenna, an 11th century Arab physician, related color to human temperament, and different colors have become linked with different qualities: without thinking, people say they are "feeling blue" when depressed, "green with envy," or "seeing red" when angry.

In addition to illuminating the scenes they portrayed, light which filtered through the stained glass of Christian church windows was believed to help the congregation pray.

In 1810 the scientist and poet Johann Wolfgang von Goethe published *Die Farben Lehre* (*The Theory of Color*), and in 1878 Englishman Edwin D. Babbitt, in his book *The Principles of Light and Color*, linked colors with elements, minerals, and functions of the body. Babbitt invented and sold aids to color healing, such as Chromo-disks, a Thermolune cabinet, and a stained-glass window that could be used for healing minor ailments. A person sat inside the cabinet while sunlight was filtered through colored glass, bathing him in red, blue, or green light.

Rudolf Steiner outlined the use of color for treatment purposes in a series of lectures in 1921, and in 1933 *The Spectro Chrome Metry Encyclopedia* was

CORRESPONDENCES CLAIMED BY CHAKRA THERAPISTS

Chakras	Location
1 Crown	Top of the head
2 Third eye	Bridge of nose
3 Throat	Thyroid
4 Heart	Center sternum
5 Solar plexus	Just below navel
6 Sacral	Lumbar region
7 Root	Base of spine

published, written by Dinshah Ghadiali.

In the 1940s Dr. Max Lüscher devised a color-based personality test after researching people's color preferences and their psychological make-up. The latest color psychology software is the PCRT (Psychological Color Assessment and Testing) system from K3 Laboratories.

At the 1990 meeting of the American Association for the Advancement of Science, neurological researchers at the University of Texas Health Science Center announced that light, in particular from the blue end of the spectrum, can heal a range of conditions, such as depression, loss of sex drive, low sperm count, jet lag, anorexia nervosa, poor ovulation, and myalgic

Attribute	Color	Effect
Spirituality	Violet	Clears the mind
Clairvoyance	Blue	Stimulates
Intelligence	Cyan	Sensitizes
Compassion	Green	Centers
Feeling	Yellow	Impassions
Sensation	Orange	Nourishes
Sexuality	Red	Reassures

encephalomyelitis (ME) and other conditions affecting
the immune system.

**SOME FINDINGS REGARDING LIGHT AND
COLOR**

- Scientists have now proved that intense light
  enters the deep organs of the body and passes
  through the skulls of sheep, dogs, and rabbits to
  activate photo-electric cells in brain tissue.
- It is also known that the level of light-sensitive
  hormone melatonin in the body is directly related
  to health. Produced by the pineal gland, high
  levels of melatonin are produced in darkness, and
  melatonin has a depressive effect on body
  functions that is appropriate to sleep. When there
  is exposure to good light, the melatonin levels
  drop and the body functions improve.
- Sexual activity is also affected by light. In
  Piccadilly Circus in central London, England, the
  birds, mostly starlings, live exposed to the
  constant glare and colors of street lights and
  advertisements. It has been found that these birds
  remain sexually potent even during the normal
  period of impotency experienced by starlings living
  in a country habitat.
- Even mammals that are color-blind are affected by
  colored light. Commercial breeders of chinchilla
  use blue light to encourage the conception of
  more females, which have thicker fur than males.
  In normal light chinchillas produce 50% males and
  50% females; in pink light they produce 70%
  males and 30% females, but in blue light the
  percentages are reversed.

TREATMENT METHODS
After taking your case history a therapist may use
extrasensory perception to tune in to your
electromagnetic field. Some therapists may use
DOWSING, others may be able to see your aura or
may use a Kirlian screen to view it (see the section
on AURA ANALYSIS). Color may be used in a
variety of ways, some of which are detailed here.

1 The therapist might use lights of different colors to
   work with very specific conditions or with the
   underlying energy states. (See the next two pages
   for examples.)
2 The therapist may suggest you modify your diet to
   include foods of specific colors.
3 You may be asked to drink water which has been
   placed in a colored container and left in sunlight so
   that it absorbs the properties of the color.
4 Some therapists may advocate breathing in
   different colored light, or using VISUALIZATION to
   imagine different colors. This is a powerful,
   autohypnotic technique.
5 You may be shown different shapes. Some
   therapists claim these support the use of particular
   colors. For example, red is often associated with
   cubes and vertical forms; blue is associated with
   spherical and horizontal shapes.
6 Rhythmic timing is also used to increase the
   harmony initiated by different colors and different
   forms.
7 The therapist may harness the properties of white
   sunlight, focusing it on a particular part of your
   body.

COLORED RAYS USED IN THERAPY

Color	Attributes	
Red	Will power Life	Vitality Courage
Orange	Practical, disciplined energy Intelligent action	
Yellow	Intellect Mental activity Creativity Wisdom	
Green	Sympathy Adaptability Harmony Diplomacy Stamina	
Blue	Serenity Consciousness Self-reliance Idealism	
Indigo	Astringency Purity Spirituality Intuition	
Magenta and violet	Spiritual and mental equilibrium	

Uses (examples)

Blood and circulation Debility and depression

Appendix	Hernias	Gall bladder
Chest conditions	Kidneys	
Digestion	Spleen	

Constipation	Liver
Diabetes	Lymphatic system
Indigestion	Nervous system
Kidney	Skin problems

Colds	Malaria
Emotional disorders	Nervous headaches
Hay fever	Syphilis
Heart	Ulcers
Influenza	

Anger	Irritations	Fevers
Bleeding	Nervous rage	Dysentery
Burns	Pain	Skin problems
Colic	Rheumatism	

Cataracts	Deafness	Eyes
Ears	Migraines	Nose
Pituitary gland	Toxicity	
Skin disorders		

Sleeplessness	Neuralgia
Rheumatism	Epilepsy
Pineal gland	Arthritis

CRYSTAL AND GEM THERAPY

Definition
The use of gemstones (including crystal) for healing.
(For additional information see the section on
CHAKRA THERAPY.)

Types
Crystal therapy involves the use of natural crystals
(usually quartz) which some believe contain positive
energy that can be channeled to clients in need.
Gem essence therapy is the use of essences made by
immersing gemstones in water and leaving them in the
Californian sunshine so that their vibrational qualities
percolate the water.

Treatment methods
Gem essences are usually self-administered by placing
a few drops under the tongue. Crystal therapists use a
variety of methods and may place crystals on a
particular part of the body that requires treatment or on
acupuncture points. Some people carry gemstones
believing them to be of value in fortifying themselves
or preventing illness.

WHAT CONDITIONS IS IT USED TO TREAT?

Crystal therapists say that all kinds of quartz are
used for physical healing, that amethyst is
particularly good for spiritual healing and that rose
quartz is suitable for emotional healing.
Gem essence therapy is believed to help improve
spiritual health and emotional well-being.

How do they work?

Therapists believe that gemstones "vibrate" with energy. Different stones vibrate with different frequencies. This energy is transferred to the water in which they are immersed to produce gem essences. Placing gemstones on or near the body (or using the gem essence in liquid form) is believed to help magnify positive qualities within individuals by helping to intensify or harmonize specific feelings (such as love, acceptance, concentration, etc.)

History

Gemstones (including crystals) have been used for centuries for healing purposes, examples of which are provided in the table, *below.*

HISTORICAL USE OF GEMSTONES FOR HEALING PURPOSES.

Gemstone	Healing properties
AGATE	• Protects against headaches and fever. • Draws out the venom of insect and reptile bites. • Cures fever and eye infections. • Improves eyesight. • Relieves inflammation and tiredness of the eyes. • Staunches bleeding. • Relieves skin irritations. • Promotes fertility.

AMBER	• Protects against indigestion, loss of teeth, deafness, the plague, the spread of infection (if held in the mouth), fits during the teething of babies. • Worn on the throat, prevents nasal catarrh, hay fever, and asthma. • Cures whooping cough, asthma, erysipelas, goiter.
AMETHYST	• Cures headaches, toothache, gout, neuralgia, and nerve troubles.
AQUAMARINE	• Prevents stomach and liver troubles. • Cures toothache.
BLOODSTONE	• Staunches bleeding • Strengthens the digestive system. • Prevents internal hemorrhage and drowning.
CARBUNCLE	• Protects against wounds, the plague, infections, and all diseases of the throat and stomach.
CARNELIAN	• Protects against fever, indigestion, and all stomach troubles. • White carnelians protect against rheumatism and neuralgia.
CAT'S EYE	• Protects against all diseases of the chest and throat. • Cures asthma. • Soothes the nerves.

CHRYSOLITE	● Cures speech impediments. ● Induces mental health and prevents madness.
CORAL	● Prevents epilepsy. ● Prevents sterility in women. ● Prevents and cures fits and whooping cough in babies. ● Eases internal pains. ● Cures ulcers and sores. ● When rubbed on gums strengthens teeth. ● Protects against madness.
CRYSTAL	● Induces peaceful sleep.
DIAMOND	● Protects against the plague.
EMERALD	● Protects against eye diseases, faintness, and loss of memory. ● Eases pain in childbirth. ● Cures epilepsy, dysentery, and fits. ● Negates the effects of snakebite. ● Touching an emerald helps sufferers of blindness. ● Relieves eyestrain and eye inflammation. ● Is a remedy for sores and ulcers.
GARNET	● Is an antidote to plague and fever. ● Wards off inflammatory diseases.
JACINTH (also called ZIRCON)	● Protects from fever, plague, dropsy and, disorders of the stomach. ● Cures indigestion.

JACINTH (continued)	<ul><li>Stimulates appetite.</li><li>Strengthens the heart.</li><li>Is an antidote against poison</li></ul>
JADE	<ul><li>Prevents nightmares and eye troubles.</li><li>Is a remedy for spleen, kidney, and digestive ailments.</li><li>Makes men potent.</li><li>Averts epilepsy.</li><li>Cures animal bites.</li></ul>
JASPER	<ul><li>Lessens pain.</li><li>Staunches bleeding.</li><li>Prevents digestive pains.</li><li>Treats epilepsy.</li></ul>
JET	<ul><li>Protects against snake bites and scorpion stings.</li><li>Prevents fits.</li><li>Cures epilepsy.</li><li>Helps treat skin diseases.</li><li>Taken in powdered form alleviates toothache.</li><li>Fumes from burning jet repel the plague.</li></ul>
LAPIS LAZULI	<ul><li>A blue stone necklace cures apoplexy, epilepsy, skin troubles, and poor blood.</li><li>Relieves the pain of neuralgia.</li><li>Allays eye inflammation.</li></ul>

LODESTONE	• Cures gout.
	• Gives health and strength to the wearer.
MALACHITE	• Protects against rheumatism and cholera.
MOONSTONE	• Cures consumption, dropsy, and kidney troubles.
	• Allays fever.
OLIVINE	• Cures speech impediments.
OPAL	• Improves eyesight.
PEARL	• Sleeping with a pearl beneath the pillow helps childless couples conceive.
	• Treats madness, jaundice, snake and insect bites.
PERIDOT	• Cures speech impediments.
RUBY	• Prevents stomach ache.
	• Is an antidote against snake poison.
	• Heals wounds.
SAPPHIRE	• Preserves sight and helps draw foreign bodies from the eyeball.
	• Strengthens and stimulates the heart.
SARDONYX	• Protects against plague and the bites and stings of poisonous reptiles and insects.

	• Lessens pain during childbirth.
TOPAZ	• Used to treat disorders of the lungs, nose, and throat. • Worn over the stomach protects against disorders of the ailmentary system. • Averts epilepsy and asthma. • Cures gout, sleeplessness, lunacy, and sudden death.
TURQUOISE	• Prevents headaches. • Cures weak sight and eye inflammation.

GEM ESSENCES

Manufacturers and therapists interpret the qualities of gem essences differently. Listed below are a selection of gem essences and *some* of the qualities *one* manufacturer asserts they promote.

Gem essence	Qualities promoted by the essence
Amethyst	Release of emotional tension Purification
Diamond	Ability to realize ideas and dreams Clarity Vision
Emerald	A sense of balance Ability to release stress Inner healing

Rose quartz	Openness
	Self-acceptance
	Self-esteem
	Self-love
Ruby	Self-assurance
	Successfulness
Sapphire	Concentration
	Determination
	Discipline
	Stamina
	Strength
Topaz	Awareness
	Broadmindedness
	Problem-solving abilities

CUPPING

Definition
A method of heat stimulation in which small warm
cups, bowls, or drums are placed on the skin in order to
increase local blood supply.

Types
There are two types of cupping: dry cupping, in which
the cups are heated, left in place and then removed, and
wet cupping, in which shallow cuts are made in the
raised skin and cups applied to draw blood into them.
Early practitioners believed that poisons would be
drawn out of the body in this way, along with the blood.

History
Cupping has been used since ancient times and was a
popular practice in both Western and Eastern medicine.

Equipment
Cups are made from glass or bamboo.

Use of
cupping in
medieval
times

WHAT CONDITIONS IS IT USED TO TREAT?
- Abscesses
- Arthritis
- Boils
- Bruises
- Colds
- Chills
- Rheumatism

Treatment methods

Heated cups are placed on the patient's skin and as it cools creates a partial vacuum which draws flesh into the cup. Blood flow increases in the area within the cups, which are left in place for 5–10 minutes according to the type of condition being treated. Sometimes the process is repeated on different parts of the body within the same treatment. After treatment the cups are removed by pressing the skin around them.

How does it work?

It was believed in the West that the increased blood flow caused by cupping helps remove impurities from nearby tissues and organs.

The Chinese believe that cupping draws unwanted Qi—life energy—to the body's surface, where it is dispersed.

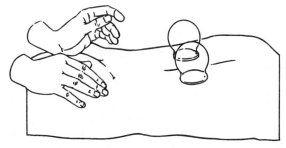

CYMATICS

Definition

The use of sound waves to heal.

History

People all over the world have been using the healing power of sound for centuries. Chanting, drumming, shaking, and dancing have always formed part of primitive ceremonies. Among North American Indians, these ceremonies were a sounding board for their Great Spirit, with whom they placed their faith.

Other cultures use the repetitive sound of chanting, drumming, or rattling to bring about healing; for example, Kiddo, a practice used by Korean Zen Buddhists, induces an ecstatic state of consciousness. Attained by chanting with percussion instruments for as long as 12 hours a day, the chanter is said to become one with the Bodhisattva of Compassion, who will bring about healing.

Austrian thinker and scientist Rudolf Steiner believed in the healing power of spoken verse that had a regular meter and he was the inspiration for contemporary

---

WHAT CONDITIONS IS IT USED FOR?

Cymatics has been used in the treatment of:

- Arthritis
- Back pain
- Bone disorders
- Fibrositis
- Fractures
- Muscular conditions
- Rheumatism
- Slipped disc
- Sprains
- Strains

research into the healing shapes of sounds. Simple sounds are often repeated as part of prayer or healing rituals in different cultures. For example, many people chant the mantra "OM" while meditating, Christians and Jews say "AMEN," and Muslims, "AMIN."

An instrument called a "tonoscope" was developed by Dr. Hans Jenny to visualize sound in three dimensions. Dr. Jenny used the human voice to show that the spoken letter "O" produced a spherical pattern on the tonoscope.

The healing effect of various sounds and the images they induce have been researched in London by musician Lawrence Ball and healer Isobel McGilvray (see box, *on the next page*).

In modern times, music therapy is used to heal the disturbed mind and body. High frequency sound waves have been harnessed in the form of the ultrasonic scanner, commonly used as a diagnostic tool and to monitor fetal development in pregnancy.

How does it work?

The heart is known to generate electrical impulses which can be monitored using an electrocardiogram. Cymatics is based on a theory that *all* the molecules within our bodies (not just some of the heart muscle cells) transmit minute signals which deviate according to their structure: each organ is believed to vibrate at a different frequency. Illness is thought to affect the frequency at which organs and cells in the body vibrate. Practitioners of cymatics assert that when an organ is in disharmony and not vibrating correctly, micro-organisms, viruses, and cancer cells may flourish. By

ACOUSTIC IMAGES AND THEIR EFFECTS

Acoustic images	Description	Effect of image
	Lines	Clears the mind
	Helix	Stimulates
	Rose	Soothes
	Four-leafed clover	Brings hope
	Triangles	Releases emotion
	Circles	Nourishes
	Squares	Reassures

using the vibrational qualities of different sounds, practitioners claim to be able to reinforce the healthy frequencies of tissues, helping to bring about healing.

Treatment methods

Practitioners aim to restore "healthy" frequencies at which cells and organs vibrate by using different sounds transmitted via a hand-held electronic device. The device is very much like a massage vibrator and can be aimed at a specific part of the body. The sound waves that are chosen to be transmitted are those practitioners feel are unique to a particular body organ and can therefore help stabilize that organ's vibrational frequency.

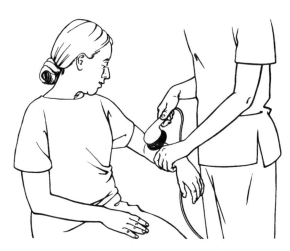

DANCE MOVEMENT THERAPY

Definition

The use of movement to bring about positive changes in a person's emotional, cognitive, and social integration.

History

Dancing seems to be a natural response to music and has been used for thousands of years. It is still widely used in tribal communities. However, the use of dance as a therapy was not much used in the West until after World War II when in America the approach to the treatment of people with emotional disorders changed. Dance as a group activity began to be used in the treatment of certain kinds of mental and emotional illness. At this time, pioneers of modern dance—such as Liljan Espenak, Blanche Evans, Trudi Schoop, and Mary Whitehouse—incorporated the theories of psychoanalysts into their therapeutic dances.

Dancer Marian Chase was hired to work at the St. Elizabeth Hospital in Washington, D.C., where, using dance movement therapy, she made progress with some of the hospital's more difficult patients. Dance therapy was pioneered by Rudolph Laban, whose freer dance forms were designed to promote harmony between body and mind and to inspire creative interaction between members of a group.

Creative eurythmy, established by Rudolf Steiner, is a therapy that blends movement with vocal sound and specific exercises, designed to benefit various parts of the body such as the digestive tract, respiratory system, and the skin, as well as to alleviate many psychiatric conditions.

WHAT CONDITIONS IS IT USED FOR?

Dance movement therapy is used by a range of clients including:

- People with learning difficulties
- People with autism
- People with behavioral difficulties
- People who are physically disabled
- People with dementia

It is used to help treat a variety of conditions including:

- Addictions
- Anorexia
- Anxiety
- Bulimia
- Depression
- Manic depressive disorder
- Schizophrenia

How does it work?

There are many benefits to dance movement therapy. On the next two pages are listed some general benefits of this type of therapy, as well as the benefits to patients suffering from schizophrenia.

Treatment methods

Dance movement therapy may be practiced on a one-to-one basis or in groups. There are many different approaches although most therapists argue that movement reflects an individual's patterns of thinking and they will work with clients to encourage new movement patterns, offering support to clients who may experience strong emotions as part of the therapy.

BENEFITS OF DANCE MOVEMENT THERAPY: General

Benefits of working in a group
- Participants learn to function as a social unit.
- Working in a circle helps promote feelings of oneness and security.
- Participants learn to touch themselves and each other.

Physical benefits
- Provides an opportunity for exercise.
- Provides a medium for the release of tension and energy.

Psychological benefits
- Clients gain an increased awareness of their body image.
- Dance facilitates role playing, valuable for self-expression.
- It can be used to act out hidden fears and emotions.
- It is an invaluable tool for non-verbal expression.

**BENEFITS OF DANCE MOVEMENT THERAPY:
For patients suffering from schizophrenia**

Access
- Provides a means of access to withdrawn or non-verbal patients.
- Bypasses communication problems associated with thought disorder.

Builds a sense of self
- Improves body image.
- Helps set ego boundaries.
- Helps a patient stand his/her ground.

Improves relationship to the external world
- Helps patients focus on the present
- Provides relief from their preoccupation with anxieties and fantasies.

Reduces psychomotor abnormalities
- Increases the range of movements available to the patient.
- Improves coordination.

Improves volition
- Develops initiative.
- Develops leadership.

Reconnects with affect
- Helps patients reconnect with their feelings as a result of group interactions.

DIETARY THERAPIES

Definition

Therapies which aim to improve health and well-being by altering the combination of foods regularly eaten by a person.

How do they work?

Each type of diet works differently. Specific diets are designed for specific reasons. For example, there are low-fat diets for people with gall bladder problems, muscle-building diets for athletes, and diets in which the amount of carbohydrate is restricted, for people who suffer insulin-dependent diabetes. Nobody yet agrees what is a correct diet, except that fresh fruit and vegetables are better than large quantities of refined, sugary food.

Can diet cure disease?

Diet has been shown to have important effects in the causation of many diseases, so it may be equally vital in maintaining remission or even curing them. A whole list of disturbances have been connected with food allergies: for example, sensitivity to food additives such as preservatives and colorants. A food additive is any substance not normally consumed as the food itself, which is added to the food to preserve it, or to enhance its flavor, color, or texture. The majority of foods contain additives, and there are around 3500 of them currently in use worldwide.

Symptoms of additive intolerance are wide-ranging, and may include asthma, rashes, headaches, and a general feeling of malaise. In children, such intolerance may also be an important contributing factor in behavior problems—research has pointed to the artificial azo dyes such as Tartrazine (E102), for instance, as a possible cause of hyperactivity. As a result, many doctors now recommend that the diet of a hyperactive child be modified to exclude all food and drink containing synthetic colorings and flavorings. Some people are also concerned about the process of irradiation—the practice of passing small quantities of radiation through food to render harmless the bacteria that cause deterioration. There are fears regarding the long-term effects of radiation as some people argue that it is not known how changing the molecular structure of the food we consume may ultimately affect our health. There has also been much research into the health and longevity of some primitive communities in relation to the claims that animal fats have a debilitating effect on human circulation. It was discovered that some tribes ate large quantities of animal meat, yet remained healthy and free from circulation problems. In the 1980s, studies of healthy tribes such as the Masai and Eskimos, who had not become Westernized, showed that while both tribes ate more meat than the average Westerner, the proportion of polyunsaturated fats to saturated fats eaten was three times greater than by the average Westerner. The primitive diets were also ten times richer in vitamin C than recommended standard intakes in the West.

It was also discovered that the meat of wild animals eaten by these tribes contained eight times less fat than the average farm animal and contained the important fatty acid, eicosapentanoic acid (EPA).

EPA protects against the dangerous over-production of the saturated acids in the system. It has also been suggested that EPA itself is involved in the prevention of malignancies and arthritis as well as cardiovascular conditions. EPA is present in fish oil and in the meat of

---

TYPES OF DIET

Detoxification diets

Strict diets which eliminate foods regarded as polluting (such as salt, sugar, meat, saturated fats, alcohol, coffee, and tea). They are designed to cleanse the body of toxins and enable it to fight back against diseases such as cancer. Beneficial effects may take a while to appear, and it is not uncommon for patients following a detoxification diet to feel briefly unwell before beginning to respond. This sort of reaction is taken to indicate that the body is being effectively cleared of harmful toxins.

Diets to control allergens

Those which restrict certain foods to which individuals may be allergic.

Fasting

Eliminating all solid foods from the diet for short periods of time in order to cleanse the body of toxins.

Lacto-ovo-vegetarian diets

Vegetarian diets in which some animal products are eaten, such as milk, cheese, eggs, and honey.

Macrobiotic diets

Those based on the correct balance between foods classified as yin and those classified as yang.

Megavitamin therapy

The use of large doses of vitamins for the prevention and treatment of specific illnesses.

wild animals, but not in the meat of farm-bred animals.

Types

There are many different types of dietary therapy, some
of which are described here.

Vegan diets
Those which exclude all foods of animal origin.

Vegetarian diets
Diets which exclude the meat of any mammal, bird, or
fish. They include vegan and lacto-ovo-vegetarian
diets. Reasons for vegetarianism vary from society to
society and individual to individual. It has been
advocated for religious, philosophical, moral,
economic, and health reasons, and also at times
adopted as a necessity. Many primitive peoples, for
example, have lived on a diet of fruit, nuts and
berries, with meat only when it could be obtained.
Some argue that a vegetarian diet is cheaper than a
diet that includes meat; others are against the use of
meat on moral grounds. Many people are now
concerned that the methods of farming used to
produce meat on a large scale may make it
unhygienic or dangerous for human consumption.
There are concerns that some meat may contain crop
pesticides, antibiotics, and hormones that are
damaging to the health of humans.

Weight-reducing diets
Any diet which aims to help individuals reduce their
level of body fat.

DO-IN

Definition
A form of Chinese self-massage.
How does it work?
The Chinese believe that disease is caused by a disturbance in life energy—known as Qi—which flows around the body via meridians. Do-in exercises are believed to prevent disease by strengthening these meridians, which are linked to different body organs. The exercises may encourage the brain to release endorphins, the body's pain-relieving hormones, and may stimulate the flow of blood and lymphatic fluid which helps release toxins and tension from muscles.
Treatment methods
Illustrations show six basic do-in exercises, each designed to help strengthen different organs.

Before you begin the exercises
1 Hold your knees with your hands and rock gently backwards and forwards.

2 Cross your legs and hold your toes for a few seconds.

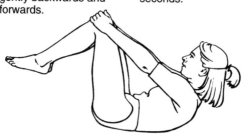

Heart–small intestine

1 Sit with the soles of your feet together as shown. Put your hands around your toes. Breathe in.

2 Keeping your back straight, slowly bend forward. Breathe out.
3 Return to start and repeat.

Stomach–spleen

1 Stand facing a wall placing your outstretched left hand on it. Hold your right foot with your right hand as shown.
2 Gently bend your head backward, stretching the front of your body.
3 Change position by placing your right hand on the wall and holding your left foot with your left hand.
4 Bend your head gently backward again.

Circulation–pericardium

1 Begin with your arms and knees crossed.
2 Gently try to press your knees to the floor.
3 Change position by re-crossing your arms and legs the other way.
4 Again try to gently press your knees to the floor.

Lung–large intestine

1 Begin by standing with your feet hip-distance apart, thumbs locked together. Breathe in. Breathe out as you stretch your arms behind you.
2 Gently lean forward.
3 Return to the start position.

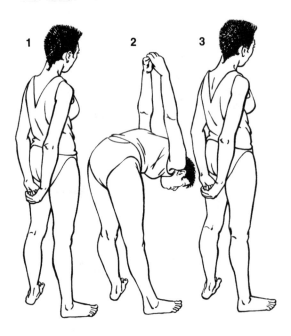

Kidney–bladder

1 Begin by stretching your hands above your head. Breathe in.
2 Breathe out as you bend gently forward to touch your toes. Take three deep breaths and then repeat.

Liver–gall bladder

1 Begin by breathing in and reaching gently over to your left leg. In this position, take two deep breaths.

2 Repeat on the other side.

After the exercises

1 Lie on the floor with arms and legs outstretched.
2 Carefully raise your head and look at your feet.

3 Lower your head, shake your body gently, and rest for five minutes.

1

2

3

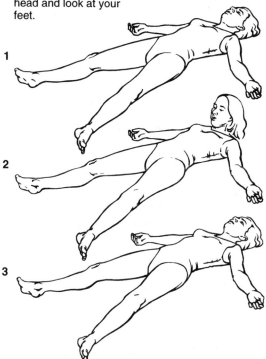

DREAM THERAPY

Definition

Using dreams to help analyze and overcome emotional problems.

History

For thousands of years people have been interpreting dreams for the purposes of healing. The ancient Egyptians thought dreams were based on real things that could not be seen or heard when the conscious mind was in control; ancient Greek priests interpreted the dreams of a sick person, giving health care advice, and Greek thinker Aristotle believed premonitory dreams of sickness could be caused by the dreamer's unconscious recognition of the symptoms.

Viennese psychiatrist Sigmund Freud believed dreams work on two levels: a straightforward level reveals surface events as they are remembered, and a hidden level in which objects and actions in the dream symbolize sexual and aggressive feelings and ideas—an individual's wishes that are normally repressed.

Austrian Alfred Adler, a disciple of Freud, argued that dreams reflect the individual's desire to move towards goals of success and superiority.

Carl Jung believed dreams reflect unconscious memories and instincts shared by all people across all cultures, represented by symbols (such as the monster, the hero, the mother, etc.)

Fritz Perls, founder of Gestalt therapy, believed that characters and objects in our dreams are projections of ourselves and represent those parts of our personality we do not accept or acknowledge.

Dr. Montague Ullman developed the use of group dream therapy to help people interpret their own dreams rather than relying on interpretations from a therapist.

Treatment methods

Dream interpretation often forms part of psychological therapies. In Gestalt dream therapy the dreamer retells a dream, taking the part of each person or object in the dream. For example, in a dream about a car, the client may choose to speak of himself: "I am driving to work in an old wreck," and as the car: "I am an old wreck being driven to work." In this way new insights are often gained.

In group dream therapy each member of the group brings along details of a recent dream which is related to each other member one at a time. Each group member has an opportunity to comment on the dream as if it were *his or her* dream. The purpose of the session is to provide each member with a variety of dream interpretations.

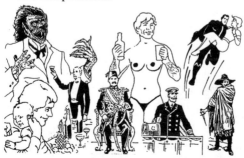

ELECTROTHERAPY

Definition
The use of electricity to treat medical disorders.

History
In AD 46 a Roman medical practitioner known as Scribonius Largus is said to have claimed he could cure headaches using the electrical charge from an electric torpedo fish or an electric eel. The electric eel was placed on the head and gave the patient a high voltage electric shock.

The idea of using an electrical charge to cure pain was not new even then; there is some evidence that it was used by the ancient Egyptians.

In the nineteenth century doctors sometimes discharged electric currents through their patients to relieve pain and dentists later used the method also.

Today, some beauty clinics use TENS (Transcutaneous Electrical Nerve Stimulation) machines as a slimming aid and make muscles twitch with the hope that this will help burn calories.

Some acupuncturists use electro-acupuncture, in which fine needles are stimulated using an electric current. Modern electroconvulsive therapy used for psychiatric disorders may be under greater control but is, in effect, the same as electric eel treatment. Known as ECT (electroconvulsive therapy) it was used for treating patients with severe depressions.

Equipment
TENS is a modern treatment used to treat pain. A small machine, known as the TENS machine, produces a

controlled electrical charge which is fed through silicon
electrodes attached to the skin with a harmless gel.

How does it work?

Research has shown that the electrical message arrives
at the central nervous system before the pain message
and prevents it from being received. This phenomenon
is known as the gate control theory.

Stimulation by a low voltage electrical charge (the
TENS method) is even more effective. It was
discovered that TENS, like rubbing, also stimulates the
body to produce more endorphins, the body's own
natural painkillers.

What conditions is it used for?

The TENS machine seems to work best with chronic or
stable, persistent pain. It is also said to help childbirth,
lumbago, and sciatica.

Giant Power Heidelberg Electric Belt for curing all
pains, from the 1902 Sears, Roebuck & Co. catalog

ENCIRCLING

Definition
The use of circles for healing purposes.
How does it work?
Methods of outlining the sickness seem to be a form of contagious magic; the person is divested of the sickness by contact with the earth or a tree round which a circle had been drawn. People relied on these methods for curing certain kinds of disease, so perhaps the real

Navaho healing mandala

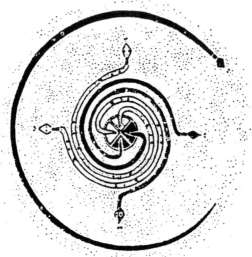

healing came about by the power of suggestion and
through a lapse of time.

People holding hands in a circle can sometimes detect a
charge of something akin to electrical power passing
round from person to person through their arms,
especially where they are involved in something active
like deep breathing or chanting.

The circle can build tension or share group energy,
depending upon the collective circumstances. Circular
arrangements involve the participants and do not easily
allow individuals to withdraw. The circle with a central
focus such as a totem pole or a fire is far more engaging
than the theater-style arrangement of many modern
gatherings, which encourages detached voyeurism.

History

Since ancient times the circle, and its variant the spiral,
have been used in rituals, buildings, and symbolism
because they were thought to have powerful magical
qualities.

Outlining the diseased part of the body was a very
common folklore practice among early communities in
South America, parts of North America and Southern
Europe.

Encircling a person to cure sickness

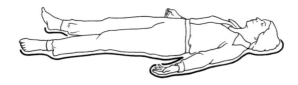

Treatment methods

Circles and encircling are used in a wide variety of
ways for healing and may involve circular healing
mandala, encircling an ailment, or taking part in tribal
dancing in which members form a circle.

In some parts of Spain, lung diseases were treated by
outlining the whole body. A boy suffering from "air
disease" in Pontevedra was taken to the top of a hill
overlooking the sea and laid on the ground while a line
was drawn round him. The earth within the edge of the
line was dug up, carried home with the child and then
thrown to the back of the fire. When it was burnt, the
child was supposed to be cured.

People suffering from tuberculosis had similar
treatment. In one case reported from Galicia, a healer
scattered sand on the ground and asked the sick man to
lie on it. The healer drew the man's outline in the sand.
The man was then moved and the line of the drawing
was cut away with a knife, to cut away the disease.

In Chilean folklore, the foot is used to represent all
parts of the body, its outline drawn on the bark on the
trunk of a tree. This may be done for foot injuries or
body problems, such as a hernia. The piece of bark is
then cut away from the tree, leaving a bare patch.
Healing is said to take place to the extent that the bark
grows to fill the space. When the bark is completely re-
grown, healing is complete.

Encircling the ailing part is also found in American
folklore. In Pennsylvania bunions and other foot
problems were said to heal if a piece of turf was cut out
round the foot and turned upside down to dry. In

Louisiana, childhood croup was cured by taking the
child to the south side of a tree where a print of the foot
was cut in the bark. In this case the bark was left intact
because the child would recover from his attacks of
croup when he outgrew the footprint.

North American Indian tribes, such as the Navaho and
the Sioux, use the circular sweat lodge for self-
purification at the start of their healing rituals. The
lodge is similar to a sauna held inside a hogan, where
the participants sit in a circle and offer fire, water,
herbs, and prayers to the Great Spirits.

ENCOUNTER THERAPY

Definition
A form of group therapy the aims of which are to help individuals improve their relationships with others.

History
Encounter group therapy developed from the humanistic psychology of the 1960s and the work of people such as Wilhelm Reich, Fritz Perls, Abraham Maslow and Carl Rogers.

How does it work?
The support and encouragement people experience during encounter group therapy is believed to help individuals identify their true feelings, more truthfully express these feelings, and therefore relate to other people in a more open and honest way.

Treatment methods
An encounter group session usually involves ten to fifteen people who sit on the floor in a circle. There does not have to be a "leader" and no set direction is established, the aim being for events to develop

naturally. During encounter group therapy individuals are encouraged to experience genuine inner feelings and to express such feelings verbally or physically in an open and honest way with other people. Individual openness is of paramount importance.

Members may be encouraged to use eye contact, physical contact, or to engage in group games. During the session all kinds of emotional responses may be revealed, including anger and hostility, and it is the purpose of the group to help individuals examine why they may be feeling angry or hostile and how such feelings can best be expressed.

The length of an encounter session may vary from several short sessions over several days to one long therapy session lasting up to 48 hours.

WHAT CONDITIONS IS IT USED FOR?

Encounter group therapy is helpful for:
- People who find close relationships difficult.
- People receiving mental health care.
- People needing to increase their confidence.
- People who find business relationships difficult.

FAITH HEALING

Definition

Also called spiritual healing, this is when the power of a god or spirit serves as a healing force.

History

Records show that appeals for healing were made of the gods of Egypt, Mesopotamia and classical Greece. The Egyptians, for example, believed the body could be divided into 36 parts and that different gods could be invoked to heal specific limbs and diseases. Famous for his healing powers was Jesus of Nazareth, the messiah of the Christian religion. In the Gospels, which describe

---

Faith healers

Some healers believe they are successors to the early Christians and carry a divine healing force, (See the LAYING ON OF HANDS section). They use prayer and meditation to channel their divine healing powers to bring about a positive change in a person's life force.

Others believe that the human personality outlives physical death and that spirits of the dead can communicate with the living and do so to help us. Such people believe they are a medium through which a spirit (usually that of a doctor or someone who was a healer in their lifetime) provides them with information they need to heal, even going so far as to guide their movements. For example, famous British healer, Harry Edwards, believed that Louis Pasteur was one of his healing guides.

his work, there are several occasions where he cured people of paralysis, blindness, leprosy, and various crippling diseases. Sometimes he did this by touching; sometimes by simply commanding the sickness to leave; sometimes he spat on the person, and usually the faith of the person, their family and friends was important. He also brought some people back to life from recent death. His healing activities were called miracles (see the next four pages) and are the best-known examples of miracle healing.

The disciples of Jesus retained his ability to heal and cure diseases and, later, illness was treated not only by the laying on of hands but through the power of prayer. In the 12th century St. Francis of Assisi and St. Bernard of Clairvaux are said to have achieved many cures. In the 14th century St. Catherine of Siena was renowned for her healing abilities, and this was true of St. Francis Xavier in the 16th century.

In the 17th century the Society of Friends, or Quakers, was founded by George Fox, a man who performed cures in England and America, details of which he kept in his unpublished *Book of Miracles*.

Belief in the power of a monarch to cure illness flourished during the 17th century. The laying on of hands was used by kings who touched the sick and gave them coins to hang around their necks. (Interestingly, in the 3rd century B.C. King Pyrrhus of Epirus cured colic by the laying on of toes.)

Then, as touch-healing among early Christians declined, the use of relics of the saints and martyrs became more popular.

EXAMPLES OF JESUS'S HEALING MIRACLES

Healing miracle	Matthew
Blind Bartimaeus (**a**)	20:29–34
Blind man at Bethsaida (**b**)	-
Centurion servant (**c**)	8:5–13
Epileptic boy (**d**)	17:14–21
Gadarene demoniac (**e**)	8:28–34
Jairus's daughter (**f**)	9:18–26
Lazarus (**g**)	-

Miracle	Brief description
Blind Bartimaeus	Jesus touches the eyes of two blind men and they instantly regain their sight.
Blind man at Bethsaida	Jesus spits on a blind man and puts his hand on him and the man instantly regains his sight.
Centurion servant	Via absent healing, Jesus cures a centurion servant from paralysis.
Epileptic boy	At the request of a father, Jesus drives out a demon from a boy suffering from epilepsy.

Mark	Luke	John
10:46–52	18:35–43	-
8:22–26	-	-
-	7:1–10	-
9:14–29	9:37–43	-
5:1–20	8:26–39	-
5:21–43	8:40–56	-
-	-	11:1–44

Miracle	Brief description
Gadarene demoniac	Saying "Go!" Jesus drives out the demons from two men into a herd of pigs.
Jairus's daughter	Jesus takes the hand of a girl he is told is dead and she gets up.
Lazarus	Jesus calls, "Lazarus, come out!" into the tomb of a dead man and Lazarus comes out alive still wrapped in strips of burial cloth.

EXAMPLES OF JESUS'S HEALING MIRACLES
(continued)

Healing miracle	Matthew
Lepers, ten healed	-
Man blind from birth	-
Paralyzed man	9:1–8
Paralyzed woman	-
Peter's mother-in-law	8:14–15
Two blind men	9:27–34

Miracle	Brief description
Lepers, ten healed	Ten men with leprosy ask Jesus to have pity on them and Jesus cures them saying, "Go show yourselves to the priests."
Man blind from birth	Jesus spits on the ground, mixing his saliva with mud which he puts on the eyes of a blind man telling him to "wash in the pool of Siloam," after which the blind man regains his sight.
Paralyzed man	Jesus tells a paralyzed man to "get up, take your mat and go home," at which the man gets up, cured of paralysis.

Mark	Luke	John
-	17:11–19	-
-	-	9:1–12
2:1–12	5:17–26	-
-	13:11–13	-
1:29–31	4:38–39	-
-	-	-

Miracle	Brief description
Paralyzed woman	Jesus says to a woman bent over and unable to straighten up, "Woman, you are set free from your infirmity," and puts his hands on her and she is able to straighten up.
Peter's mother-in-law	Seeing Peter's mother-in-law lying on a bed with fever, Jesus touches her and the fever is gone.
Two blind men	Jesus touches the eyes of two blind men and their sight is restored.

During the nineteenth century spiritualism was in vogue. Many people took part in what may now be seen as nothing more than parlor games during which objects supposedly materialized and de-materialized. Later, organizers claimed to be able to contact the spirits of those who had died.

How does it work?

No one knows how faith healing works, as there are many different methods used by followers of this type of healing. Some (such as Christian Scientists) believe that cures result from the healing power of a God, so that faith in God is particularly important. Some believe healing occurs as a result of guidance by spirits, from the Virgin Mary, or the relics of dead saints.

Believing that you will get well from an illness may in itself affect the outcome of the illness, as doctors have discovered who give patients placebo medicines.

Ancient peoples often had little else to rely upon other than optimism. The act of doing something, such as reciting a magic formula or drawing a magic circle, gave shape to the hope for a cure.

In the 1960s, Maxwell Maltz, an American skin-graft surgeon, was puzzled as to why some of the people who had suffered great disfigurement in accidents recovered quickly and others didn't.

He found that patients behaved according to what they believed to be true. Badly disfigured people who believed in themselves and were optimistic about their future were successful, and people who had no self-respect and only wanted to cling to things as they used to before the accident, failed to recover, even when no disfigurement remained.

Treatment methods

Some spiritualists aim to make contact with their spirit
guides and they do this by going into a trance which
may or may not be apparent to their patient. Once in a
trance the spiritualist may be taken over by the spirit
guide and may not be able to recall events which take
place during the healing process. In some cases the
guide may simply take over the healer's movements.
A healer may place his or her hands on the patient's
head or some part of the body. Some healers may use
deep breathing, yoga, Christian prayers and the use of
mantras.

For some patients the
presence of a healer
is unnecessary—
they may use the
power of prayer
(either alone or
as part of a
congregation)
to bring about
healing or may
visit a healing
shrine for a
cure.

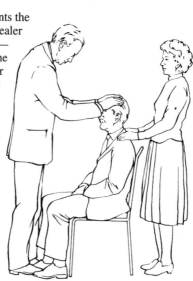

FELDENKRAIS METHOD

Definition
A series of exercises designed to realign the skeleton
and make the body move with minimum effort and
maximum efficiency, improving posture and general
health.

History
Moshe Feldenkrais was a Russian-born Israeli. As an
engineer and physicist he was interested in the way
things worked—including the human body. He was a
keen footballer and judo teacher, and troubled with a
recurring knee injury, he began a life-long study of the
mechanics of human movement, eventually combining
methods inherent to the Alexander Technique, Oriental
martial arts, and yoga to produce a series of movement
exercises designed to realign the skeleton and improve
general health.

WHAT CONDITIONS IS IT USED FOR?

- Arthritis
- Back pain
- Cerebral palsy
- Chronic pain
- Injury trauma
- Muscular pain

- Paralysis
- Scoliosis
- Strokes

Also used for general fitness and by actors, athletes,
dancers, musicians, and those with learning
disabilities.

How does it work?

The theory behind the Feldenkrais method is that by
helping people to become aware of their body and how
it moves, they can learn to bring about physical changes
that may result in an improvement in a physical—or
emotional—condition. For example, people suffering
from depression often stoop and have hunched
shoulders. Teaching people new patterns of
movement—to straighten up and pull his or her
shoulders back—improves posture and may also
alleviate their depression.

TREATMENT METHODS

The Feldenkrais method has two components:

1 Awareness through movement. This is a series of
exercises taught to groups of pupils and involves slow,
simple movements designed to make pupils aware of
their habitual patterns of movement, and to enlighten
them as to new patterns. The exercises may be
performed in a lying, sitting, or kneeling position and
help people identify and respond to areas of muscle
tension.

2 Functional integration. In cases where a person
requires more assistance than that available during an
awareness through movement class,
they can choose to receive gentle manipulation from a
Feldenkrais teacher on a one-to-one basis. Teachers
identify problem areas and prefer to work on them
indirectly as they feel that a direct approach often
evokes those patterns of movement that cause pain in
the first place.

FENG SHUI

Definition
The positioning of buildings, rooms and, objects to achieve harmony with nature.

History
Feng shui originated in China about 3000 years ago and was originally used to determine the most auspicious site to place a tomb so that the deceased spirit would be in harmony with heaven and earth. The principles of the science were first described in the *I Ching*, a classic book of Taoist philosophy. It is now used to help people achieve more harmonious living and work environments.

How does it work?
Feng shui practitioners inspect an area to determine lines of Qi (energy flow) and suggest ways in which buildings, rooms, furniture, and objects might be positioned in order to maximize the flow of Qi. This is believed by some to bring increased health, happiness, and prosperity.

WHAT CONDITIONS IS IT USED FOR?

Feng shui is not used to treat specific disorders but to help people achieve an overall harmonious environment in which to live and work. As a result, practitioners claim feng shui can help with:
- Emotional problems
- Lack of confidence
- Stress-related problems

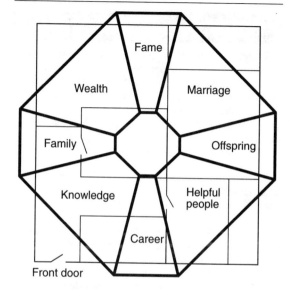

Fame

Wealth

Marriage

Family

Offspring

Knowledge

Helpful people

Career

Front door

Procedures

Feng shui practitioners use an octagonal "map" (ba-gua) superimposed on the floor plan of homes and offices (see illustration, *above*). Each segment of the ba-gua relates to a different aspect of life, and practitioners may advise changing the use of certain rooms or moving the position of furniture and objects, and changing the pattern of lighting and color schemes in order to facilitate a more harmonious overall environment. Plants and mirrors may be suggested to boost the energies of an office or home.

FERTILITY AMULETS & RITUALS

This section deals with amulets and rituals that are used to increase fertility. An amulet is an object made of wood, stone, metal, or other substance which protects against evil and may be inscribed with a magical character or figure. It is expected to invoke the help of great spirits associated with a culture or religion.

History

In almost all primitive cultures, the power of men and women to procreate was often of crucial importance to their status in the tribe and to the continuation of the tribe. Human fertility was also linked with good harvests and good fortune in battles and other situations.

A barren woman would be obliged to take all the shame for her condition and would be rejected or even expelled from the community because it was feared her influence would ruin the crops or cause animals to die. Women were generally treated as chattels in this context.

Fertility amulets

The most common way of encouraging the spirits to bestow fertility was by wearing a charm or amulet. In the religion of the Maoris of New Zealand, Tiki was the great Creator, and the Hei-Tiki, an amulet carved from greenstone, was very popular as a fertility charm. It is a small, round figure with an enormous head tilting to one side, thought to represent the fetus. Originally, it was said to give protection against the spirit of the unborn, who was placated by being offered parents.

FERTILITY AMULETS

1 Hei-Tiki carved from greenstone
2 Hei-Tiki carved from a skull—this is an unusual carving and may also represent Tiki the creator
3 Mistletoe growing on the trunk of an oak tree
4 A corn dolly fertility charm

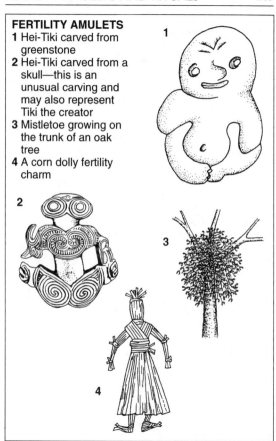

Among ancient Britons and other early European settlements, mistletoe was a very powerful fertility symbol because it apparently grew without roots and flourished with green leaves and white berries throughout winter when all other things appeared to be dead. In later centuries, mistletoe was carried into homes to ensure fertility, and later still the practice of kissing under the mistletoe was supposed to bring good luck to the lovers. Sometimes the oak tree on which the mistletoe grew was also regarded as potent, and oak twigs were carried as fertility symbols.

Fertility was often thought to be contagious, so a barren woman would ask for the gift of a brooch, shawl, or carved figure from a woman who had had many children in the belief that contact with the mother would result in her own conception. Some went to great lengths to weave fertility amulets from the hair of a woman who was already pregnant. Corn dollies were also woven from ripe corn and hung in the house or over the bed to encourage conception.

Rice or barley, being prolific plants, would be thrown over a couple as they retired to their marriage bed. Horseshoes, because they had been in contact with the earth, were thought to transfer fertility. Eggs and rabbits, too, are universal symbols of fertility. Rabbits' feet were popular good luck charms. Easter bunnies mark the new life of springtime and the Christian resurrection, while Bunny girls in clubs have a more sexual nuance.

In many cultures, the fox was associated with fertility, and amulets of fox skins would be hung in precise patterns to ensure a conception in Ancient Egypt. Foxes

were also buried in vineyards or hung about the fields
to propagate plants.

Some fertility rituals

Male fertility rights have included stabbing the ground
with spears, a ritual common to Bronze Age people and
contemporary aborigines. Many springtime festivities,
such as maypole dancing, originate as fertility rituals
for humans and plants. The Swedish Midsummer
Festival was originally a fertility dance, the maypole
representing the male, the garlands representing the
female.

In 16th-century Yugoslavia, there were several methods
a bride could use to ensure she would have children.
She could place an unlocked padlock in her bodice
when dressing. Having decided how many children she
wanted, she would take the same number of steps from
the door of her house and then snap the padlock closed.
If she was wise, she would also have a ladder ready.
When her groom arrived to take her to the wedding
ceremony, she would climb the same number of rungs,
in case the spirits had got it wrong the first time.
However, if any barley grains fell into her shoe after the
ceremony, her first pregnancy would be delayed as
many years as there were grains.

Fertility ritual in
Swedish rock
painting, 1000 B.C.

FLOTATION THERAPY

Definition
Floating in a tank of warm water in order to induce a state of deep relaxation.

Equipment
A flotation tank is used at a specially equipped therapy center. The tanks are large and the water, which is maintained at 34.2°C (93.5°F), is packed with Epsom and other mineral salts to enable clients to float.

History
Flotation therapy evolved from studies carried out by American psychoanalyst and neurophysiologist Dr. John C. Lily who, together with Dr. Jay Shurley, observed the effect floating had on the brain. Lily and Shurley theorized that when the brain was free from outside distraction, it would turn inward to the body's own biological and mental processes.

WHAT CONDITIONS IS IT USED FOR?

Stress-related conditions such as:

- Addiction
- Anxiety
- Back pain
- Cardiovascular disease
- Headaches
- High blood pressure
- Immune system suppression
- Insomnia
- Migraine
- Muscle fatigue
- Pain control
- Stress
- Ulcers

By the 1970s the two doctors had developed a flotation tank similar to those in use in therapy centers today.

How does it work?

During a session of flotation therapy external sensations—such as sound and light—are minimized. This induces a state of deep relaxation and is thought to be effective at reducing stress biochemicals and affecting endocrinal and psychological states.

Experiences of pain relief and mild euphoria are due to the release of endorphins, the body's natural painkillers.

Treatment methods

After a shower, some people choose to float naked in the tank. Once in the tank the door is closed and the light switched off so you remain in semi-darkness. Earplugs are sometimes available to protect against the salts and minerals in the water. Some tanks have speakers so hypnotherapy or meditation tapes can be listened to. Clients remain in the tank for a set period of time.

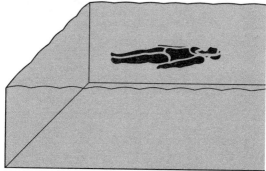

HEALING AMULETS

This section deals with the use of charms for the prevention and cure of disease and illness. See also the section on FERTILITY AMULETS & RITUALS.

History

Magical protection from the spirits of disease was big business among communities in the past. Folk medicine would be used only if an illness became a physical reality, but prevention was better than any cure. Charms, amulets and talismans abounded and were not so different from the charms and mascots we use today;

DEFINITIONS

Charms A charm is anything that will protect against evil. Some modern charms are a sprig of heather, a four-leaved clover, a rabbit's foot or a pendant of St. Christopher, the patron saint of travelers.

Amulets An amulet is an object made of wood, stone, metal, or other substance which protects against evil and may be inscribed with magical characters or figures. It is expected to invoke the help of great spirits associated with a culture or religion.

Talismans A talisman is an amulet that has been engraved with characters that attract occult influences. Hence the zodiac signs made into rings or brooches could be regarded as talismans.

Mascot A mascot is a person or an animal, or a thing in the form of a person or an animal, that will bring good luck.

---

they were also intended to stir the spirits of good
fortune and bring the wearer luck in the casino of life.
Many charms had a religious origin. The Ancient
Egyptians had a pantheon of gods that controlled every
detail of daily life. The talismans and amulets
associated with their gods were therefore thought to
have great powers.

The color red has had magic properties since prehistoric
times. The Roman believed coral to have healing
powers because of its pink color. In the Middle Ages in
Europe, a cure for sickness was to wrap a clipping of
hair or nails from the sick person in a red cloth and
bury it in the ground.

Some Ancient Egyptian amulets for health

Amulets were known in Ancient Egypt by the name
udjau, meaning "that which keeps you safe." Most
Egyptian amulets were not only worn by living
individuals but were placed in tombs to ensure the souls
of the dead would have protection, good health, and
long life when the time came for resurrection.

One of the oldest and most significant of the Ancient
Egyptian amulets is the scarab, which was dedicated to
Ra, the Sun God, the giver of life and protector of the
heart. The scarab is a representation of the dung beetle,
which lays its eggs in animal dung, rolls it up into a
ball, and pushes it to a place where the eggs will hatch
in the sun. The scarab symbolizes how the power of the
sun can be harnessed by even the most lowly of
creatures.

Another ancient amulet is the *ankh*, which represents
life itself. It is thought to be a representation of a scroll

of papyrus doubled over and tied with a strip of
papyrus. On the scroll was written the spell which
restored life to the Egyptian god Osiris.

Two other amulets that were carried to guard against
ill-health are the "two fingers" amulet, which would be
carried by a person in danger of falling, such as a stone
mason, and the *ba* amulet, which was a small, red
model of the heart and was carried by people with heart
problems. In a tomb it would bring to life the
mummified heart.

The ouser was a magic wand with enormous powers. In
many healing rituals, sick people would hope to be
touched by the ouser and its healing spirit.

It was a straight stick about four feet long with two
prongs at one end forming a U-shape. At the other end
was a T-cross. The magic rod given to Moses to lead
the Israelites out of Egypt was probably an ouser.
According to the Old Testament stories, he used his rod
to turn water into blood, dust into lice, and to produce
hail, fire, and spring water. The ouser may be the origin
of the modern magic wand.

The physician's amulet

The caduceus is a very ancient amulet used for healing
sickness, healing quarrels, and bringing peace. It
appeared in Sumeria at about 2600 B.C. and was also
used in Egypt, India and Ancient Greece. The two
entwined serpents are said to represent the balance
between good and evil, while in Buddhist terms they
are regarded as symbols of Kundalini, the life-force that
lies coiled at the base of the spine.

In later Greek times the caduceus acquired a pair of

wings, attributed to the story of how Mercury, the
messenger of the gods, calmed the two fighting snakes
with his silvery eloquence. The wings are those from
the feet of Mercury.

1 A scarab
2 An ankh
3 An ouser
4 The caduceus

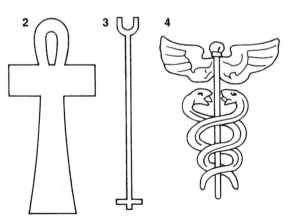

PRIMITIVE HEALING AMULETS
1 Horseshoes were said to ward off nightmares.
2 An amulet made from the hair and dried skin of a
   deceased person would protect the mourners from
   pain.
3 Moles' feet would give protection from rheumatism
   and were carried in a small bag.
4 The Ancient Egyptians wore a glass necklace as an
   amulet against the Evil Eye, the cause of all
   disease.

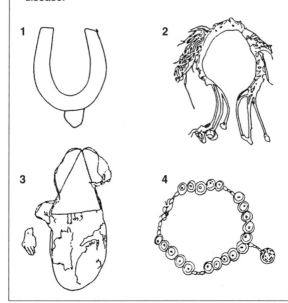

5 Amulets to prevent toothache and sore or bleeding gums: (**a**) cowrie shells (Russia); (**b**) orris root (Poland); (**c**) a fossil shark's tooth (Holland); (**d**) bag of alum (Russia).

6 Teething amulets served a double purpose as children could also chew on them: (**e**) ivy wood necklace; (**f**) seed necklace; (**g**) shell necklace used in Jersey, Channel Islands.

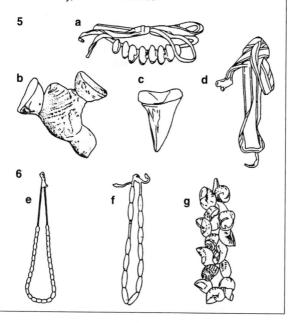

HEALING SHRINES

Definition

Places believed to have healing properties.

How does it work?

It is a belief in both Christianity and Islam that by making a journey to a distant holy place one can acquire the grace of God, symbolized in the tree of life. This belief is still firmly held by thousands of people who undertake modern pilgrimages, such as to the shrine of Our Lady of Lourdes, in France.

Belief in the healing power of the pilgrimage to a shrine is strong, despite the very small numbers of actual cures that have been claimed and recognized. For example, in 1929, 8 million people visited the grave of an American priest, seeking cures, yet only 100 claimed any kind of relief. Over 3 million people visit the Christian shrine of Lourdes every year, yet of the 5000 who have claimed to be cured during the last 120 years, the church has officially accepted less than 100 as miracles of healing.

History

Sick people often made annual pilgrimages to a favored shrine. Many visited one shrine after another, casting lots to decide which one to visit next, believing that the hand of God was directing even random choices. Their journeys branched from home like the branches of a tree. They returned home after each pilgrimage before embarking on the next, although a round trip might often have been shorter and less tiring in the long run. One medieval European text, a medical journal of the time, records a person making pilgrimages for 14 years before a partial cure was granted and another who visited 84 shrines, collapsing with exhaustion at the last, where he died.

Most pilgrims sat or lay in the church, or in the shrine itself, waiting to be healed. Often they had dreams or visions during which they were visited by angels or saints.

Sometimes women had to wait outside the shrine or even outside the church. For example, in the 12th century, St. Cuthbert of Durham was reputed to be a misogynist who punished females who dared to enter his church. People often sang or prayed aloud and when the crowd was gripped by hysterical fervor, people were knocked down or crushed.

Canterbury Cathedral

Perhaps the best known place of pilgrimage is to the tomb of St. Thomas à Becket in Canterbury Cathedral in Kent, where he was murdered in 1170. *The Canterbury Tales*, written by Geoffrey Chaucer (c.1340–1400), are a collection of stories told by a group of pilgrims.

The shrine of Bishop St. Thomas Cantelupe

A less well known shrine was that of Thomas Cantelupe at Hereford Cathedral, where, in the years around 1290, hundreds of suffering, crippled pilgrims would make their way. Some would be carried on litters, paying a penny to be brought to nearby villages, while one person is recorded as traveling from London in a wheelbarrow, pushed by family and friends for over 100 miles.

Miracles of healing had occurred at Cantelupe's tomb

and people gave offerings both in hope and gratitude. At its height, Cantelupe's shrine had a reputation that spread all over England and beyond. Papal records show an enormous hoard of offerings had already accumulated only 22 years after his death. See box, *below*, for inventory at the shrine on August 29, 1307. While the poor made wax images, the rich fashioned their images from precious metals to represent the part of the body that needed healing. When the image was

---

ITEMS FOUND IN SHRINE OF THOMAS CANTELUPE

- 170 silver ships
- 129 silver images of diverse human limbs
- 436 wax images of men
- 1200 wax images of parts of the body and limbs
- 77 wax figures of horses and other animals
- Large numbers of wax ears, eyes, breasts, teeth, etc.
- 95 children's shifts (dresses)
- 108 walking sticks for cripples
- 10 candles as large as a man
- 38 cloths of silk and gold with many girdles (belts)
- 520 gold or silver rings
- 96 gold or silver brooches and pins
- Diverse precious stones
- Lances
- Swords and spears
- Iron chains offered by prisoners
- Uncountable numbers of coins and candles

of a whole person, the pilgrim was either sick all over or taking precautions against the spread of disease. The clothes and jewelry would be from the sick person and the walking sticks indicated that some, who had arrived needing a crutch, had left able to walk again. Sick prisoners had only their chains to give and the weapons came not only from soldiers but also from the common man who necessarily carried a weapon for protection on any journey.

Papal commissioners stayed at Hereford for 78 days, noting that in the two months of September and October 1307, 86 more images, three more ships, two more children's shifts and hundreds more coins and candles were added to the collection.

The very existence of so many offerings would be taken as proof by some people of the miraculous powers of the dead Thomas Cantelupe, who was not canonized until 1320. Since Hereford is a long way inland, the reputation of the shrine must have spread far, as the presence of images of ships indicated that sea-going families from coastal settlements had also made a pilgrimage there.

The miracle of Lourdes

In 1844, mill worker François Soubirous and his wife had their first child whom they named Bernadette. Times were hard in the village of Lourdes and became harder for the family when Sourbirous lost the use of an eye and was sacked from his job. By then there were other children to feed and an outbreak of cholera had almost claimed the life of Bernadette, leaving her asthmatic.

Due to famine, Bernadette went away to work as a nanny for a while until January 1858, when, aged 14, she returned to Lourdes and went to the free school run by the Sisters of Charity.

Three weeks after her return, she was out early with her sister and a friend, collecting firewood as usual. In a grotto in the rocks, above a rose bush at Massabielle, she saw a glow of light and the vision of a beautiful woman she later referred to as *Aquero*, meaning "that one," in her local dialect.

Her claims to have seen a vision of the Virgin Mary on two occasions drew public disapproval, but one prosperous woman thought the vision must have been the ghost of a pious child who had died the previous year and took Bernadette back to the grotto, where she saw the vision again.

Between February 18 and March 4, Bernadette saw the vision of *Aquero*, Our Lady, 13 times and her audience grew from a few local villages to a crowd of 8000. *Aquero*, it is claimed, told her secrets, showed her the sacred spring in the grotto and carried out several healing miracles. Political and religious problems arose and there were increasing battles between the authorities.

On Wednesday, April 7, Bernadette saw the vision again, burning her hands in a candle flame in her ecstasy. Afterwards her hands were examined by a doctor, Pierre Dozous, who was present throughout, and declared her hands unharmed.

She last saw the vision on July 16 and at the age of 22 became a nun in the town of Nevers. She died at the age of 35 after long illnesses in 1879.

After her death, Lourdes' reputation grew as a healing shrine. In the region around Lourdes were at least four other shrines that had been dedicated to Our Lady. The stories were similar; at one, a shepherdess had seen a vision of a Lady that led to a cult following, a chapel being built, and the appearance of a spring of holy water. Our Lady of Lourdes and Our Lady of Garaison, of Poëylanun, of Héas and of Piétat are all shrines within the Lourdes area of the Pyrenees where miraculous healing is said to have taken place.

Pilgrims at Lourdes waiting for Mass in the Grotto

HERBAL MEDICINE

Definition
The use of certain plants for medicinal purposes. A
herb is usually defined as a plant with a non-woody
stem that dies down after flowering. Chinese herbalists
also use non-plant substances such as the bone, hair,
horn, or skin.

Types
A wide variety of herbs are used. Sometimes the whole

FIVE WAYS IN WHICH HERBALISM AIMS TO HEAL

1 By eliminating waste products
For example, senna contains anthraquinone
glycoside, which irritates the bowels and causes
elimination. Other plant remedies useful for
constipation are alder, blackthorn, fennel, licorice,
molasses, prunes, and slippery elm.

2 By adjusting and balancing body processes
For example, the foxglove and, to a lesser extent, the
lily of the valley for normalizing heart rate; also
dandelion root for the liver, coltsfoot for the lungs, and
couch grass root for the kidneys. Fruit of the
chasteberry tree is thought to balance the production
of progesterone and estrogen by its action on the
pituitary gland. Mistletoe, rose hips, and lady's mantle
help to normalize the menstrual flow.

3 By stimulating natural body responses
For example, chili, ginger, and mustard contain acrid
glycoside, which stimulates the blood vessels and
improve circulation. Gentian and other bitter herbs

herb is used, sometimes part of it, such as the root, bark, seed, fruit, flower, leaf, or stem.

Herbs are used in a variety of forms, including tinctures, where one part of the herb is mixed with five parts of diluted alcohol. Herbs are also administered in the form of infusions, inhalants, pills, tablets, and lotions.

Equipment

The traditional equipment used by herbalists is a pestle and mortar—a small bowl and a smooth-headed club used to grind up parts of plants. Commercially prepared

---

stimulate the digestive processes. Comfrey has many herbal uses and is particularly helpful in clearing lung congestion and stimulating the lungs to work more efficiently. Oil of basil stimulates a brighter outlook.

4 By protecting against undesirables

For example, marshmallow root soothes and gives a mucilaginous protection against irritation. Witch hazel, tannin and other astringents form antiseptic coatings over tissue surfaces. Garlic fights both bacterial and fungal infections, and wormwood works against internal worms. Onions are also useful.

5 By sedating body processes

For example, oats for nervous exhaustion and valerian for sedation. Hawthorn slows the heart rate yet increases blood flow, and licorice is excellent for calming stomach ulcers. Some herbs are useful against pain, such as oil of cloves for toothache and oil of peppermint for cramps and other pains.

herbal remedies may be available in raw form or as
pills, lotions, ointments, etc.

How does it work?
Herbalists aim to detect and restore normal functioning
rather than attack a pathological condition. Only if the
pathology is well entrenched may orthodox methods be
recommended. Herbalists claim their remedies restore
normal functioning by one or more of five basic
approaches (see box, on the previous pages). It is
thought that the combination of substances in herbal
tinctures is more important than any single constituent.
Tinctures themselves may also contain more than one
herb.

An ancient
Japanese
herb gatherer

History

This branch of folk medicine has been developing as
herbal medicine for over 5000 years.

Manuscripts giving lists of herbs and their uses have
been found in Ancient Egypt and China. The Chinese
Pen Tsao (3000 B.C.) lists around 1000 herbal remedies
and a papyrus dating from 1500 B.C. lists hundreds of
herbs that were used in the city of Theses, including
cinnamon and caraway seed.

A 16th-century herb gatherer
and a herbalist preparing his
mixture with pestle and
mortar

Roman conquerors of Britain brought Mediterranean
herbs with them, such as lavender and rosemary.
Then, during the medieval period, superstition and
sorcery became a necessary part of ritual healing
ceremonies. For example, to ensure a herbal infusion
would work properly, the patient might be required to
walk seven times around a gravestone while reciting a
Latin incantation.

Published in 1640, John Parkinson's *Theatrum
Botanicum* contained descriptions of more than 3800

TREATMENT METHODS
Herbs are used in a variety of ways, depending on
the kind of practitioner using them.

Types of herbal practitioners
- Retail herbalists who sell remedies and give
  advice on their use.
- Professional medical herbalists who are trained
  and recognized by a professional institute. Many
  of these are orthodox doctors or recognized
  paramedics.
- Aromatherapists who use herbs distilled into
  essential oils and apply them externally during
  massage.
- Specialist herbalists in cultural medical systems,
  such as Chinese acupuncturists who use
  herbalism as an adjunct and the Hakims of Islam
  who practice Indian medical systems.
- Alternative medical practitioners, such as
  osteopaths, radionic technicians, dowsers,
  naturopaths, and others who may include
  herbalism as part of their practice.

plants, grouped according to their medicinal properties.
In 1653 London's most famous herbalist—Nicholas
Culpeper— wrote his famous herbal, *The English
Physician Enlarged*, which is still in print today. In
1864 the National Association of Medical Herbalists
was founded in order to maintain standards of practice
and to fight attempts by the orthodox medical
profession to have herbalism banned. People such as
Samuel Thompson and Dr. Benedict Lust popularized
herbalism in the United States. Dr. Lust opened the first
health food store in America in 1896.

During the 19th century herbal folklore spread widely,
when European emigrants arrived in America and
brought with them their native herbal folklore. This,
together with the ancient knowledge of the American
Indians, forms the basis of much modern herbalism in
the USA.

Primitive tribes continue to rely on their traditional
knowledge of herbs and their healing properties.

Herbs form the major part of Ayurvedic medicine in
India, and are widely used in Chinese medicine also.
Today, the work of medical herbalists is sometimes
been termed *phytotherapy*.

What conditions is it used for?

Herbalists treat all kinds of conditions. A list of
common conditions and the herbs which are used to
treat them can be found on the next six pages. This is
provided for information only and is not intended as a
treatment guide.

Always consult a qualified herbalist.

COMMON AILMENTS AND REMEDIES PROPOSED BY HERBALISTS

Ailment	Herbal remedy	
Acne	Burdock	
	English walnut	
	Valerian	
Asthma	Aniseed	Ground ivy
	Celandine	Gum plant
	Coltsfoot	Hyssop
	Comfrey	Licorice
	Elder flower	Mullein
	Fennel	Sloe
	Garlic	Valerian
	Garden thyme	Willow herb
Bladder problems	Barberry	Chickweed
	Birch	Cowberry
	Camomile	
Blood pressure	European mistletoe	Onion
	Garlic	Parsley
	Hawthorn	Rue
	Mistletoe	
Boils	Burdock	Sanicle
	Camomile	Scarlet pimpernel
	Flax	Slippery elm
	Linseed	Thyme
	Marjoram	Wild indigo
	Marshmallow root	
	Nasturtium	

Ailment	Herbal remedy	
Bronchitis	Coltsfoot Comfrey Gum plant	Licorice
Bruises	Arnica Marjoram oil	
Burns	Burdock Coltsfoot Comfrey	Onion Potato
Colds	Agrimony Catnip Camomile Cinnamon Coltsfoot Ginger	Marjoram Peppermint Sunflower seed oil Thyme Yarrow
Constipation	Alder Blackthorn Dandelion Fennel Licorice	Molasses Prunes Senna Slippery elm
Coughs	Calamint Elder blossom Hyssop	Sunflower seed oil

**COMMON AILMENTS AND REMEDIES PROPOSED
BY HERBALISTS** (continued)

Ailment	Herbal remedy	
Cramps	Cayenne Fennel Rosemary	Rue Wild yam Wormwood
Diarrhea	Agrimony Blackberry root Cinnamon fern Oak bark	Silverweed Spotted cranebill
Dyspepsia	Caraway Camomile Dandelion	Peppermint
Eczema	Burdock root (internal) Chickweed (external)	
Fatigue	Agrimony Marjoram Peppermint	Rose hips Yeast
Fever	Aconite Fenugreek Slippery elm	Sorrel
Flatulence	Caraway Cardamom Charcoal biscuits	Fennel Garlic Turmeric

Ailment	Herbal remedy	
Gout	Celery seed Colchicum Hyssop Juniper	Meadowsweet Nettle
Headache	Camomile Hops Lavender Mint	Poppy Willow Wood betony
Influenza	Catnip Garlic Ginger	Peppermint Yarrow
Insomnia	American valerian Aniseed Bergamot Hops Lime flowers	Passion flower Valerian
Menstrual cramps	Blue cohosh Camomile Lady's mantle Marigold Mistletoe Passion flower	Rose hips Sorrel St. John's Wort Wild lettuce
Nasal congestion	Fenugreek	

**COMMON AILMENTS AND REMEDIES PROPOSED
BY HERBALISTS** (continued)

Ailment	Herbal remedy	
Nausea	Black horehound Caraway Camomile Clove	Ginger Lemon balm Peppermint
Nervousness	Peppermint Rosemary	Sage
Neuralgia	Hops Passion flower Wild marjoram Willow Wormwood	
Piles	Lesser celandine Plantain	
Rheumatism	Agrimony Black cohosh Borage Camomile Celery seed Cuckoopint Ground elder Hyssop Juniper	Meadowsweet Mugwort Onion Rosemary Wintergreen Wood betony
Sore throat	Cayenne Poke root Raspberry Sage	Stinging nettle Thyme Wild indigo

Ailment	Herbal remedy	
Toothache	Elder Oil of cloves Tansy Yarrow leaves	
Ulcers	Camomile Lemon balm Licorice Peppermint	
Vomiting	Black horehound Camomile Lemon balm Peppermint Spearmint	
Wounds	Comfrey Lovage	
Sprains	Arnica Comfrey Marjoram oil	
Stings	Burdock Garlic Goosegrass	Horseradish

HOMEOPATHY

Definition

A system based on the principle of "like curing like," which aims to treat the whole person and is the opposite of allopathic (orthodox) medicine in that it does not aim to suppress symptoms of illness.

The principle of similars—like cures like—is the basis of the medical system called homeopathy.

History

Hippocrates, the Greek physician who lived in the fifth century B.C., was the first to record in his medical books the homeopathic principle that like cures like. However, it was not until 1810 that Dr. Samuel Hahnemann, from Leipzig, published his *Organon*, a textbook of a practical system of healing based on this principle.

Hahnemann was interested in the effect of substances of animal, vegetable, and mineral origin or even disease products. He was experimenting on himself with an extract of quinine from the Peruvian cinchona bark which was the common treatment for malaria and was surprised to observe that the substance produced in himself the same symptoms as it was used to cure.

Over several years he tested hundreds of substances on himself and healthy volunteers, observing any deviations from the norm that were produced. These deviations he listed as symptoms, in some cases as few as five or six, in others as many as 300 or more.

He then matched the symptoms of his patients with the symptoms produced by the tested substances. To do this

accurately, he had to devise a thorough method of
diagnosis, which involved recording the patient's
answers to many detailed questions.

EXAMPLE OF HAHNEMANN'S OBSERVATIONS

Scarlet fever produces delirium, hot dry red skin, and throbbing pains in a healthy person.

Belladonna produces these same symptoms in a healthy person and Hahnemann deduced that belladonna could therefore be used to treat scarlet fever.

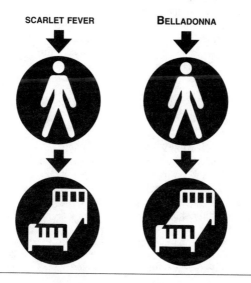

SCARLET FEVER   BELLADONNA

The new skills of homeopathy practiced by Hahnemann were successful except in a few cases, when the doses given seemed to make the disease worse. Since his aim was to cure without adding to the harm already caused by a disease, he began to give smaller and smaller doses, diluting the substances in pure water and alcohol.

Unfortunately, the more dilute the solution, the less effective it was therapeutically. At least this was the case until Hahnemann made a startling discovery. He was testing different ways of preparing the homeopathic solutions when he found that by shaking the dilutions violently, they retained their medical potency despite repeated dilution. A substance might be diluted 100 times, yet be more effective than a stronger solution, provided it has been shaken very thoroughly during its preparation. This process was called potentization and the diluted remedies were known as potencies. A typical homeopathic practitioner would have in excess of 2000 remedies in a range of potencies from which to choose one or more suitable for a particular patient.

How does it work?

Homeopathy is the process of treating a disease in such a way that the symptoms of the disease would be induced in a normally healthy person. For example, a fever would be treated by a drug that increased the fever slightly, thus mobilizing the body's own system to fight the sickness.

Correct homeopathic treatment has regard for the whole person and his or her way of life. The assumption is that the body can fight the sickness, so the treatment

It is thought that environmental factors contribute to many chronic diseases and homeopathic doctors recognize that some people are simply luckier than others and are born with potentially better basic health balance. Some doctors claim there are no incurable diseases, but that there are some incurable people. Three different and healthy people may therefore respond differently to the same disease.

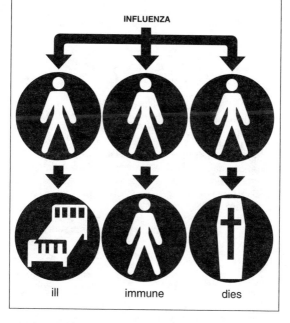

INFLUENZA

ill   immune   dies

aims to help stimulate the body to do its natural job. Different treatments are selected for different people, even though they may be suffering from the same disease.

It can be demonstrated in the laboratory that while a large dose of poison kills, a minute dose of the same poison can stimulate the cellular function vital to produce a natural antidote.

How can it be that a solution that may no longer contain any molecules of a substance can still be therapeutically potent? Modern nuclear physics is now providing evidence that a molecule can leave its mark in a diluent, that substances can leave an imprint of themselves upon a diluent, providing there is enough energy available for them to do so.

MAKING HOMEOPATHIC REMEDIES

After its extraction, usually from a plant, the substance under preparation is diluted by either mixing it with pure alcohol or lactose powder, depending whether it is a liquid or a solid.

Titration is the fairly vigorous grinding process used to mix solids which are at first diluted. Further dilutions are made by the same process of titration. Succession is the process used to mix the liquid substance with pure alcohol by violently shaking together one part substance with nine parts alcohol. Higher dilutions such as 5c or 10c contain very little of the substance yet become more potent.

The grinding and shaking of substances increases the
energy potential of their molecules, so while remedies
may be given to patients in low concentration, they
contain high energy states, patterned in the same way as
the original molecules. It has been also suggested by
physicists that imprinted patterns can replicate
themselves. If this is so, it would explain the increased
potency of a remedy even beyond the dilution.
Hahnemann always treated the patient not the disease.
He found that different combinations of potencies were
required for different people who at first glance
appeared to be suffering from the same disease. He also
found that while acute conditions were easily cured,
only temporary relief was gained in many chronic
situations. He concluded that there were inherited and
acquired disease tendencies that he called miasmus.
His opinion that some people had a lower natural
vitality, and therefore greater vulnerability, led him to
state that there could be no such thing as disease
without the ground in which it could grow. Disease only
occurs when the vital principle of a person's body
cannot cope with changes occurring in the body.

What conditions is it used for?

A list of common ailments and homeopathic treatments
can be found on the next four pages. These are provided
for information only and are not intended as a source of
self-treatment.

Always consult a qualified homeopath.

COMMON AILMENTS AND TREATMENTS SUGGESTED BY HOMEOPATHS

Ailment	Homeopathic treatment
Abscesses	Lachesis
Acne	Lycopodium
Arthritis	Calcarea Rhus tox
Asthma	Ipecac
Back pain	Arnica Ipecac
Black eyes	Ledum
Bleeding	Ipecac
Boils	Lachesis
Burns	Hypericum
Bruising	Arnica
Catarrh	Dulcamara Euphrasia Gelsemium

Ailment	Homeopathic treatment
Colds	Aconite Allium Arsenicum Eupatorium Gelsemium Lycopodium Nux vomica Pulsatilla
Cold sores	Hepar sulph
Conjunctivitis	Hepar sulph
Constipation	Calcarea Nux vomica
Coughs	Drosera Gelsemium Pulsatilla
Cramp	Nux vomica
Cuts and grazes	Hypericum
Cystitis	Nux vomica

COMMON AILMENTS AND TREATMENTS
SUGGESTED BY HOMEOPATHS (continued)

Ailment	Homeopathic treatment
Digestive problems	Nux vomica
Dizziness	Gelsemium Glonoinum
Drowsiness	Gelsemium
Earache	Belladonna Gelsemium
Eczema	Calcarea
Faintness	Gelsemium Ipecac
Fever	Belladonna
Food poisoning	Arsenicum
Gastric complaints	Aconite
Hay fever	Allium Pulsatilla

Ailment	Homeopathic treatment
Headaches	Belladonna Glonoinum Lachesis Pulsatilla
Heartburn	Lycopodium
Indigestion	Calcarea
Influenza	Hepar sulph Nux vomica
Insect bites	Hypericum
Insomnia	Gelsemium
Joint stiffness	Ledum
Menopausal problems	Glonoinum
Menstrual problems	Calcarea Gelsemium Lachesis Nux vomica

COMMON AILMENTS AND TREATMENTS
SUGGESTED BY HOMEOPATHS (continued)

Ailment	Homeopathic treatment
Migraine	Nux vomica
Motion sickness	Nux vomica
Mouth ulcers	Hepar sulph
Muscle pain	Lachesis
Nausea	Ipecac
Nosebleeds	Arnica Ipecac
Pain	Pulsatilla
Panic attacks	Arsenicum
Phobias	Gelsemium
Piles	Nux vomica
Premature ejaculation	Lycopodium
Ringing in the ears	Rhus tox

Ailment	Homeopathic treatment
Sciatica	Rhus tox
Sinusitis	Hepar sulph Lachesis
Sore throat	Gelsemium Lachesis
Sprains	Arnica Rhus Tox
Sunburn	Hypericum
Swelling	Pulsatilla

HYDROTHERAPY

Definition
The use of water to heal.
Types
Water may be used in its various forms—as solid ice, liquid, steam, or gas. It is used either hot or cold (or in combinations of both). Some treatment centers are located around hot or cold springs or mineral springs (called spas) where hot or cold baths, compresses, showers, or wraps may be used. For descriptions of different types of hydrotherapy treatment see "Treatment Methods" at the end of this section.
History
Many Greek temples honoring the god of medicine, Asklepios, were built at the sites of hot springs. In the 4th century B.C., Greek physician Hippocrates advocated bathing in and drinking spring waters, and baths were an essential part of daily life for Romans. In Europe in the 16th century practitioners suggested that water could be used as a "cure."
In the 18th and 19th centuries hydrotherapy became exceedingly popular. Water treatment was of two kinds: hot or cold. Some doctors who ran hydrotherapy programs at various spa centers that developed in Europe in the 19th century swore by heat treatments; others insisted that cold water was the only valid water treatment. One infamous cold water spa was at Gräfenberg, 2000 feet up in the mountains of Austrian Silesia (now known as Jesnik, in Czechoslovakia). It was run by Vincent Priessnitz, a farmer's son, who

---

WHAT CONDITIONS IS IT USED FOR?
Different hydrotherapy treatments are helpful for
different disorders, some of which include:

- Anemia
- Arthritis
- Asthma
- Back pain
- Bronchitis
- Colds
- Constipation
- Cystitis
- Digestive problems
- Gallstones
- Headaches
- Joint problems
- Menstrual problems
- Piles
- Rheumatism
- Skin disorders
- Sprains
- Strains

---

became famous for his hydrotherapy cures-without-
drugs, and rich in the process. He combined cold water
treatments with lengthy exercise and mountain air.
Priessnitz claimed his cures made people fitter than
they had ever been, although according to rumor, a
person had to be fit to undertake his water cures. *The
Journal of Health*, of 1852, reporting on his methods,
called him the "Water Demon."

Priessnitz reasoned that if a cold compress cured a
sprained ankle then why not a cold compress for the
whole body to cure a deep disorder? Warm water and
sweat blankets were only used to add shock to the
consequent application of icy cold water.

Sebastian Kneipp, a Dominican monk from Bavaria,
believed water could help stimulate the body's own
healing powers.

A TYPICAL DAY AT GRÄFENBERG

A certain Captain Claridge, who suffered from rheumatism, listed his first day of treatments at Gräfenberg as follows:

4 a.m.	• Dip in the cold spring • An hour in the sweat blanket • Cold plunge for three minutes followed by a long walk • Breakfast, with cold spring water to drink
10 a. m.	• Five minutes under cold douche • Warm sitz bath and foot bath for fifteen minutes each • Another cold douche • A long walk
1 p.m.	• Lunch • Wet-sheeting (skin massage with wet sheets) • An ascending cold douche for the genitals • Another long walk, a head-pack and cold sponge-down • Warm sitz bath and foot bath for fifteen minutes each
9.30 p.m.	• In bed with feet and legs bound in cold, wet bandages

It is said that after three months the Captain had walked 1000 miles and was cured of rheumatism.

How does it work?

Water in its various forms may be used to:

- Aid relaxation
- Ease pain
- Ease stiffness
- Stimulate blood flow
- Remove impurities
- Treat disease

Water brings about different bodily changes according to its temperature:

Hot water:

- Dilates blood vessels
- Encourages sweating
- Relaxes muscles and joints
- Draws heat to the surface of the body

Cold water:

- Constricts blood vessels
- Reduces sweating
- Reduces inflammation and congestion
- Stimulates the flow of blood to internal organs

When cold water is used, blood vessels in the skin constrict. This causes an increase in blood flow in deeper blood vessels. When the cold water is removed and hot water applied, the blood vessels dilate and flood the area with blood. It is known that the simultaneous application of hot and cold in this way improves circulation.

TREATMENT METHODS

Balneology

This is the therapeutic use of natural spring waters or
mineral waters, so called because they contain
inorganic salts such as chlorides and carbonates. Spring
water may be naturally hot or cold.

European spa towns are those that were developed
when natural springs were available. The ancient city of
Bath, England, has had public mineral baths since
Roman times.

Other well-known spas include Baden-Baden in West
Germany, Spa in Belgium, Vichy in France and
Marienbad in Czechoslovakia.

Research has shown that it is probable that some
minerals can be absorbed directly through the skin.
Visitors would also drink the mineral water while
relaxing after bathing.

Baths, hot

Hot baths—with water temperature just above 38°C
(100°F)—are used in hydrotherapy to relax muscles,
ease pain, and promote sweating. Epsom salts are
sometimes added to help drive off chills and colds,
while adding sea salt helps fresh injuries to heal.
Bags of oats or bran are sometimes added to help
eczema.

Baths, cold

Cold baths—with water temperatures about 16–20°C
(60–68°F)—are used in hydrotherapy to reduce
inflammation and improve circulation.

Baths, sitz

A sitz bath consists of two small baths, one filled with hot water, the other with cold. For three minutes patients sit in one part of the bath with hot water covering abdomen, with their feet in the cold water bath, then they change positions and sit in the cold bath for one minute with their feet in the hot water.

Baths, steam

Turkish baths and sauna baths promote sweating and help disperse impurities form the body. In a sauna people sit around a room that is heated to a high temperature—perhaps to 38°C (100°F)—and then go for a swim or shower in very cold water.

Compresses

Cold compresses are used to constrict blood vessels and reduce inflammation. Hot compresses are used to increase blood flow to a diseased area or organ and flush out impurities by promoting sweating.

Inhalation

Inhalation of steamy air is often used as part of home hydrotherapy treatments for colds where a few drops of eucalyptus or menthol oil are added to the water to aid decongestion.

Physiotherapy

Hydrotherapy is an essential part of some physiotherapy treatments. Patients may be immersed in a pool of warm water, usually at 33–36°C (92–97°F) and allowed either to relax, to exercise, or to be gently massaged using water. Exercising gently in water helps

to increase the strength of muscles and improves
general mobility. The warm water dilates blood vessels,
increasing oxygen flow to areas where it is needed for
healing. Hydrotherapy treatment of this kind is
particularly beneficial after injury or surgery or
following disease or stroke.

Thalassotherapy

From the Greek word *Thalassa* meaning sea,
thalassotherapy is the tonic effect of time spent in the
sea or in sea water.

External sores, wounds, skin burns, and skin ulcers all
benefit from regular bathing in the sea (providing, of
course, the sea water is not too polluted).

Thermalism (see box, *right*)

In health care, this term describes the use of the
pressure of moving water of various temperatures to
massage the muscles and stimulate the circulation.
When a person is immersed in water the body becomes
almost weightless, and this helps the massaging action
of water to have more effect on relaxed muscles.

Wrapping

When wrapping is used as part of a hydrotherapy
treatment, a sheet dampened with cold water is
wrapped around the body. Next, a dry sheet is applied
and then a warm blanket is wrapped around the dry
sheet. A patient remains in the wrap until the original
wet sheet dries out, after which the body is sponged
with tepid water and rubbed dry.

THERMALISM IN ETHIOPIA

Ethiopia is situated in the African Rift Valley, an area of historic volcanic activity that now has some of the world's most spectacular hot springs.

According to traditional Ethiopian medicine, rheumatism, skin diseases, leprosy, and venereal diseases were all said to be cured by regular thermal bathing.

It was also a belief that spring water was of divine origin, so miracle cures for serious terminal conditions were sought. The outstanding feature of all thermal baths in Ethiopia was their high temperature. They were known as *felwaha*, meaning boiling water. Anything from 49–60°C (120–140°F) was common.

Patients used to stay at the baths for several days, drinking the spring water mixed with honey and linseed. This produced copious sweating, an important aspect of the treatment.

People with different diseases were segregated: there was the leprosy pool, the scrofula pool, the rheumatism pool and there was always a pool reserved for ordinary, healthy bathers.

Most of the treatment pools were covered with straw and bamboo thatch, which protected the bathers from too much direct sunlight and enclosed the heat, producing steam which also induced sweating.

HYPNOTHERAPY

Definition

Using hypnotism to improve physical and psychological health.

One view of hypnosis is that it involves an altered stated of consciousness that can be induced by oneself or by another person and during which conscious control is relaxed, making the contents of the unconscious more accessible. In most measurable physiological respects, it does not differ from the waking state.

History

There is evidence that hypnosis was used in the temples of Aesculapius in ancient Greece as well as in ancient medicinal and religious practices—such as shamanism, voodoo, faith-healing and Druidism. Hypnotism has been known as "mesmerism" after Anton Mesmer who, in the 18th century, induced trance states for the purposes of healing. (See the section on MAGNETISM AND MESMERISM.) Mesmer believed that he was utilizing magnetic energy to heal his patients. It was French physician Alexandre Bertrand and Scottish surgeon Dr. James Braid who independently arrived at the conclusion that it was not animal magnetism that contributed to the cure of patients, but suggestions made by the practitioner which were somehow adopted by the imagination of patients. In his book *Neurypnology*, published in 1843, Dr. Braid argued that the combined states of enhanced awareness and relaxation should be called "hypnotism." He is credited with being the founder of medical hypnosis.

In Calcutta, surgeon James Esdaile performed operations using hypnosis with no anesthetic, and Sigmund Freud made use of hypnosis while investigating the unconscious.

In the 1890s hypnotherapy went into decline; its reputation suffered from misuse in the hands of charlatans.

Types

The type of hypnosis used by Sigmund Freud is now known as classical hypnosis, in which a trance-like state is induced either by the sound of the therapist's voice, or using a bright light, metronome or pendulum. The hypnotherapist uses direct suggestion and other hypnotic procedures in order to reduce a symptom.

In the United States particularly, a somewhat different approach is used, based on the work of Dr. Milton H. Erickson who made greater use of subtle, indirect suggestions, allowing a greater freedom of response from patients.

WHAT CONDITIONS IS IT USED FOR?

- Alcohol addiction
- Angina
- Anxiety
- Arthritis
- Asthma
- Childbirth
- Dentistry
- Drug addictions
- Emotional problems
- Insomnia
- Irritable bowel syndrome
- Migraine
- Overeating
- Pain relief
- Peptic ulcers
- Phobias
- Rheumatism
- Skin disorders
- Stress

How does it work?

Although we may pride ourselves on our ability to stay in control of our own minds, we are all, fortunately, open to suggestive healing. Hypnotic suggestion is not, despite popular belief, available only to weak, emotional people.

Since women were supposed to be the weaker sex, most early illustrations show a male hypnotist putting a female subject into a trance, although there is no reason why it should not occur the other way around.

This biased attitude still causes people to ignore the potential of hypnotic suggestion for healing and to continue to regard hypnosis as some kind of power the strong have over the weak.

No one really knows how hypnotism works. Understanding how the mind works is a help in exploring the latent powers of hypnosis.

There are many theories on the effect hypnotism has on the brain's functioning. These are rigorously contested by experts. One of the most plausible theories is as follows (see illustration, *right*).

When we concentrate our attention on a swinging ball, messages received through the eyes are relayed by visual pathways to the midbrain. Areas of the brain affected include the reticular formation (**a**), pons (**b**) and medulla (**c**), but the incoming messages primarily influence and inhibit the midbrain centers, so that the responses of the motor and sensory areas, and memory areas of the cerebrum (**d**) are influenced and modified.

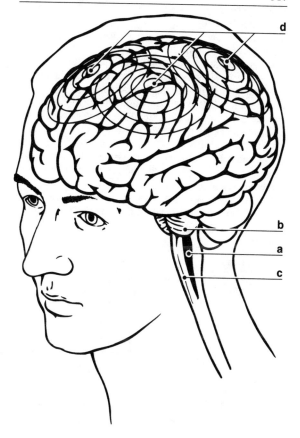

Treatment methods

There are normally five basic steps to attain hypnosis, although actual methods vary.

1 The subject sits or lies comfortably; this limits physical tension and anxiety. This is the first stage of withdrawal from "normal" consciousness.

2 The subject is told to concentrate on the hypnotist's voice and actions to the exclusion of everything else. This reduces the number of environmental distractions.

3 The subject is asked to listen passively and comply with what is said. This limits the complex internal mental processes of evaluation and decision-making.

4 The subject may be asked to stare at a single object (**a**). This produces retinal fatigue, precisely what is required in hypnosis, so that the eyes are ready to close.

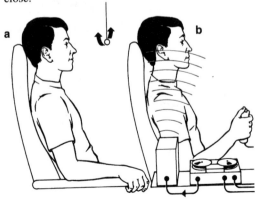

5 A relaxed (trance-like) condition is suggested, and the hypnotist may make some trial suggestions to confirm that the subject has slipped into a hypnotic trance.

Self-hypnosis
The hypnotist's voice may be recorded on tape and played back by the subject. After each suggestion, the subject presses a remote control device to go on to the next stage (**b**). This puts control of the procedure in the hands of the subject and shows that hypnosis is a more simple technique than many practitioners might like to admit. However, this is not a commonly used method. A cue word or other signal is often used to train people to achieve self-hypnosis.

Hypnosis for insomniacs
It is possible to induce sleep in insomniacs simply by using a device which sends low-frequency current through the brain (*right*), affecting sleep control centers. Similar electrical input devices may affect brain waves to produce hypnotic states.

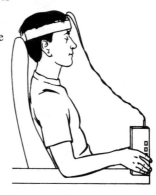

ION THERAPY

Definition
Using ions (charged air particles) to prevent and cure illness and disease.

WHAT ARE IONS?
Ions are particles that carry either a negative or a positive electrical charge, owing to the loss or gain of an electron.
The air we breathe has a natural, very small ion content, the balance of which can easily be disrupted by pollution such as fumes or by central heating and air conditioning. Some natural phenomena also cause negative ion-depletion; pre-thunderous weather, during solar radiation, humidity, and temperature changes, and in certain warm winds such as the Föhn in Germany and the Sharav in the Near East.

History
It was established in the 1920s that air with a low ion count adversely affects humans. In the 1950s Professor A.P. Kreuger of the University of California established that the bacteria which cause colds and influenza to spread could be killed off utilizing negative ions. In 1960 he suggested that positive ions caused an over-production of serotonin in animals.

How does it work?
The conditions which cause negative ion depletion are known to cause a general malaise, sometimes called "serotonin hyperfunction syndrome" because the

WHAT CONDITIONS IS IT USED FOR?

Ionizers are said to help people suffering:

- Allergies
- Burns
- Catarrh
- Claustrophobia
- Common respiratory disorders
- Depression
- Hay fever
- Headache
- Hypertension
- Insomnia
- Irritability
- Stress

neurotransmitter serotonin moves out of its bound form in the cells into a free form in the body fluids. This results in stress reactions, depression, constricted breathing, and other unpleasant effects. Increasing the negative ion proportion in the air will reverse these effects, causing the serotonin to return to its healthy bound form inside the cells of the body.

The atmosphere can regain its own ion balance, given a lack of pollution. High concentrations of negative ionization exist naturally near waterfalls, on the coast, in some mountain areas, and wherever there is fresh air and fine rain.

Equipment

Small machines called "ionizers" can be bought in electrical stores and some health food shops.

Treatment methods

Ionizers, using a high electrical voltage to produce a flow of negative ions, can be used in rooms, cars, by the bed, or in the office to keep the ion balance healthy. Aromatherapy may be another way of increasing the negative ion balance in the body.

IRIDOLOGY

Definition
Examining the eye's iris to diagnose conditions of the body.

Types
A full iridology assessment usually includes sclerology, in which the sclera (white) of the eye is also examined.

Equipment
Various equipment is used to examine the iris, including a magnifying glass, a penlight, and an iris microscope (similar to an optician's slit lamp); photographs may be made and an iridology manual or chart used for reference.

How does it work?
Iridologists believe that changes in the iris reveal changes in body structures, and that abnormalities in these structures may show up in the iris before the physical symptoms of disease begin. There are various ways the iris may reflect bodily changes: (1) The fine nerve filament of the iris may receive impressions from every part of the body, and abnormalities in the body may throw these nerve fibers out of alignment; (2) Bloodflow in the capillaries within organs and tissues may cause alteration to the pigments in the surface layers of the iris; (3) Since the iris is linked to the sympathetic nervous system, fibers in the iris may move their position in response to stress.

History The Chaldeans of Babylonia recorded readings of diseases from the eyes around 1000 B.C., and the process of iris diagnosis was known to the Ancient

WHAT CONDITIONS IS IT USED FOR?

Dr. Ignatz von Peczely believed that examination of
the iris could reveal a variety of conditions including:
- Chemical imbalances
- Endocrine disorders
- Structural defects
- Tensions
- Toxemias
- Weaknesses

Chinese, Japanese and Indian cultures. The medical
writings of Hippocrates also refer to iridology.
The most comprehensive study of iris diagnosis was
undertaken by Hungarian physician Dr. Ignatz von
Peczely, who published his "map" of the eye in 1886, a
chart linking diseases and conditions of specific organs
in the body with markings on the iris. As a boy he
accidentally broke the leg of an owl and noticed a black
streak appear in one of the owl's eyes. After he
qualified in medicine in 1867, Peczely began to
examine the irides of patients before and after surgery
and claimed to have discovered a correlation between
the markings in his patients' eyes and their diseases.
Many others began to investigate iris analysis,
including Dr. Bernard Jensen, who developed the
technique in America in the 1950s and produced
diagrams of the left and right irides (see *overleaf*)
which resemble a clock face, with different areas of the
body featured at specific locations around the dial.

Treatment methods

To obtain a thorough diagnosis, iridology should be
carried out by a trained practitioner. Some of the
markings they may look for are shown on pages
326–329.

Charts for the left and right irides developed by Dr.
Bernard Jensen.

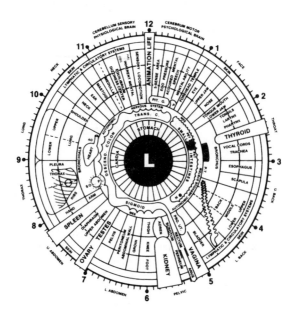

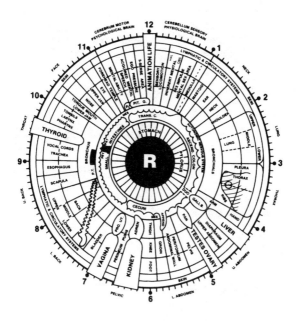

RINGS

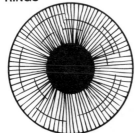

Stress rings are associated with problems such as depression, insomnia, stiffness and tension, painful periods, headaches, migraine, etc.

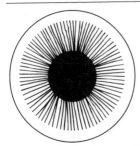

A lipaelnic ring is associated with fluid retention, kidney problems, and high blood pressure. It is caused by poor liver function. It also infers poor fat metabolism and raised uric acid.

Scurf rims indicate a poor skin, poor peripheral circulation, and lung congestion.

SPOTS

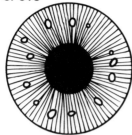

Drug spots These relate to a past intake of chemicals or drugs and indicate poor metabolism. They also indicate poor liver and pancreatic function.

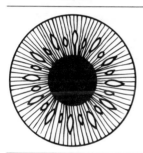

A daisy iris resembles the petals of a flower and can be associated with diabetes and hypoglycemia, poor endocrine and exocrine function, postural problems, reproductive weakness, and gastro-intestinal disturbances.

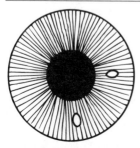

Lacunae indicate a deficiency in the associated organ and may be open or closed. They are often found in heart, kidney, lung, brain, or pancreas zones.

MARKINGS

Asthenic ridges suggest depression, irritability, nervousness, a low level of energy, headaches, and toxins eliminating from the bowel.

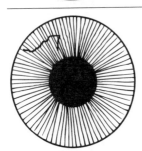

A transversal can indicate trauma, damage, or a tendency towards malignancy.

Arcus senilis the arc of old age, also known as a "semi-arc," indicates lack of oxygenated blood to the brain area.

A **tulip sign** indicates asthma, ear inflammation, meningitis, or sinus problems.

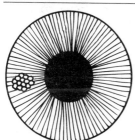

The honeycomb is associated with disorder in the zone in which it appears and is formed of tiny hexagonals. It indicates disturbed local cell metabolism, the result of poor tissue nutrition.

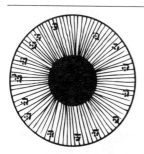

Lymphatic rosary indicates congestion, retention of toxins, and a poor lymphatic system. It may be formed from a single bead-like marking or a full ring of beads.

KINESIOLOGY

Definition

A system of assessment and treatment based on the reaction of muscles to light touch.

TYPES

Kinesiology was originally used by psychotherapists to test a person's range of movement and the tone of his or her muscles.

Today these techniques are used alongside others in a system known as applied kinesiology, which uses muscle testing in relation to all body functions.

How does it work?

Kinesiologists believe that groups of muscles are related to different parts of the body—to bones, circulation, glands, organs, and the digestive system. The ways in which a muscle responds to certain tests is indicative of how the rest of the body is functioning. Points on a muscle which are sore, for example, suggest the build-up of toxins which prevent nerve impulses from traveling between the brain and the muscle. Therapists believe that the application of light pressure to troubled spots increases blood flow to muscles and helps balance the lymphatic system. This in turn helps revitalize areas where there may be an imbalance in nutrition or energy, for example.

Also, therapists believe that our bodies contain energy circuits which may become upset during times of illness or stress. These energy circuits are the meridians which are used in acupuncture and believed to carry the

---

WHAT CONDITIONS IS IT USED FOR?
- Allergy
- Back pain
- Catarrh
- Colds
- Depression
- Headaches
- Neck pain
- Tension
- Tiredness
- Weak immune system

---

body's life energy, Qi. By using muscle testing, kinesiologists say they can identify imbalances before they become serious, and can also "reset" those circuits found to be affected.

History

Kinesiology was developed in 1964 by an American chiropractor, Dr. George Goodheart, who discovered that massaging certain spots on a patient's body strengthened weak muscles. He painstakingly discovered links between each spot and the muscles to which they were related.

Treatment methods

After taking a full case history the therapist carries out a series of muscle tests in order to locate physical problems or to discover imbalances or deficiencies in bodily energy. You may be asked to hold an arm or leg in a certain position while the therapist applies light pressure. Once a trouble spot is located, the therapist applies light massage to pressure points.

Some people experience slight soreness for a few days after treatment, which therapists say is the result of toxin dispersal.

Nutritional deficiencies are assessed by placing a small amount of food in your mouth while certain muscles are being tested.

LAYING ON OF HANDS

Definition

A technique used in spiritual healing and other types of healing in which the healing power of a god or spirit is channelled through the hands of the healer to the patient.

History

Ancient Egyptian priests used their hands for healing as did Buddhas, messiahs, shamans, kings and their chosen disciples who often gave blessings by placing their hands on the heads of supplicants. The toucher was recognized as being more powerful than the recipient, so that those being touched felt blessed. Famous for his healing by the laying on of hands was Jesus of Nazareth, the messiah of the Christian religion. In the Gospels, which describe his work, there are several occasions when he cured people of paralysis, blindness, leprosy and various crippling diseases. Sometimes he did this by touching, sometimes by simply commanding the sickness to leave.

One famous story tells of Jesus ordering the evil spirits that were making a man insane to jump into a herd of swine that consequently ran off screaming into the river. He also brought some people back to life from recent death. His healing activities were called miracles.

In the Middle Ages, tubercular disorders were commonplace and showed up especially in the glands of the neck (an illness known as scrofula). For centuries, European monarchs undertook the ritual of touching the sick on the head to show their power. People suffering from this sickness believed that being touched by the king would cure them. The disease became known as King's Evil and the ritual was called "touching for King's Evil." Edward the Confessor is said to have received the ability to heal through touch as a divine gift which he passed on to subsequent rulers. The last monarch to touch sufferers in this way was Queen Anne, who reigned until 1714.

Henry IV of France touching for King's Evil

LEECHING

Definition
Using blood-sucking animals called leeches for medical purposes.

Types
Hirudo medicinalis, the gray, German variety and the most common leech, is an aquatic blood-sucking worm which has been used for 2000 years to suck "bad blood" from people with severe fevers. It became so popular in Europe in the early 19th century that its price rose, and it became an endangered species. Although the Hirudines were the most popular, other parasitic species were sometimes used, such as the *Haementeria costata*; however, these were not as effective. When supplies of the *Hirudo medicinalis* ran short, the Hungarian variety, *Hirudo officinalis* was used.

a The *Hirudo medicinalis* or common leech.
b The smaller *Haementeria costata*.

a

b

How does it work?

The leeches' saliva contains a host of potential medicines, including hirudin. Hirudin is an anticoagulant—it may be of use in preventing blood clots during surgery, in those with blood disorders, or in patients confined to bed. Hirudin is now mass-produced from genetically-modified bacteria and yeasts. Leech saliva also contains other anticoagulants, an anesthetic, and antihistamine.

What conditions is it used for?

Leeches are currently in accepted medical use for the care of skin grafts and for fingers that have been surgically re-attached after injury. If the return of blood from the skin graft or re-attached finger is insufficient, the graft becomes congested with blood. Leeches placed on the skin graft of finger drain the congested blood, allowing normal circulation to resume. Fresh leeches are attached until the congestion subsides—this may take several days.

History

Blood-letting was a standard procedure in many parts of the primitive world, ranging from pricking warts and cutting boils to more magical actions such as scoring the skin of the head to let out the spirits of madness.

In the fifth century in Europe and Asia, a "leech" was a physician and leechcraft was the art of healing. The first records of the medicinal use of leeches was in the Benares area of India. Leeches were popular in Ancient Egypt and were mentioned in Greek, Roman and Arabic medical texts. Translations filtered into Europe during the Middle Ages.

In 16th century Europe, the leech had been abandoned

in favor of mechanical blood-letting with lancets and artificial leeching tools. Many prominent physicians, however, preferred to continue using live leeches because they were more delicate, took less blood, and never caused infections or vascular damage.

During the 18th century physicians learned how to apply leeches to specific areas by using a leech glass to control exactly where the leech would suck. Leeches were very popular and effective for reducing the swelling of black eyes, removing tooth abscesses, and many other small applications where the removal of inflammation, pus, and excess fluid were indicated. They were invaluable for the relief of pressure after delicate eye operations.

Both rich and poor, the famous and the infamous, were familiar with the leech. The French chemist Louis Pasteur, who had a brain hemorrhage at the age of 40, was treated by the application of 16 leeches behind the ear. He recovered from the hemorrhage but was paralyzed on his left side.

In 1827 imports of leeches for medical use in the military hospital at Val de Grâce, in Paris, totalled 30 million. They were the main treatment against typhus, dysentery, enteritis, and other fevers.

The head of the hospital was military physician François Joseph Victor Broussais, who believed that these diseases were caused by internal irritations and that leeching would reduce the localized inflammation. So convinced was Dr. Broussais of the efficacy of the leech that every new patient at the Val de Grâce hospital was given a fresh batch of 30 leeches, regardless of the diagnosis. Leeches were most often placed on the skin of the hands, arms, feet, legs, or neck of the patient.

By the 18th century blood-letting was so common that English physicians were called "leeches," and the word began to acquire its derogatory meaning: physicians charged very high fees for draining a person's blood. In the 19th century when leeching was at its peak, Sweden gained a reputation for producing the best and most hardy leeches. However, in 1834 stocks dwindled and leech ponds were developed in an area outside Stockholm. Unfortunately, no restraint was placed on exports, and supplies became scarcer. The new leech ponds had been stocked with 25,000 leeches; yet only 2000 were harvested in four years. At that time it was not known that leeches only reach sexual maturity after seven or eight years. Sweden exported a million leeches a year, and countries such as England and Germany would often have to import 100 times more than they could produce themselves.

Treatment methods

Leeches attach to the skin by two muscular suckers, at each end of their body. Three teeth inside the front sucker give a painless bite. Each leech feeds for 30 minutes to an hour, removing 10 to 20 milliliters, (about a teaspoonfull) of blood before falling off, although bleeding from the wound can result in further blood loss. The side-effects of leech therapy include excessive blood loss, and infection with the bacteria found naturally in the leech's gut. To avoid infection, patients are often given antibiotics during leech therapy. Cross-infection between patients is prevented by disposing of each leech after use.

MACROBIOTICS

Definition
A Japanese term to describe a dietary system.
How does it work?
It is a macrobiotics belief that most illness is caused by
an imbalance of yin-yang in the diet. A diet balanced in
yin and yang foods is claimed to cure illnesses and keep
people healthy, as well as ensuring good sleep and
freedom from worry.
History
In the 1880s Japanese doctor, Sagen Ishizuka, treated
many of his patients' health problems by moderating
their diet. His ideas were later put into practice by
George Ohsawa, who termed Ishizuka's dietary system
"macrobiotics."
Treatment methods
It is for each person to find his or her own macrobiotic
diet from local foods, which will vary between regions.

A BASIC MACROBIOTIC DIET
This includes 50% brown rice plus grains, such as
whole wheat, rye, barley, oats, millet, buckwheat,
and maize. Vegetables, legumes, and soy bean
products are added. It may include seaweeds,
salted pickled plums, sesame seed salt, green tea,
grain coffees and mu tea, a special blend of 15 roots
and herbs. Foods that are avoided include alcohol,
butter, cheese, eggs, meat, milk, processed
products, and refined flour and sugar.

YIN AND YANG FOODS

Yin foods	Yang foods
• Generally acidic	• Generally alkaline
• Grown in a hot climate	• Grown in a cold climate
• Grown above ground	• Grown below ground
• Foods that are purple, blue, or green	• Foods red, yellow, or orange in color
• Foods with a high water content	• Foods with a low water content
• Foods that perish quickly	• Foods that dry and store well
• Sweet foods	• Salty foods
• Hot foods	• Bitter foods
e.g. • Fruits • Leaves	e.g. • Roots • Seeds • All those of animal origin, cereals and some vegetables

MAGNETISM AND MESMERISM

This section explains the use of magnetism for healing purposes which was used by Franz Mesmer in the 1760s, a man who some believe was the originator of HYPNOTISM.

History

The use of a magnetic charge for healing is an ancient treatment that was revived by Paracelsus, who was born Theophrastus Bombast von Hohenheim in Zurich in 1493. He took the name Paracelsus and many of his ideas from the Roman physician Celsus, some of whose writings had been discovered 50 years earlier.

Paracelsus developed his own ideas and is thought to have tried to use the magnetic forces of magnets to heal illnesses of the mind.

The full exploitation of magnetism began in the 17th century, when many magnetic healers worked with the sick and were often given full recognition.

The Irish healer Valentine Greatriks would gently stroke the sick body with a magnetized iron bar and give massage with his own hands. He is reputed to have cured certain paralyzing afflictions, restoring the use of previously useless hands and feet.

The idea that a healer could stroke away pain was commonplace until the Swiss healer Father Gassner suggested that it was the power of the magnetic force that healed, and the healer was merely a medium. The young Franz Mesmer watched Father Gassner at work and expanded the idea.

Mesmer was convinced that the healing element was
animal magnetism which, like mineral magnetism,
could be stored in iron bars. He worked in Vienna,
where he was a close friend of Mozart. A girl musician
who had been struck blind had been taken under the
wing of the court, and through Mozart, Mesmer
contacted her and offered her treatment. She went to
live in Mesmer's house, and after several sessions her
sight began to be restored. The girl was delighted, but
others were not so happy. Local doctors were jealous
and tried to discredit Mesmer.

Mesmer left Austria to settle in Paris where he tried
new methods, and his magnetic bath became the talk of
Paris society.

In addition to his magnetic bath (see box, *below*),
Mesmer also put on other shows to demonstrate the
healing power of magnetic fields, sometimes drawing
magnetism directly from the moon. Mesmer believed
that the healing magnetic force came from the planets,
and his devices were only a means of channelling the

MESMER'S MAGNETIC BATH

Into a large wooden tub of water were placed
several magnetized iron bars. Those who were ill or
merely in need of revitalization were invited to join
hands in a circle around the tub. Mesmer then spoke
to them, going through various rituals and making
stroking movements above their heads to indicate
The flow of magnetic fluid through the air. Many
people went into trances, some had convulsions,
and many heard voices speaking to them.
Whatever their experiences, most felt much better.

energy force. He had no knowledge of what we call hypnosis and would not have recognized the link that has been made between it and mesmerism.

Mesmer might have been more sympathetic to the idea that the natural energy life-force in humans could be enhanced by magnetism, but his work was closer to spiritual healing than to hypnosis.

Eventually he was investigated and his "mesmerism" was called into question. The Paris commissioners concluded that any healing that took place could only be attributed to the imagination of the patients.

Mesmer continued to believe that his results were due to the effect of animal magnetism.

Unfortunately, after his death, egocentric individuals claimed to have personal magnetic powers, and stage shows demonstrating magnetism were born; they often discredited Mesmer's work. The power to induce a trance state in another person was called mesmerism, but in reality that is what we now call hypnosis.

Mesmerism was, however, the beginning of our understanding of an important phenomenon that has been used for centuries: the power of the imagination while in a trance state.

The illustration (*right*) was made by a cartoonist who makes fun of Mesmer, showing him capturing the magnetic power of the moon and some of the devices used, such as the tub under the table.

Modern developments

Today, the use of magnets is known as Magnetic Field Therapy and has many applications for healing.

WHAT CONDITIONS IS IT USED FOR?

Today, magnets are used in the treatment of:

- Cancer
- Circulatory problems
- Environmental stress
- Fractures
- Infections
- Inflammations
- Insomnia
- Migraine
- Pain
- Rheumatoid disease

Types

There are many different types of Magnetic Field Therapy. Some involve pulsating magnetic fields produced by electrical devices; others involve static magnetic fields generated by artificial or natural magnets.

Equipment

Magnetic healing devices range from small, hand-held instruments to large machines generating high-energy fields. Magnetic blankets help induce sleep, and specially designed ceramic magnets are used to help healing when placed over various organs of the body.

How does it work?

Practitioners believe that the body has certain magnetic "poles," just like the poles of the Earth. The head, upper body, front of the body, and right hand relate to the North Pole; the feet, lower body, back of the body, and left hand, correspond to the South Pole. When these poles are unbalanced, illness may result.

THE BODY'S MAGNETIC POLES

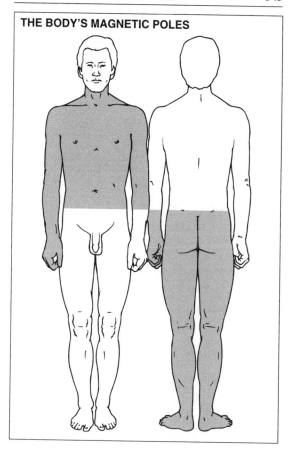

HOW MAGNETS WORK

Magnets have two poles: one positive, one negative

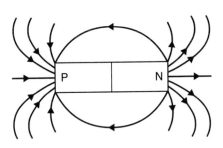

The positive pole	• Has a stress effect • Interferes with normal metabolic functioning • Produces acidity • Reduces cellular oxygen supply
The negative pole	• Has a calming effect • Helps normalize metabolic functioning • Reduces acidity • Promotes oxygenation of cells

USE OF MAGNETS FOR SPECIFIC CONDITIONS

Condition	How magnets can help
Infections	Use of a negative magnetic field lowers the body's acidity and promotes oxygenation, factors which are harmful to disease-causing microorganisms which do not like well-oxygenated, alkaline environments. In this way magnets are used like antibiotics.
Nervous system disorders	Placing a negative magnetic field over an area of electrical activity in the brain may help to reduce delusions, hallucinations, panic, or seizures.
Pain relief	In addition to the pain caused by infection, a negative magnetic field may be used to help conditions such as edema (swelling of the cells), cellular acidosis (excessive acidity of cells), and lack of oxygen to cells by normalizing the metabolic processes that cause these conditions.
Stress	Applying a negative magnetic field to the top of the head stimulates the brain to induce sleep.

MANIPULATIVE THERAPIES

Definition
A group of therapies in which practitioners use their hands to bring about positive changes in a person's physique.

Types
For examples, see the box (*below*).

EXAMPLES OF MANIPULATIVE THERAPIES

- Alexander Technique
- Bone setting
- Chiropractic
- Feldenkrais method
- Kinesiology
- Laying on of hands
- Massage
- Osteopathy
- Polarity therapy
- Reflexology
- Rolfing
- Therapeutic touch

History
Until the 20th century, daily life in the Western world was filled with physical activity, much of it extremely hard labor. The body, especially the back, must have ached and suffered dislocation and damage frequently. Almost everyone was adept at some kind of massage and manipulation. More can be found about modern manipulative therapies in the relevant sections of this book. Older techniques are described here.

Back-walking

By the Middle Ages back-walking was well established
as part of folk medicine throughout Europe. An
effective way of manipulating the spine, it was a ritual
undertaken by women, usually by the mother of twins
or a virgin. Young girls were taught how to stamp hard
as they walked up the backs of hard-working peasant
women, and older women used their strong legs on the
backs of men who were sick or whose muscles had
been strained.

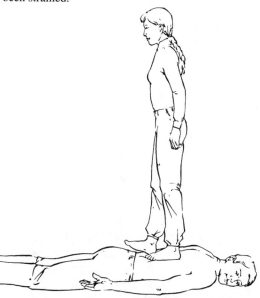

The bone-setters

Bone-setting was not just related to setting broken bones but involved reorganizing the skeleton by pushing and pulling on it. Usually, it was a special skill passed down through a farming family. It was believed that pains were due to one small bone, often one of the vertebrae, being out of place. The bone-setter manipulated the bone back into place. The click of the neck, wrist, or back indicated that the devil causing the pain was being forced out. One of the most famous bone-setters was a woman called Mrs. Sarah Mapp, ridiculed by Hogarth.

Traction and pressure

Traction is used to relieve the pressure of the vertebrae on the spinal cord. The illustration shows how traction was achieved by the Ancient Greek doctor Hippocrates. The bindings are pulled on sticks used as levers, and a man tramples on the back muscles . . . a common way of giving massage.

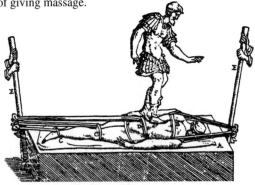

An 18th-century caricature showing bone-setter Sarah
Mapp (middle of the top row) by Hogarth who called
this *The Undertaker's Arms, or a Consultation of
Physicians.*

ET PLURIMA MORTIS IMAGO

MASSAGE THERAPY

Definition
A manipulative therapy designed to relax, stimulate, and invigorate the mind and body by kneading, stroking, and pressing the soft tissues of the body.

Types
There are many different types of massage (see box, *right*) Some of these focus on just one part of the body, others treat the whole body; some are vigorous and may be uncomfortable, others are gentle.

Equipment
Oil is the usual medium used by therapists, although talcum powder may also be used.

History
Massage has been practiced in the Middle and Far East since 3000 B.C. and in the fifth century B.C. daily massage was advocated by the Greek physician

---

WHAT CONDITIONS IS IT USED FOR?
Massage is believed to be useful in the treatment of a variety of conditions including:

- Anxiety
- Asthma
- Back pain
- Blood pressure
- Circulatory problems
- Constipation
- Depression
- Headaches
- Heart disorders

- Hyperactivity
- Insomnia
- Irritable bowel syndrome
- Muscle tension
- Neck pain
- Sciatica
- Sinusitis
- Sprains

Some types of massage

Aromatherapy	Using essential plant oils as part of the massage treatment.
Marma	Part of Ayurvedic medicine. The therapist attempts to press *marmas* (107 points on the body which in Ayurvedic medicine correspond to organs and functions).
Oriental	Examples are Indian *marma* massage, Japanese *reiki* or *tuina* massage, Thai massage.
Reiki	A form of touch therapy. The therapist senses which parts of the body are emitting weak energy and lays his or her hands on or close to the site.
Sports	Massage commonly used for the treatment of sports people and sports injuries.
Swedish	A popular form of Western massage which combines massage with exercise techniques.
Tuina	Used in China alongside acupuncture or herbal medicine, this is a form of intense deep massage used to balance energy flow.

HOW DOES IT WORK?
Massage is believed to:
- Improve circulation
- Improve the flow of lymph
- Reduce blood pressure
- Reduce heart rate
- Reduce muscular pain
- Stimulate the digestive process
- Stimulate the release of endorphins

Hippocrates as a means to attaining health.

In 1563 at Trento, in North Italy, the Council of Trent produced a long declaration designed to help the Roman Catholic Church regain its status lost during the Reformation. Many practices were denounced as evil, including surgery, bone manipulation, and massage.

Swedish Movement Treatment (popularly known as Swedish massage) was developed by Swedish gymnast Per Henrik Ling who combined therapeutic massage with exercises for muscles and joints.

During the First World War massage was used as part of the rehabilitation of injured soldiers.

Massage methods formed the basis of physiotherapy until therapists became attracted to the use of gadgets.

In 1970 American massage therapist George Downing published *The Massage Book* in which he combined massage techniques with those of reflexology and shiatsu and put forward the notion that massage as a therapy should take into account a person's physical, mental, and emotional disposition.

Treatment methods
Usually the therapist takes a case history and may

examine you to observe any obvious
strength/weaknesses in your musculo-skeletal system.
Treatment depends on the kind of massage you are
receiving. Different techniques are used (see box,
below) throughout the treatment.
After treatment some people may feel light headed.
Massage can also be an emotional experience and
occasionally people feel weepy. After particularly
vigorous massage some people may feel stiff the
following day. This usually passes in a day or two.

FOUR MASSAGE TECHNIQUES

Technique	Description
Effleurage	Stroking with the palms of the hands. This movement is usually used at the start and end of treatment, and to link other techniques. It is gentle and calming.
Pétrissage	Kneading fleshy areas to help stretch and relax muscles.
Frictions	The application of pressure to a small area, often using small circular movements. This is used where muscles are particularly tight and need to be encouraged to relax.
Hacking	A stimulating technique in which the sides of the hands are used in a chopping motion to invigorate and increase blood flow to an area.

MAZDAZNAN

Definition
A practice of healing based on the philosophy of two
great prophets and of the Ahura Mazda, the Creative
Intelligence of ancient Middle Eastern thought.

History
The prophetess Ainyahita, 9600 B.C., and the prophet
Zarathustra, 6900 B.C., were Iranian sages who both
preached a belief in one God and a philosophy of right

HOW DOES IT WORK?/TREATMENT METHODS
In practice there are five linked areas:
Mazdaznan breathing
The function of breathing is to maintain physical and
spiritual life. There are exercises to develop the
twelve senses, including extrasensory perception and
spiritual inspiration.

Deep, rhythmical breathing is taught to improve
general health and intelligence. The aim is to achieve
inhalation and exhalation that lasts for seven seconds
each, with a pause of one second in between. This is
said to calm, slow down, and steady the heartbeat.

Mazdaznan dietetics
Raw, lacto-vegetarian foods form the basic diet, and
such cooking as is needed is done in ways designed
to preserve the vitamin and mineral content. In many
ways, Mazdaznan methods are naturopathic, making
use of fasting for inner cleansing, bathing, and herbal
remedies.

The amounts of different types of food are carefully
balanced according to individual body types.

living, now adapted into Mazdaznan.

The modern Mazdaznan Association was founded in 1902 by Dr Otoman Zar-Adusht Ha'nish, who spent his youth in a remote community in Iran, where he overcame a heart complaint using breathing techniques. He studied medicine in Europe and lectured in healing in Europe and America, translating the philosophies of the prophets into a viable modern New Thought movement, known as the Mazdaznan or Master Thought.

Mazdaznan personal diagnosis
Self-understanding is encouraged through a very complex form of personality-typing, taking account of body- and head-shape, thought modes, strengths and weaknesses, and family background.

Glandular science
Endocrine function is regarded as vital to intelligence and spirituality. The thymus and the pineal gland are given particular attention. Slow exercises, rhythmical breathing, and humming are performed daily in the belief that they will improve glandular functions.

Eugenics
The study of the regeneration of the individual and the procreation of children is the fifth area in which Master Thought is practiced, mainly as education of the young and of young parents. Much attention is given to choosing compatible partners, who are then encouraged to build a strong family unit on which a Mazdaznan civilization can be perpetuated.

MEDICAL ASTROLOGY

Definition

The use of astrology to aid diagnosis and treatment.

History

During the seventeenth century astrologers cast horoscopes in which they predicted the onset of disease, the course the disease was likely to take, and the best moments for its treatment. Astrological physicians traditionally provided herbal preparations and suggested changes in lifestyle that were often highly ritualistic.

How does it work?

Medical astrologers believe that an individual's birth chart can be examined to determine his or her physical constitution and emotional make-up. Some believe that each of the twelve signs of the zodiac is associated with diseases affecting different parts of the body.

Treatment methods

Because medical astrologers believe they can predict when a person is likely to suffer an illness or when an illness may worsen, they are able to recommend that a person take appropriate action at these times.

WHAT CONDITIONS IS IT USED FOR?

Medical astrologers claim their diagnosis is useful for chronic conditions where the underlying cause is difficult to pinpoint. It tends to be used for psychotherapeutic counseling and not for the alleviation of specific physical ailments.

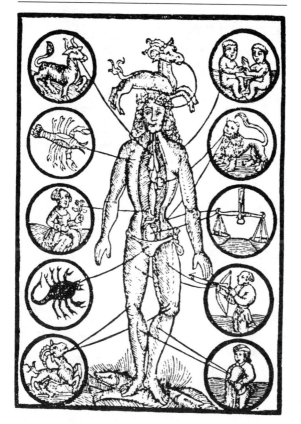

SIGNS OF THE ZODIAC AND THE DISEASES
RELATED TO THEM

Sign	Area of the body influenced	Diseases
Aries	Face Head	Apoplexy Convulsions Epilepsy Headache Measles Paralysis Ringworm Small pox
Taurus	Neck Throat	Scrofula Tonsillitis Tumors
Gemini	Arms Shoulders	Aneurisms Frenzy Insanity
Cancer	Breast Stomach	Asthma Cancers Consumption Dropsy
Leo	Back Heart Neck vertebrae	Fevers Jaundice Plague Pleurisy

Sign	Area of the body influenced	Diseases
Virgo	All viscera surrounding the internal organs	Diseases of the internal organs
Libra	Kidneys	Diseases of the kidneys
Scorpio	Sexual organs	Diseases of the sexual organs
Sagittarius	Hips Muscles	Gout Rheumatism
Capricorn	Knees	All cutaneous diseases (e.g., leprosy) Melancholy ailments (e.g., hysteria)
Aquarius	Ankles Legs	Cramp Lameness Swelling
Pisces	Feet	All diseases of the feet

MEDITATION

Definition
Training your attention or awareness to bring mental processes under voluntary control. In the West, meditation is used as a self-help technique to improve well-being by allowing the mind and body to relax and does not require particular religious beliefs.

TYPES
There are many different "schools" of meditation:
- Transcendental meditation involves repetition of a mantra.
- Buddhist meditation. Techniques include *anapana-sati* (focus on in-and-out-breathing) and *metta-bhavana* (the development of loving kindness).
- Practices involving movement—yoga sequences, K'ai Men and T'ai Chi, for example.
- It has been suggested that visualization therapy is a form of meditation.

History
Buddhist meditation has been practiced for over 2500 years in Asia. In the East, meditation developed into yoga while in the West it developed into prayer. In the fourteenth century, Christian writers referred to withdrawing from ordinary consciousness to contact God and the repetitive prayer "Lord Jesus Christ, have mercy on me" was used by the Byzantine Church. Transcendental meditation was founded in 1957 by the Maharishi Mahesh Yogi, guru to the Beatles pop group, and is now used by many prominent business people.

How does it work?

It is not clear exactly how meditation works. Some believe that it enables us to get in touch with our inner beings and draw on this source of inner strength. Others suggest that being able to focus the mind allows for greater productivity in problem solving—we can learn what is and what is not important and what we should or should not be focusing on. The table (*below*) lists some of the physiological and psychological changes brought about by meditation.

CHANGES BROUGHT ABOUT BY SOME FORMS OF MEDITATION

Physiological changes
- Slowing of the heartbeat
- Slowing of the breathing rate
- Lowering of blood pressure
- Lowering of metabolism
- Change in brainwave frequency to the long alpha waves signifying deep relaxation coupled with mental alertness.
- Reduction in cholesterol
- Increased energy

Psychological changes
- Increased inner calm
- Heightened powers of creativity
- More efficient decision making
- Increased work efficiency
- Decreased mental tension
- Decreased negative emotions
- Increased reactions
- Improved memory

WHAT CONDITIONS IS IT USED FOR?

As a form of therapy (rather than spiritual development), meditation is used in the treatment of a variety of conditions including:

- Alcohol dependency
- Anxiety
- Chronic pain
- Drug dependency
- Headaches
- High blood pressure
- Insomnia
- Nervous tension
- Phobias
- Stress-related ailments

Treatment methods

There are many different ways of meditating. Some examples are provided here.

Some suggested seated positions

a Kneeling
b Lotus position
c A relaxed sitting position

MEDITATIVE TECHNIQUES

Meditation requires practice and the correct environment. *Briefly* described here are some of the different methods used in meditation. Many people find that they need the assistance of a teacher in order to master these techniques properly and may attend one or more classes to familiarize themselves with such techniques.

Mantra meditation A mantra is a letter, word, sound, or phrase repeated continually in meditation as you breathe in or out. The best-known mantra is "Om." Other words can be used and popularly include those such as "peace," or "one." The word may be specifically chosen for you if you follow transcendental meditation.

Concentrative meditation This involves steady gazing, known in yogic tradition as "tratak." Choose a small static object—such as a candle flame—and focus on it without blinking. Then close your eyes and try to visualize the object.

Focused breathing This involves centering your awareness on the rise and fall of your breathing. The idea is to observe your breathing with quiet detachment.

Breath counting method This method involves counting your breaths, beginning with one, and moving to ten before starting again at one. This is designed to focus attention in one area, away from all other thoughts.

MEGAVITAMIN THERAPY

Definition
Also once termed "orthomolecular medicine," this is
the use of large doses of vitamins and minerals to
improve physical and mental health.

History
The term "orthomolecular" was coined by an
American, Dr. Linus Pauling, who was the 1945 Nobel
Prize winner for chemistry. He was interested in the use
of vitamin C to prevent and cure the common cold.
Later he became involved with others in
orthomolecular psychiatry, which treats depression and
schizophrenia with large doses of the C and several of
the B vitamins, both of which are essential to brain and
nerve cells. Early practitioners of orthomolecular
psychiatry were Dr. Abraham Hoffer and Dr.
Humphrey Osmond.

WHAT CONDITIONS IS IT USED FOR?

Advocates claim megavitamin therapy has been
successful in the treatment of a variety of conditions
including:
- Alcoholism
- Certain drug addictions
- Depression
- Hyperactive children
- Neuritis
- Osteoarthritis
- Psychiatric disorders

In the 1970s, Dr. R.F. Smith, an alcoholism expert, claimed to have a 77% recovery rate over a two-year period with 507 alcoholics at the Brighton Hospital, Detroit, using massive doses of vitamin B complex.

How does it work?

Advocates of megavitamin therapy claim that the doses of vitamins and minerals recommended by doctors and health practitioners is far below that needed for most individuals. They argue that the amounts of vitamins and minerals we are able to absorb from the foods we eat may not be optimal for preventing illness and disease and that additional quantities need to be taken. Dr. Abraham Hoffer regards many mental diseases as being due to vitamin dependency states. Vitamin dependency is described as a condition in which the body is unable to absorb or metabolize certain vitamins from food normally containing those vitamins.

Evidence that absorption may be the problem points to the changes in the digestive tract suffered by those who have celiac disease. Celiacs are given large doses of vitamins because it has been shown that they have difficulty absorbing certain vitamins in the gut. Some long-term schizophrenias are accompanied by changes in the gut lining that are similar to those seen in celiac disease. Of course, there must be other factors at work, since people with celiac disease are not schizophrenic.

Treatment methods

To correct vitamin dependency states in individuals with mental disease, orthomolecular psychiatrists prescribe extremely large doses of specific vitamins so that at least some will be absorbed in the blood stream.

METAMORPHIC TECHNIQUE

Definition
Also called prenatal therapy, this is the manipulation of
the feet, hands, and head to help people come to terms
with long-term problems.

How does it work?
Practitioners believe that our physical, mental,
emotional, and spiritual structures are established
during the nine months in which we are in the womb.
By manipulating the feet, hands, and head, say
therapists, it is possible to release the body's healing
processes as well as those of the mind and spirit.

History
The metamorphic technique was developed in the
1960s by British naturopath Robert St. John, who
believed that disorders of childhood and adulthood are
traceable to experiences in the womb.

Treatment methods
Practitioners do not work all over the foot, for example.
Instead they concentrate on points on the foot which
they believe correspond to different stages of the nine-
month, prenatal development period (see chart, *right*).

WHAT CONDITIONS IS IT USED FOR?
Practitioners say that this technique is helpful for
anyone who is unable to shake off long-term health
problems or who feel unable to make necessary
changes in their lives. The technique is said to help
children with autism and Downs syndrome.

THE PRENATAL PATTERN
This chart shows the weeks spent in the womb (**a**) (from 0, conception, to 38, birth), which correspond to areas of the foot, which in turn correspond to spinal vertebrae (**b**), shown as a "time line" down the side of the foot (**c**).

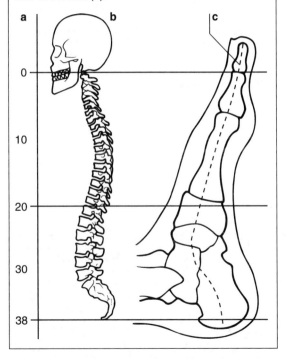

MOXIBUSTION

Definition
A method of heat stimulation in which burning moxa
(the dried leaves of Chinese wormwood) is placed on or
near the skin, or to the top of acupuncture needles.

History
Moxibustion was practiced almost two thousand years
ago in China. It is now regularly used as part of
acupuncture treatments.

TREATMENT METHODS

 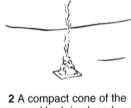

1 Moxa can be wrapped
in small papers and
attached to the top of
acupuncture needles so
the heat travels down the
needle.

2 A compact cone of the
ground herb is placed
over the acupuncture
point and set alight so it
glows. The cone moxa
burns very slowly and
gives out great heat. It is
removed long before it
could burn the skin.

WHAT CONDITIONS IS IT USED FOR?
Chronic conditions such as arthritis.

How does it work?
Moxibustion is believed to stimulate certain body
functions such as circulation and metabolism. It also
dilates the blood vessels. Chinese therapists believe it
helps to regulate the flow of Qi—the body's vital
energy.

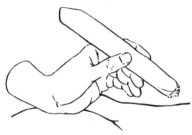

3 Moxa can be piled onto
a slice of ginger, or
leaves of the herb can be
rolled into a cigar-shape.
The glowing end of the
moxa cigar is then held
close to the acupuncture
point and can be moved
along the course of the
meridian.
Moxa is forbidden at
certain points because its
effect is too radical.

MUSIC THERAPY

Definition
A means of promoting self-expression through improvised music-making with the aim of facilitating positive changes in behavior and emotional well-being. Music therapy is different from sound therapy (which relies on sound vibrations to heal) and voice therapy (aimed at retraining the vocal chords).

Equipment
Music making involves the use of a whole range of simple instruments as well as the voice.

History
Music has been used for centuries to assist the healing process. Ancient Egyptian priests sang medical scriptures in specific tones which were believed to be curative.

The Greek mathematician Pythagoras suggested that for some patients music might be used to restore balance among the four humors and their associated temperament, and in Homer's *Odyssey* Autolycus sings

---

HOW DOES IT WORK?
Music therapy helps to:
- Alleviate anxiety
- Alleviate depression
- Alleviate pain
- Enhance memory recall
- Enhance positive emotions
- Enhance positive mood states
- Promote physical rehabilitation
- Provide opportunities for interaction
- Reduce stress

WHAT CONDITIONS IS IT USED FOR?

Music therapy is used to treat those people with:

- Alzheimer's disease
- Brain injuries
- Chronic illnesses
- Disabilities relating to autism
- Emotional disturbances
- Learning disabilities
- Mental illness
- Physical disabilities
- Sensory disabilities
- Speech and language impairments
- Substance abuse problems

It may also be used for people:

- Who are elderly
- Who wish to investigate personal growth and their relationships with others

a magic song to staunch the flow of blood when Ulysses is wounded during the siege of Troy.

For centuries the spiritual healers (such as shamen) of tribal peoples have used music to induce fits and help people shake off their illnesses. Bells, drums, and rattles were often used to frighten demons and disease from the body.

During the eighteenth century Dr. Richard Brocklesby argued that music might be used to help treat insanity, yet music therapy was regarded as something of a joke among the medical profession at this time and it was not until 1958 that Heinz Graupner drew attention to the Schüssler Sanatorium in the Hartz mountains where

music therapy was being used with some success for
their patients.

Austrian scientist and philosopher Rudolf Steiner, a key
figure in the development of anthroposophical
medicine, advocated the use of eurythmy, a form of
therapy in which movement is linked to the sounds of
speech. Steiner's approach was aimed at improving a
person's physical constitution, whereas modern music
therapists—who may work to help people with severe
physical disabilities—recognize the importance of
providing an environment that is safe for the release of
emotions.

Treatment methods

Clients do not have to have any experience of music in order to participate, and are not taught how to play an instrument. Although practices may vary, most therapists assess clients, design sessions for them, and monitor their progress.

TREATMENT METHODS

Assessment
Therapists assess:
- Cognitive skills
- Communication abilities
- Emotional well-being
- Physical health
- Social functioning

Session design
Therapists design sessions based on client needs. Sessions may involve:
- Learning through music
- Lyric discussion
- Music and imagery
- Music improvization
- Music performance
- Receptive music listening
- Song writing

Treatment
Therapists participate in:
- The treatment of clients
- The ongoing evaluation of clients
- The follow-up of clients.

NATIVE AMERICAN HEALING

Definition

The healing concepts and rituals of North American Indian tribes.

History

The Oglala Sioux tell of the spirit of the White Buffalo who appeared to their ancestors as a beautiful woman, bringing the sacred pipe and knowledge of the seven rituals to be used in times of need. The pipe contained the spirit of peace and was to be smoked as a sign of goodwill between people. The seven rituals were sacred ceremonies which, if carried out regularly and correctly, would ensure a healthy and good life for all the tribe.

SEVEN NAVAHO RITUALS	
Ritual	**Uses**
1 The Sweat Lodge	For purification
2 Calling the Vision	For boys entering manhood
3 The Sun Dance	For renewal of strength
4 The Rites of Relationship	With people and spirits
5 Preparing for Womanhood	For girls
6 Ball Throwing	For seeking wisdom from the spirits
7 Soul Keeping	For purifying the souls of the dead

How do they work?
Healing rituals are based on a belief in the power of the
Great Spirit and the many spirits which reside in
people, animals, plants, and all objects. The Navaho
take a holistic view, and their ceremonies may work due
to the power of suggestion and as the concentrated
concern of every member of the community.

CAUSES OF NAVAHO ILLNESSES
The Navaho Indian makes little distinction between
what Western medicine would call physical and
mental illness. To the Navaho there are three main
causes of all sickness and three kinds of ceremony
to cure them.
1 Undesirable behavior determined by evil winds,
such as how the braid on a water-bottle is made or
which way a poker is left by the fire, and more
serious behavior, such as incest, which results in
Moth Craziness. Evil Way ceremonies, such as the
Moth Way Sing, are used to cure sickness caused
by evil.
2 An attack by a malevolent spirit or witchcraft, for
example, Ghost Sickness, or being frightened by an
animal, such as a bear, an antelope, or a coyote, or
burning a snake, toad, or porcupine. The Holy Way
ceremonies are used to fight the witchcraft and cure
the sickness.
3 Accidental hurts, such as arrow wounds, broken
bones, or cuts. These are cured by Life Way
ceremonies during which some natural medication
may be used.

Descriptions of Navaho Moth Craziness and Navaho
Ghost Sickness can be found on the next two pages.

Treatment methods

Ceremonies often last several days and rejuvenate
everyone who takes part, although the rituals are
directed toward one sick and often elderly person. The
patient has the support of the whole community; he is
not held responsible for his illnesses, except one,
known as Crazy Violence, the sickness let loose by

TYPES OF ILLNESS
Navaho Moth Craziness
Intermittent fits, during which the patient froths at the
mouth, is incontinent and, afterward does not
remember what has happened, indicate that moths
have taken over the body and are thrashing about
inside.

Moth Craziness is linked with an old Navaho legend
which tells of a time when parents refused to give
their children in marriage, so the children married
each other, breaking the taboo against incest.

When this happened, moths were sucked in by the
soul-wind, flew about inside the head, made a nest
in the stomach, and became more and more violent,
making the patient throw himself into the fire.

The cure is to remove the moths by making the
patient vomit them out. Ritual vomiting is induced
during a Moth Way ceremony when the patient
vomits real moth wings.

Navaho Ghost Sickness
Weakness, anxiety, bad dreams, fainting,
depression, loss of appetite, night-time terror,
delirium, and hopelessness are attributed to Ghost
Sickness.

drinking large quantities of alcohol.

The Navaho do not humble themselves, nor do they analyze their own behavior; they believe that a named ceremony, correctly performed, will put the power of the gods at their disposal. The sick person has only to participate in the ceremony to be healed.

The sickness is caused by the malevolent ghosts (bad winds) that inhabit certain plants. If a person picks any of the plants, then the sickness will travel from him to anyone he touches with his hands. When the sickness becomes severe, the patient dislikes everyone and picks fights, although it is not his fault; it is the fault of the bad winds inside him. All evil things are bad winds.

The cure for an attack of Ghost Sickness is the Blessing Way Sing, a purification ceremony during which there is singing and everyone smokes mountain tobacco. The tobacco wind chases away the bad winds from inside.

Navaho Crazy Violence

While alcohol is seen as firewater, drinking it is seen as deliberately self-determined and not the will of the wind-soul. The reason for this is that when drunken Navaho men go on the rampage, they inflict violence on others and often end by committing suicide. Wanton destruction and violence against others of one's community and against oneself is alien to the Navaho belief in the inner reality of the wind-soul, which is a life-positive force. Restraint and isolation are the treatment for Crazy Violence.

NAVAHO HAIL CHANT RITUAL

The preparations may take as long as two weeks. A tepee is cleared, and sprigs of oak and corn pollen are placed around the walls. Sacred water is sprayed over the walls and ground, and a herbal fumigation is the final cleansing process. Little cakes made of corn and resembling hailstones are made for relatives and friends who will take part in the ceremony, for no one will be allowed to eat anything else. Many other things are forbidden during the ritual, such as urinating while facing north.

The ceremony begins at sundown, as the world enters the time of dreams. For the next two days, all the participants purify themselves in the sweat lodge. Then the patient is made to vomit and clean out his bowels by taking herbs. The soapy yucca cactus is used to wash him, and he is then anointed with fragrant oils and herbs.

The ritual drumming, rattling and whistling then begins, each sound being made with a special object, to help the patient and make his spirit leap. The patient is eventually emotionally moved to make a spontaneous confession of his misdeeds and the taboos he has violated.

During the third day, songs are chanted while the air is filled with smoke from tobacco, burning herbs, and feathers. The chanter tells the ancient Navaho story of Black Rainboy and his sister Blue Raingirl, recounting their many adventures at great length as they are destroyed and then restored to wholeness. On the fifth day, the patient is kept out of the tepee while a picture of the story is made with colored sands. At sunrise, the patient re-enters and sprinkles cornmeal on the picture and recites prayers. As the chanting and drumming reach fever pitch, the medicine-man puts his wet hand on the sand picture and touches the patient who instantly becomes one of the holy people. He repeats the words of the chanter, and happiness and feelings of pleasure and beauty flow into everyone present.

On the seventh day, the chanting and drumming reach a final climax and everyone withdraws, leaving the restored patient to rest and return to his whole self.

Often many other sick people are restored to health by contact with him.

Navaho sand-painting used in healing ceremonies

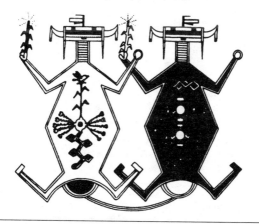

NATUROPATHY

Definition
A system which aims to treat the underlying cause of illness by encouraging the body to cure itself.

How does it work?
Naturopaths believe that disease is the result of a breakdown in the body's normal balance and may be brought on as the result of a variety of factors such as restricted breathing, poor posture, poor eating habits, emotional fears, etc. Their aim is to restore vitality and energy to the body. Their three basic principles are:

1 All disease is due to the same cause (i.e. the accumulation of waste materials in the body).
2 Symptoms of disease are part of the body's attempt at healing.
3 The body is able to return itself to a state of balance and may be assisted with the use of certain methods (see box, *right*)

History
In 400 B.C. the Greek physician, Hippocrates, argued that cures should work with the body rather than against it and should be as natural as possible.
In the early 19th century many others contributed to the

WHAT CONDITIONS IS IT USED FOR?
- Anxiety
- Arthritis
- Colds
- Diarrhea
- Emphysema
- Skin disorders
- Tiredness
- Ulcers

practice of naturopathy, including Vincent Preissnitz, who believed that water had miraculous healing powers and founded what we now call hydrotherapy.

Father Sebastian Kneipp was a Bavarian monk who recommended water as a cure for all kinds of aches and pains. Towards the end of the century Benedict Lust (who had studied under Kneipp) founded his own form of naturopathy.

Treatment methods

Naturopaths take detailed case histories and carry out routine medical examinations before recommending appropriate treatment (see box, *below*).

TYPES OF NATUROPATHIC TREATMENTS	
Type of treatment	**Examples**
Biochemical	Diets, fasting, herbal medicine, homeopathic remedies, vitamin and mineral therapy.
Neurological	Acupuncture, acupressure, reflexology, shiatsu, spinal manipulation.
Physical	Alexander Technique, manipulation of joints and soft tissues, massage, personal hygiene, postural exercises.
Psychological	Biofeedback, counseling, hypnotherapy.

ORGONE THERAPY

Definition
Part of Reichian Therapy designed to restore the body's energy.

History
Austrian-born Wilhelm Reich qualified as a doctor in 1922 and worked with Sigmund Freud in a psychoanalytic unit in Vienna. By 1939 when Reich moved to America he was already an accomplished author. He believed that the repression of emotions and sexual instincts could result in rigid patterns of behavior (character armor) and the tightening of certain muscles (body armor), both of which were caused by blockages to the body's energy, called bioenergy. Ill-health would result if blockages were allowed to remain untreated.

How does it work?
Reich believed that character armor prevented people from discharging their sexual energy during orgasm (which he called "orgone") and that this led to anxiety, neuroticism, and sadism, feelings that prevented orgasm on subsequent occasions. He identified sexual energy with the life force and called it "orgone energy," and claimed to have observed "bions" (units of this energy) under a microscope.

Equipment
Reich developed a box he called the "orgone accumulator," in which patients were supposed to have their orgone energy restored. The boxes were shaped

like slim telephone booths, made of steel encased in wood, and Reich believed they allowed orgone to enter but not to leave, so that it became concentrated.

Treatment methods

Three methods were used by Reich to help loosen character armor.

1 First he used analysis,

2 Next he used physical means such as deep massage and manipulation.

3 Finally he developed the orgone accumulator. He believed that the sick could sit in one of his orgone boxes and would be healed as the concentrated orgone irradiated their bodies.

THE NATURE OF ORGONE
Also called Primordial or Cosmic Orgone Energy

Reich believed orgone:
● Was a new form of energy
● Was always in motion
● Moves in waves
● Moves from east to west
● Travels at the speed of light
● Surrounded us all like electromagnetic waves
● Is different from electromagnetism
● Penetrates everything at varying speeds
● Flows from weaker to stronger parts (the opposite of kinetic energy)
● Is reflected by metal
● Is attracted to vegetable matter

OSTEOPATHY

Definition

A therapy aimed at restoring proper movement and functioning to the body by manipulating the musculo-skeletal system (bones, joints, muscles, ligaments, and connective tissues).

Types

Cranial osteopathy is not a branch of osteopathy but one of several techniques used by osteopaths in which the eight bones of the skull are gently manipulated. Craniosacral therapy may be practiced by therapists who are not necessarily trained osteopaths. It involves manipulation of body tissues in order to bring about a balance in the body's cerebrospinal fluid. A comparison between cranial osteopathy and sacrocranial therapy can be found at the end of this section.

History

Osteopathy was founded by a physician from Missouri, Dr. Andrew Taylor Still. At that time, bone-setting was a common practice among physicians, used to realign broken bones and to break down lesions occurring around joints and old fracture sites. Still took the practice of bone-setting much further. He believed that if the structure of the body was altered in any way, the function would alter as well. In his view, a person could be disturbed biochemically, psychologically, and structurally and in order to return a person to normal balance, a therapist may have to adjust these three levels of body function.

In 1874 Still announced his theory of osteopathy in

Osteopaths are commonly thought to treat mainly disorders of the spine. They do, however, treat a wide variety of conditions resulting from disruption in the skeletal (**a**) and muscular (**b**) systems.

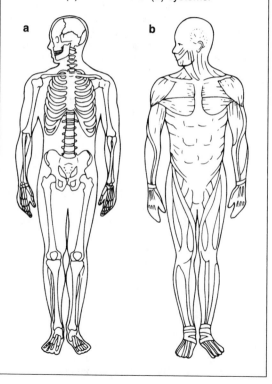

order to gain the acceptance of medical doctors. He was
rejected by them, denounced by his Methodist minister
for being in league with the devil and forced to leave
the area. He moved to Kirksville in Missouri to open
the first school of osteopathy in 1892.

John M. Littlejohn, from Glasgow, Scotland, attended
Andrew Still's school. He had already studied
physiology for three years at Glasgow University as
part of a course in forensic medicine. Later he put
osteopathy on a firmly physiological basis and opened
the first British School of Osteopathy in 1917.

Cranial osteopathic techniques were developed at the
turn of the century by William Garner Sutherland, an
osteopath trained by Still.

How does it work?

Modern osteopathy is based on three fundamental
principles:

1 The body has a natural tendency to heal itself.
2 There is an intimate relationship between the body's
  structure and its function.
3 The body will function best if it is structurally and
  mechanically sound.

Osteopaths believe that the force of gravity causes
particular problems for the spinal vertebrae and the soft
disks that cushion them, owing partly to the fact that
humans now walk upright rather than on all fours.
Mechanical faults in the spine cause spasms in the
surrounding muscles and this in turn sends irritating
nervous impulses to the local area of the spinal chord.
Nerves in that part of the chord become oversensitive
and abnormal nervous stimulation may reduce proper
blood flow to an organ. Osteopaths aim to restore

WHAT CONDITIONS IS IT USED FOR?

Osteopathy is used in the treatment of a variety of conditions including:

- Asthma
- Bronchitis
- Constipation
- Digestive problems
- Dislocations
- Headaches
- Lower back pain
- Menstrual pain
- Neck pain
- Osteoarhtritic symptoms

Cranial osteopathy is used for a variety of conditions including:

- Colic
- Glue ear
- Headaches
- Jaw pain
- Middle ear problems
- Sinus problem

Craniosacral therapy is used for a variety of conditions including:

- Anxiety
- Arthritis
- Asthma
- Digestive problems
- Fatigue
- Headaches
- Post-viral syndrome
- Spinal curvatures

normal blood flow and may use a variety of techniques to achieve this.

Treatment methods

After taking a detailed case history the osteopath will make a full examination, perhaps observing how you sit, stand, and move. Treatment may involve:

1 Massaging stiff muscles

2 Manipulating of joints

3 High-velocity thrust techniques

4 Indirect techniques (such as cranial osteopathy, see next two pages).

COMPARING CRANIAL OSTEOPATHY AND CRANIOSACRAL THERAPY

Cranial osteopathy

There are eight sections of bone in the human skull (cranium) which houses the brain, bathed in cerebrospinal fluid. The eight cranial bones are believed to be ever so slightly moveable and may change position slightly during birth, for example, or after a blow to the head or dental work that displaces the jaw bone. Slight misalignment of cranial bones distorts the passage of cerebrospinal fluid in the brain, resulting in pressure on the brain. This pressure may cause problems elsewhere in the body. One of the techniques used by osteopaths is to apply very gentle pressure to the head in order to realign cranial bones, relieve any pressure to the brain, and thereby restore normal functioning.

Craniosacral therapy

Following the work of American osteopath, Dr. John Upledger, craniosacral practitioners believe that the body has a craniosacral rhythm which is caused by the flow of cerebrospinal fluid around the brain and spinal cord. Physical and emotional disorders may result if the symmetrical rhythm of cerebrospinal fluid is strained. Craniosacral therapists say that such disorders may be relieved by gently pulling and twisting connective tissues all over the body, as this restores symmetry in the flow of cerebrospinal fluid.

The skull showing divisions between bones

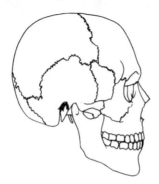

Cross section through the head showing
cerebrospinal fluid (colored black)

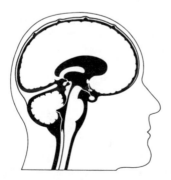

PAST LIVES THERAPY

Definition
A therapy based on the belief in reincarnation and that by addressing troublesome events in former lives clients may be helped to resolve present problems.

History
Belief in reincarnation was central to ancient Egyptian religion and forms a major part of Hinduism and Buddhism. Leibniz, Plato, Plotinus, Pythagoras, Schopenhauer, and Socrates all believed in rebirth. Many cases of reincarnation were investigated by Dr. Ian Stevenson of the School of Medicine at the University of Virginia. Research into the experience of reincarnation as a therapy has been pioneered by the founder of the Institute for Past Lives Awareness, Dr. Morris Netherton, and Dr. Helen Wambach.

How does it work?
It is not clear how past lives therapy works, as it is impossible to prove the existence of reincarnation and practitioners say that it is not necessary for clients to believe in reincarnation for the therapy to be effective. Critics suggest that the therapy may simply be a way of accessing a patient's subconscious, helping them come to terms with buried fears.

Treatment methods
The object of therapy is to help clients come to terms with things that may be bothering them which therapists may do by regressing patients back to their former lives. There are various methods of regression (see box, *right*).

SOME REGRESSION METHODS

The people who first formulated the particular methods listed are named in brackets. Many of these therapies are discussed elsewhere in the book.

Primal therapy (Dr. Arthur Janov) A highly structured and controlled individual process which increases the pressure upon early (primal) emotions until they explode outward, often culminating in a "primal scream." This is followed by a re-integration program.

Re-birthing (Dr. Elizabeth Lehr) Access to repressed attitudes and emotions is gained by deep breathing techniques and a re-enactment of the birth process.

Clinical theology (Dr. Frank Lake) An active form of psychotherapy to resolve traumas that occurred during birth.

Gestalting (Dr. Fritz Perls) Allowing the two parts of oneself to talk and resolve conflicts between them.

Peer group bonding (Dr. Daniel Casriel) Loud, wholesome screaming is used to stir long-forgotten feelings. The work proceeds in couples, one of each sex, who hold each other closely, thus enabling the unfinished emotions to be tolerated that were related to the original parent.

Reichian therapies (Dr. Wilhelm Reich) A variety of regression methods based on Reichian Character Analysis have been devised by many people including Dr. Elsworth Baker, Dr. Karen Kent, Dr. Alexander Lowen, Dr. John Pierrakos, Stanley Keleman, Gerda Boyesen, Jenny James, Nadine Scott and Charles Kelly.

PATTERN THERAPY

Definition
Using certain shapes, proportions and, positions to
positively influence the well-being of people. (See also
PYRAMID HEALING.)

How does it work?
No one is really sure how pattern therapy works,
although there are numerous examples of the effect of
patterns. For example, sick mice living in spherical
cages heal more quickly than those living in any other
shape and the bacterial action that makes tasty yogurt is
said to increase when it is in a conical container.

History
Patterns have been used for thousands of years by
artists and architects and are now also used by some
healers to aid the healing process. During the 1950s Dr.
T.A. Westlake, an English psionic doctor, claimed 300
cures by patterning homeopathic remedies. He and his
colleagues devised a series of two-dimensional patterns
and three-dimensional shapes and tested them with
homeopathic and herbal remedies.

A small phial of the remedy was placed on the pattern
or within the shape and transmitted mentally to the
patient. With the correct pattern, the remedy was
effective. With the wrong pattern, the same remedy was
ineffective. It was discovered that in some cases it was
only necessary to write the name of the remedy on the
pattern. Dr. Westlake suggested that all patterns are
forces in their own right, just as the nature of an atom
or molecule is related to its shape.

SOME PATTERNS AND THEIR EFFECTS
a Vertical lines are dynamic and rousing
b Horizontal lines are passive and restful
c A triangle on its base is stable and secure
d A triangle on its point is unstable and stimulating

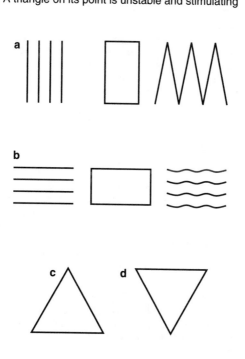

POLARITY THERAPY

Definition

Use of diet, self-help techniques, and manipulation to re-balance the body's vital energy flow.

History

Born in Australia but working in the United States, Dr. Randolph Stone developed the concept of polarity therapy over a period of 50 years, having studied both Eastern and Western medicine. Stone trained as chiropractor, osteopath, and naturopath, and studied the theories underlying acupuncture, Ayurveda, herbal medicine, shiatsu, and yoga. He adopted the Oriental belief in "life energy," known in India as *prana*, and in China as *Qi* (or *Chi*), believed to govern our physical, mental, and emotional processes.

How does it work?

According to polarity therapists, energy flows through the body in a series of channels that are linked together. This energy links every cell in the body and all body organs. Energy is polarized at the head and palm of the right hand (where it is positive) and at the feet and palm of the left hand (where it is negative). The middle of the body—from the crown of the head down through the spinal cord—is the neutral pole.

Harmony is achieved when physical, mental, and emotional elements of this energy are balanced. Illness results from stress, dietary imbalances, and life's traumas which tighten muscles, causing energy blockages.

WHAT CONDITIONS IS IT USED FOR?
Practitioners claims that anyone can benefit from
polarity therapy.

Therapists believe they can unblock energy in a variety
of ways. As blockages are broken down, toxins are
eliminated through breath, sweat, feces, urine, or
emotions.

Treatment methods
Polarity therapists believe that it is possible to improve
health by relieving blockages in energy flow. This is
achieved in a variety of ways:

1 Diet By eating "live" foods such as fruit and
vegetables, and by drinking plenty of liquid, a person
may cleanse and purify his or her body.

2 Exercise Yoga postures and other muscle-stretching
postures help to remove energy blocks and tone the
body generally. (Examples of some of the exercises
used are shown on the next two pages).

3 Manipulation Similar to shiatsu, hand pressure is
used at certain pressure points in order to alleviate
tension and remove energy blocks and then to
"polarize" the body. There are three types of pressure:
neutral pressure (light touch using the fingertips) is
soothing and balancing; positive pressure (direct
manipulation) creates movement; negative pressure
(painful manipulation, deep into the tissues) disperses
blockages.

4 Attitude change A person must be willing to change
his or her attitude where it is blocking the free flow of
energy.

EXERCISES USED IN POLARITY THERAPY TO BALANCE THE BODY

The Squat (the "youth posture")

The Woodchopper

The Cliff Hanger

Variations on the Squat

PRIMAL THERAPY

Definition
A means of helping people come to terms with negative experiences of childhood.

How does it work?
Primal therapists believe that unpleasant experiences of childhood may be pushed into the unconscious mind and lead to emotional problems in adulthood, such as nervous disorders. They argue that until we can experience the pain that we have locked away, we are unable to heal ourselves.

History
Primal therapy was developed by an American psychiatrist, Dr. Arthur Janov whose patients produced intense cries when confronting the need for parental love that had not been forthcoming in their childhood. Janov was influenced by the work of Swiss psychotherapist Alice Miller and psychoanalyst Wilhelm Reich. Alice Miller believed that childhood could be particularly painful for many people and that feelings related to childhood traumas were often suppressed—perhaps because children were afraid of losing the love of their parents. Miller believed that suppression of feelings in childhood would later result in emotional difficulties.

Wilhelm Reich believed that mental pain gave rise to muscular tension and could alter posture and breathing. Janov developed primal therapy based on some of these ideas. Mental illness, he argued, originated from primal pain, a non-physical pain derived from unhappy childhood experiences such as isolation, humiliation, or rejection by a parent.

Treatment methods

Treatment methods vary although all are usually intensive and can be particularly traumatic. The aims of therapy are to enable adults to express the anger, needs, and hurt they may have experienced in childhood and to come to terms with such feelings. During treatment clients may give vent to a "primal scream," releasing tension pent up by a lifelong backlog of pain. Janov argued that they may also display hysterical behavior that appears to represent their experience of pain yet which is a defense mechanism used by people to prevent them from experiencing the "real" pain. Such episodes Janov called "fake" primals.

PSIONIC MEDICINE

Definition
A system that combines orthodox medicine with
RADIESTHESIA to tackle the original causes of
disease, avoiding use of synthetic chemicals.

History
Psionic medicine was developed by an English surgeon,
Dr. George Laurence, who believed that disease was
related to protein imbalance and that individuals radiate
a vibration which may be in or out of balance.

WHAT CONDITIONS IS IT USED FOR?

Psionic doctors claim to be able to treat:

- asthma
- brucellosis
- coeliac disease
- dental caries
- depression
- eczema
- Hodgkin's disease
- mental retardation
- migraine
- physical retardation
- schizophrenia
- skin conditions

How does it work?
There are four tenets to this system of medicine:

1 The body is made up of the physical body and the
etheric body (see box).

2 Either can be disturbed by miasmas—memories of
old sickness. Because the etheric body is timeless,
psionic doctors believe that miasmas cause illness in
successive generations. For example, they claim that
many modern disturbances, such as asthma, eczema,
hay fever, sinusitis, migraine, and allergies are

manifestations of an inherited tuberculosis miasma that has been passed down through families. Childhood physical disease, such as measles, may leave a miasma which can cause problems in later life.

The physical and etheric bodies
a Physical body
b Etheric body or aura (pulsation of life energy)

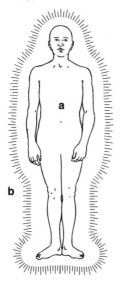

3 Some substances, such as aluminum and lead, cause etheric imbalances even when measurable blood levels are normal.
4 All diseases disrupt the body's vital energy force according to the Unity Theory of Disease as proposed by surgeon J.E.R. McDonagh.

Unity Theory of Disease
McDonagh saw physical life as transitory, because our body chemicals are always changing. The only baseline from which physical life can be built is the primitive life force or vital energy which is seen pulsing around the body as the etheric body or aura.

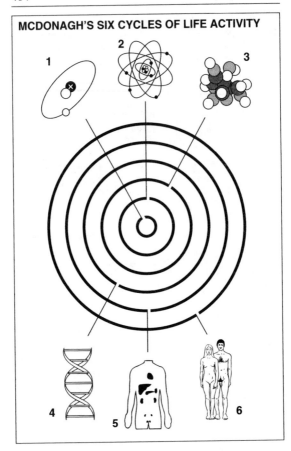

MCDONAGH'S SIX CYCLES OF LIFE ACTIVITY

McDonagh's six cycles of life activity

Primitive energy forming the aura:

1 Sub-atomic particles, such as electrons, are constantly being replenished.

2 Groups of atoms are formed.

3 Atoms like to make molecules. An imbalance is the result if the aura is disturbed.

4 Building of proteins from molecules. An imbalance is the result if the aura is disturbed. McDonagh saw all disease as a degree of protein disturbance; cancer, for example, being a serious imbalance of protein production.

5 Structuring body organs. At this stage, traditional symptoms of disease are clearly manifested if there has been a protein imbalance.

6 Building the whole physical body.

Treatment methods

Any disturbance in the primitive energy force will affect the first three cycles and result in energy imbalance. Psionic doctors claim that the potential sickness can be detected in the aura by psychic sensing (dowsing is the preferred method) before damage has begun to be manifest in any of the levels and before physical symptoms can be detected, when it is often too late to prevent the physical damage we call disease. To detect irregularities in the aura, psionic doctors use intuition combined with a series of questions asked of the pendulum during dowsing. Treatment is given both psychically by thought transference and homeopathically. Color therapy is also used; disturbances of the aura often show a change of color from a brilliant blue to dull and dirty yellow.

PSYCHIC HEALING

Definition

The use of psychic powers for healing purposes.

Types

Psychic surgery is a form of psychic healing in which healers claim to perform surgical operations, often without anesthetic or any surgical equipment, and after which there are no visible scars.

Psychic diagnosis is practiced by radionic practitioners.

TYPES OF PSYCHIC ABILITY

The ability of psychic healers to predict future events relating to health and illness fall into several different categories:

Clairaudience ("Clear hearing") Ability to divine the future by hearing it ahead of time.

Clairvoyance ("Clear seeing") Ability to see the future ahead of time.

Psychometry Clairvoyant divination about a specific person through holding an object belonging to that person.

Metagnomy Divination by sights of future events seen when in a hypnotic trance.

Precognition Inner paranormal knowledge of the future.

History

In tribal communities illness is often attributed to the invasion of a foreign substance, and a shaman or witch doctor is called on to extract it from a patient using his psychic powers. Psychic surgery is popularly performed in Brazil and in the Philippines, where healers appear to cut open their patients, causing some blood loss but no pain. European psychic surgeons are more likely to "operate" at some distance from the body, working on the body's psychic rather than physical energy.

How does it work?

It is not clear how psychic healing works. Some argue that it may be the result of an energy transfer from the healer to the patient, others suggest that healing occurs because patients believe it will—the placebo effect. Some healers say that the body has a psychic energy as well as a physical energy which exists in the form of an aura. Kirlian photography is used to make images of the aura which some healers say they can see and diagnose according to its color, size, and shape. (See also COLOR THERAPY.)

Treatment methods

There are various methods of treatment, and different healers use different types, depending on what they believe to be appropriate. For example, many psychic healers are religious and may use prayer as part of the healing process. Others may use massage and manipulation or may simply lay their hands on the patient. Some may perform psychic surgery.

PSYCHODRAMA

Definition

A therapy which aims to help individuals release their emotions by acting out real-life situations.

History

Psychodrama was developed by psychiatrist Jacob Moreno, who observed that an actress playing unpleasant stage roles became much more pleasant in real life. Moreno concluded that because of her job, the actress had an opportunity to release pent-up emotions of anger and hostility and in doing so was able to enjoy the positive side of her personality off stage.

TECHNIQUES USED IN PSYCHODRAMA	
Mirroring	One person in the group mimics the behavior of another. The person doing the mirroring expresses the emotions that his or her partner has been unable to release.
Role reversal	One person in the group attempts to become another person in the group.
Soliloquy	Individuals describe to the group how they feel about a particularly traumatic event in their life.

WHAT CONDITIONS IS IT USED FOR?

Psychodrama helps:
- People who feel inhibited.
- People who have difficulty relating to family and friends.

How does it work?

Psychodrama enables people to act out and come to terms with feelings that they may not otherwise be able to express during real-life situations. The spontaneity required during acting helps remove inhibitions, and working with others and trying to act out different roles helps develop empathy.

Treatment methods

Working in groups, clients take turns acting out real-life situations, guided by a therapist. There are various methods (see box, *left*).

PSYCHOSYNTHESIS

Definition

A transpersonal psychology in which people are helped to discover their deeper sense of Self and the meaning of their lives and to integrate this awareness into their personality and everyday life.

History

Psychosynthesis was developed by Italian psychiatrist Dr. Roberto Assagioli, who believed that we are each responsible for our own development and that we have a natural desire to develop our potential, to discover our true identities, and to attain a higher level of consciousness than that accepted by traditional psychologists.

Assagioli was prevented from promoting his ideas

WHAT CONDITIONS IS IT USED FOR?

Psychosynthesis is useful for the treatment of a variety of conditions including:
- Migraine
- Phobias
- Psychosomatic illness
- Stress

As well as:
- People suffering a "mid-life crisis"
- People having difficulty with relationships
- People wanting to learn about personal growth.
- People wanting to improve their communication skills

---

during World War II by the authorities instructed by Mussolini, but his theories were later adopted in other countries, including the United States, England, and Greece.

Treatment methods

The goals of psychosynthesis are (1) to identify the "true" aspects of your personality, (2) to take control over these aspects, (3) to realize your true self, and (4) to reconstruct your personality around your new self.

These goals are met by:
- Developing the imagination
- Developing creativity
- Becoming aware of the superconscious.

TECHNIQUES OF PSYCHOSYNTHESIS

Techniques include:
- Analysis
- Creative visualization
- Developing the use of your imagination
- Experimenting with movement patterns
- Free drawing
- Group work
- Interpersonal work
- Journaling

Fundamental to the process of psychosynthesis is the individual's desire to change.

PSYCHOTHERAPIES

Definition
Therapies which use psychological rather than surgical
or ordinary medical means to treat people suffering
from emotional or mental problems.

Types
There are more than 250 kinds of psychotherapeutic
treatment, just some of which are described here. Many
require the patient to talk to a trained therapist but
others—such as art therapy, bioenergetics, dance
movement therapy and music therapy—allow for other
forms of expression. More information about these
therapies can be found in the relevant sections of this
book.

A Psychoanalysis
A therapy based on discoveries by the nineteenth-
century Austrian doctor Sigmund Freud. The patient
relaxes on a couch and the therapist (usually a
psychiatrist) sits behind him or her, out of sight. The
patient tells the therapist all random memories and
thoughts entering his or her mind—a process known as
free association. By gradually bringing to the surface
unconscious thoughts and wishes, this technique helps
the therapist discover and resolve mental conflicts
caused by repressing childhood desires. At first,
patients usually resist telling all, and a course of
treatment to reconstruct a badly damaged personality
may involve three or four sessions a week for several
years.

B Re-birthing

Developed by British pediatrician and psychoanalyst, Donald W. Winnicott, this is a form of therapy in which therapists blame neuroses on birth trauma. Treatment involves encouraging patients to reenact their birth so that traumas can be confronted and dealt with.

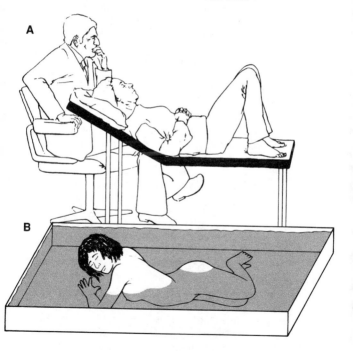

A

B

C Gestalt therapy

This aims to enable patients to re-discover elements of their personality that may have been suppressed and utilizes creative activities to bring these about. It also emphasizes learning the ability to assume control over one's life.

Gestalt is a German word meaning whole. Gestalt therapies involve the client in the whole situation in which they find themselves in the here and now.

The whole situation may be explored in a group setting, or it may be explored through a medium such as paint or clay. Clients are encouraged to use "I" and speak only of current life problems and the actual people involved. In doing so, clients may come across parts of themselves which they had not previously acknowledged. It is the aim of gestalt therapy that clients see themselves as whole, and accept these parts into themselves without making judgments.

In gestalt dream therapy a similar approach is made. The dreamer re-tells a dream, taking the part of each person or object in the dream. For example, in a dream about a car, the client may choose to speak of themselves: "I am driving to work in an old wreck," and as the car: "I am an old wreck being driven to work." In this way new insights are often gained.

D Behavior therapy

This is a specific form of therapy aimed at changing a person's behavior in the context of a situation which causes emotional difficulties, particularly anxiety. It does not explore why the problems might have arisen and is therefore of limited scope, but it has proved useful in treatment of neuroses, phobias, and anxiety attacks.

E Family therapy

This is used to explore psychological problems which are concerned with relationships between family members. It aims to help partners and children to understand each other better and find ways of living together that are less stressful.

F Counseling and co-counseling

Counseling and co-counseling aim to help sufferers

E

find out what they think is wrong in their life and assess
how it can best be changed. Some counselors operate in
specific fields such as bereavement or student
problems, while others perform more general
psychotherapeutic work.

People who are not deeply disturbed and who can easily talk about their emotions may find counseling and co-counseling particularly useful because these techniques acknowledge to some extent the contribution of social factors to mental illness. The emphasis is more on learning to help oneself than being a patient directed by a doctor, and the aim of this approach is to create greater confidence and independence. Counseling is most often short-term, lasting just a few weeks or months.

G Transactional analysis (ta)

This analyzes human emotional response and communication in terms of three "voices"—child, adult, and parent. Learning to recognize which voice is speaking, and what it signifies, can help patients to realize what their needs are and express them more clearly.

H Encounter group therapy

This may be combined with another form of therapy or it may be sought separately. Participants explore problems in their dealings with others by talking, and gain insight into how they themselves appear to others.

I Primal therapy

Therapists disturb patients until they give vent to a "primal scream" releasing tension pent up by a lifelong backlog of pain.

PYRAMID HEALING

Definition

A type of PATTERN THERAPY in which pyramidal structures are used for healing purposes.

History

The pyramid is probably the one shape that has evoked most interest since the 1930s, when Antoine Bovis, a Frenchman, was on vacation in Egypt. He observed that small animals that had died inside the Great Pyramid had not decomposed but had become mummified. Bovis made his own small pyramids and found that both a dead cat and fruit and vegetables dried out but did not decompose.

In the late 1940s, a Czechoslovakian radio technician called Karl Drbal patented a cardboard pyramid that could prolong the life of a razor blade for up to four months.

In the 1970s Bill Schul and Ed Pettit found that seeds kept in pyramids germinated more quickly than those that were kept in ordinary containers.

Experiments in the US by Kathy Coggin and Bill Kerrell have shown that the taste of food improves when it is stored under pyramids. Coffee is less bitter, the acidity of fruit is lowered, wine improves, and frozen foods regain their natural flavor. Food is said to keep fresher longer in pyramid storage.

Biofeedback experiments have shown that trained meditators, who can control their brain-wave patterns, were affected by an open pyramid being lowered over their heads. Their alpha and theta brain waves were doubled in amplitude, and they reported feeling a greater sense of warmth, tranquillity, and weightlessness and had visions; some even experienced clairvoyance and clairaudience.

How does it work?

It is not clear how pyramid healing works. Pyramids appear to concentrate certain energies, not all magnetic. It is also thought that the shape may enhance ionization balance in the air which has a healing effect.

In the case of Drbal's pyramid razor-blade "sharpener," it took ten years to discover how this worked: water reduces the strength of steel by up to 20%. Used razor-blades retain tiny droplets of water along the cutting edges, even when wiped dry. This dampness further reduces the sharpness of the blade. By placing the blade in the pyramid, with both blade and pyramid aligned north-south, the residual dampness completely dried out. Scientists speculate that some kind of electro-magnetic force field was sufficiently concentrated inside the pyramid to dehydrate the blade.

WHAT CONDITIONS IS IT USED FOR?

Pyramid shapes, constructed of cardboard, have had many claims made for them. It is said they enhance sleeping, delay aging processes, and heal minor wounds more quickly than normal.

People who spend time within a pyramid find their burns, bruises, and cuts heal particularly quickly, and may experience relief from conditions such as cramps, headaches, rheumatic pain, tension, and toothache.

RADIESTHESIA

Definition

From the French word meaning "sensitivity to radiation," radiesthesia is medical dowsing and is used as a diagnostic technique in PSIONIC MEDICINE and RADIONICS. As a technique rather than a therapy itself, radiesthesia may also be used by aromatherapists, herbalists and homeopaths to help them decide between a range of appropriate remedies.

History

Dowsing would appear to date back to at least 6000 B.C.—a cave painting of that period found in the northern Sahara shows a man holding a forked stick just as a modern diviner would do. Dowsers also appear in early Egyptian, Chinese, and Peruvian carvings.

From the fifteenth to the seventeenth century, dowsers searched mainly for metal, and were often attached to the staff of prospecting and mining expeditions. Today's dowsers may be employed by public corporations or in industry to pinpoint unmapped cables, pipelines, and so on.

French priest Abbé Mermet, a practiced dowser, wondered whether, if you were able to locate an underground stream using dowsing, you could also diagnose the condition of a patient's bloodstream, using the same technique. Mermet believed that everything emits radiations and that a rod or pendulum could be used to locate radiations and measure them.

EQUIPMENT

For medical dowsing, a pendulum is usually used and is often made of wood. An average size pendulum would be about 1–2 in (2–5 cm) in diameter, and 1–2 in (2–5 cm) long. A cavity pendulum (1) can be used to hold a sample of any specific substance being searched for.

But pendulums can be made in any material, and in any size and shape. Those shown here are some commercially available.

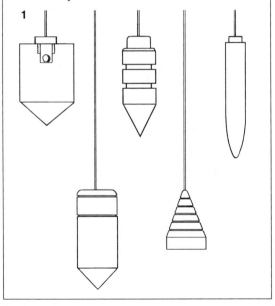

Mermet was able to accurately pinpoint causes of sickness using a pendulum and published his findings in *Principles and Practice of Radiesthesia* in 1935.

How does it work?

No one is clear how radiesthesia works although advocates claim that it involves extrasensory perception. Some people believe that the radiesthesitist may act as a kind of amplifier for radiations arising from the person or substance being dowsed.

Treatment methods

Radiesthesitists use pendulums in different ways. Often the pendulum is held over various parts of the afflicted person's body, and the radiesthesitist reads in its movements the location and diagnoses the ailment. The pendulum is believed by some to discover the onset of illness, and so to advise in preventative medicine. Some radiesthesitists work using a sample of blood, hair, or urine from a patient who is not present. Others may use a photograph. One of the commonest uses of radiesthesia on the human body is in attempting to detect the sex of an unborn child.

Detecting the sex of an unborn child

A radiesthesitist uses a dowsing pendulum (perhaps made using a wedding ring), allowing it to swing over the body of a pregnant woman. The pendulum may swing clockwise to indicate a boy (**A**) or may swing counter-clockwise to indicate a girl (**B**).

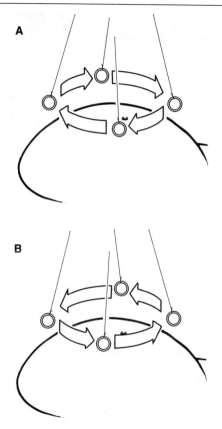

RADIONICS

Definition

Radionics is a method of treatment—often using radiesthesia for the initial analysis—to bring about positive changes in a person's energy fields, whether or not the person is present. The term "radionics" was coined by early pioneers of the technique who believed the instruments they used were akin to radio transmitters.

(More information on RADIESTHESIA can be found in that section.)

Equipment

Radionic instruments are used to analyze the health of the patient, to make remedies, and to give treatments to the patient either physically or at a distance. "Black boxes" come in all shapes and sizes, from the simple old instruments with a few dials on which a practitioner can put a corrective treatment using the radionic numerical language known as radionic rates, to fully automatic computerized systems with a database of over half a million treatments. Some instruments have a stick-pad which is a dowsing device. This is stroked by the practitioner when making an analysis of the health of the patient or to get a treatment rate; when the dial reaches the correct position the practitioner's finger sticks to the stick-pad.

Readings obtained during analysis using a black box are entered in a chart, an example of which can be found at the end of this section.

WHAT CONDITIONS IS IT GOOD FOR?

Radionics has been found helpful in alleviating a variety of acute and chronic conditions including:

- Allergies
- Arthritis
- Asthma
- Hay fever
- Hypersensitivity
- Mental illness
- Pain

How does it work?

All matter is energy, and physics now tell us that matter can be changed by altering the energy behind the physical. If this energy gets distorted by anything, say the stress of life, it will interrupt or distort the flow of energy in the energy fields, which will be manifest in the person as some form of illness. Radionics aims to correct the flow of energy by giving the patient corrective treatments and providing additional energy to help the patient correct the illness.

During the initial analysis the radionic practitioner takes readings to assess the state of health of the person in the physical, emotional, mental, and spiritual levels; any distortion in one level affects the others.

Dr. Albert Abrams, a professor of pathology, found that he could detect disease starting in the patient before it manifested itself physically, and this is an important aspect of work in radionics today.

In treating the patient the practitioner takes note of the causes for the illness, which might include toxins from previous or current conditions, stress from personal or environmental problems, such as radiation, shock from

THE SEVEN CHAKRAS (OR ENERGY CENTERS)

1 Sahasrara (on the crown of the head, associated with the pineal gland)

2 Ajna (brow chakra, between the eyes)

3 Vishudda (throat chakra, also encompassing the cervical regina)

4 Anahata (heart chakra)

5 Manipuraka (solar plexus chakra, above the navel, in the lumbar region)

6 Swadhisthana (sacral chakra, below the navel, in the sacral region)

7 Muladhara (base chakra, near the coccyx)

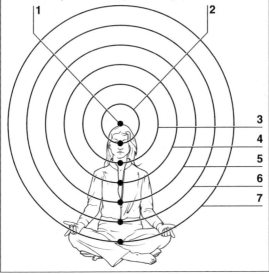

worry or grief, and infections, etc. The overall aim of radionics is to bring patients back to optimum health and to keep them healthy. During the process, named diseases are dealt with as part of overall health.

History

The antecedents of radionics, psychic and absent healing, have been practiced for thousands of years, but modern radionics grew from an observation made by American Dr. Albert Abrams in 1910. Doctors regularly "percuss" patients to assess their conditions, a process that involves tapping the middle finger of the left hand with the tip of the middle finger of the right hand while the left hand has contact with the body. It was during percussion of a patient's abdomen that Dr. Abrams noticed a dull note that could not be explained by normal anatomy and physiology. He later observed that this dull note was found in different places according to which disease a patient was suffering from and concluded that different diseases emitted different energy vibrations.

Assuming this was an electro-magnetic factor, Abrams devised a way of measuring resonances and kept records from his examinations of patients with identifiable diseases. He discovered, for example, that syphilis produced a dull note with 55 ohm resistance and cancer produced a dull note with 50 ohm resistance.

Believing that radio waves might be involved, Abrams termed his new method *radionics*.

He did hundreds of tests and found he got the same results using spots of blood from a patient. By comparing his results with healthy persons he determined measurements for a range of diseases but when he published his results the medical world was very hostile. However, in 1924, the year of his death, a medical committee ran a series of tests under controlled conditions; to the committee's astonishment the results confirmed Dr. Abrams' findings.

Few allopathic doctors would risk their reputations using an unorthodox method, but in the 1930s American chiropractor Dr. Ruth Drown pioneered radionics as an alternative to the use of drugs and surgery, arguing that it was possible to treat a patient at a distance using a blood sample. Radionics was banned in America by the Food and Drug Administration and research moved to the United Kingdom.

George de la Warr and his wife and their assistants set up the Radionic and Magnetic Centre Organization at Oxford, England, in the 1950s to explore the radionic field.

Since his death in 1969 the work was developed further by Malcolm Rae, David Tansley and others. The Radionic and Radiesthesia Trust took over the research and produced the first fully automatic computerized treatment system in 1994. It has sold in 15 countries worldwide.

Treatment methods

As radionics can be performed at a distance it is not necessary to be with the practitioner who is carrying out treatment. You will be sent a questionnaire to enable the practitioner to formulate a case history, and may need to send a sample of your hair which the practitioner will use as a connecting link. (Some practitioners may use a blood sample.)

In the analysis, the practitioner measures your flow of energy and reads your physical, emotional, mental, and spiritual states before deciding on the appropriate treatment.

The first step the practitioner takes in treatment is to decide what other therapies as well as or instead of radionics are required by patients. Assuming that radionic treatment is required, the practitioner will put the hair sample on some of the many different types of instrument available in radionics which project a great variety of different treatments. In addition patients might be provided with a radionic remedy to take physically and be given advice on diet, lifestyle, and other aspects affecting health.

RADIONIC ANALYTIC CHART
On the following pages is a radionic diagnostic chart.
The upper chart indicates the deviation from optimum health of the organs and functions of the body.
The lower chart shows the condition of the seven chakras, which are locations of concentrated life energy. Having pinpointed affected areas, such as respiration and the throat chakra, causative miasmas and toxins are sought, and the general condition of the whole person is noted.

RADIONIC DIAGNOSTIC CHART

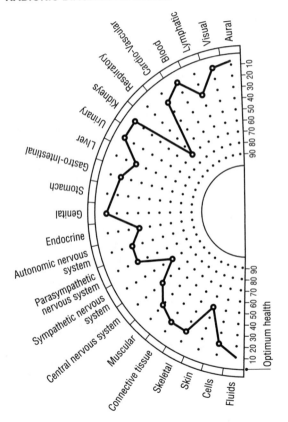

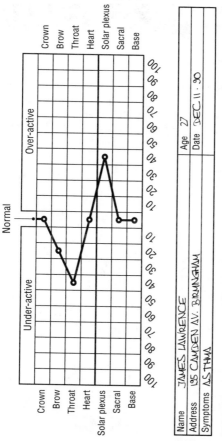

Name	JAMES LAWRENCE	Age 27
Address	195 CAMDEN AV. BIRMINGHAM	Date DEC. 11 . 90
Symptoms	ASTHMA	

CONGESTION	ETHERIC - PHYSICAL 50	MIASMUS TB 70
OVER STIMULATION —		TOXINS
LACK OF COORDINATION —		

REBIRTHING

Definition
A therapy in which clients are asked to reenact their
own birth.

How does it work?
Rebirthing therapists believe birth to be a traumatic
event which can lead to adult neuroses. By regressing
patients back to the point of birth they say that traumas
can be confronted and dealt with.

History
Rebirthing was developed by British pediatrician and
psychoanalyst Donald W. Winnicott, who observed
several of his clients in what he believed to be a

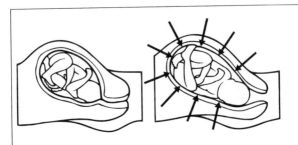

Stanislav Grof equated
life trauma with four
stages of birth.
1 The "blissful," pre-birth
stage.

2 Feelings of being
closed in or crushed. This
equates with the initial
stages of contraction.

reenactment of their births. Winnicott's patients appeared to work things out of their systems in this way and emerged as their true selves.

Other therapists added to the rebirthing theory: R.D. Laing described the struggle of a fertilized ovum to secure itself to the wall of the womb as "implantation trauma," and French obstetrician Frederick Leboyer argued that newborn babies should be allowed to bond with their mothers and should not be traumatized by noise and bright lights.

Treatment methods

The aim is to enable clients to regress to points in their early lives that were particularly traumatic and to tackle such problems. Therapists may do this through regression, taking you back the point of trauma.

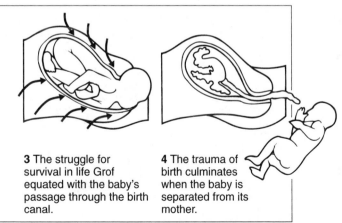

3 The struggle for survival in life Grof equated with the baby's passage through the birth canal.

4 The trauma of birth culminates when the baby is separated from its mother.

REFLEXOLOGY

Definition
A method of bringing about relaxation, balance, and healing through the stimulation of specific points on the feet, or the hands.

How does it work?
Traditionally it is believed that energy flows through channels in the body. When these become blocked or depleted, parts of the body are starved of energy and become diseased. Reflexology is believed to clear these channels and restore the free flow of energy. A more modern theory is that reflexology works through the

---

SOME PROCESSES INVOLVED IN REFLEX HEALING

No one knows how reflexology works although it is thought that its effects may involve one or more of the following processes:

- The relaxation of deep muscles bringing about relief from tension and stress.
- Improvements to cardiovascular circulation.
- Improvements to lymphatic circulation.
- A reduction in pain (as a result of gate control and the production of endorphins).
- The stimulation of pressure points on acupuncture meridians.
- The effects on the body's electromagnetic field.
- The benefits resulting from an hour's rest.
- The psychological benefits of an hour's personal attention.

---

nervous system. There are over 70,000 nerve endings in the feet which connect through the spinal cord to all parts of the body. By working on the nerve endings, reflexology stimulates the nervous system to normal healthy functioning. Other theories include interaction with electromagnetic fields, working with the body's own natural vibrations and healing potential, or breaking down waste products which collect in the feet.

Types

The various systems of reflex healing involve massaging a surface area of the body in ways designed to stimulate a response in an apparently unrelated internal organ. Acupuncture and shiatsu combine reflex healing with other methods.

History

Around 5000 years ago reflexology was practiced in India, China, Japan, and Egypt, and later spread to Europe.

In 1913 American surgeon Dr. William Fitzgerald discovered that partial anesthesia of the ear, nose, and throat could be achieved by applying pressure to certain parts of the foot. In a system known as "zone therapy," he argued that the body was divided into ten vertical zones and that applying pressure to one part of a zone could affect all other parts of that zone.

In the 1930s, American physiotherapist Eunice Ingham concentrated on the zones of the feet and developed her own method of foot massage, the beginning of Western reflexology. (Some reflex positions on feet are shown on the next four pages.)

SOME REFLEX POSITIONS ON THE FEET
These positions are approximate

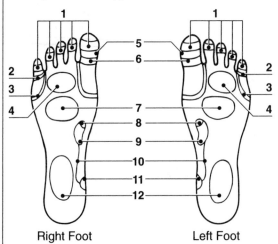

Right Foot   Left Foot

 1 Sinuses   11 Bladder
 2 Armpit   12 Small intestines
 3 Shoulder
 4 Lung
 5 Pituitary gland
 6 Thyroid and neck
 7 Solar plexus
 8 Adrenal glands
 9 Kidneys
10 Ureter

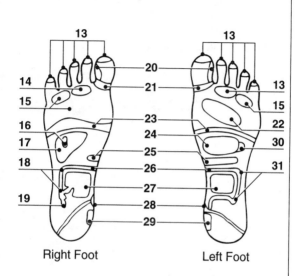

Right Foot   Left Foot

13 Head   23 Diaphragm
14 Eyes   24 Stomach
15 Ears   25 Pancreas
16 Gall bladder   26 Transverse colon
17 Liver   27 Small intestine
18 Ascending colon   28 Sciatic nerve
19 Appendix   29 Coccyx
20 Voice   30 Spleen
21 Neck, throat   31 Descending colon
22 Heart

SOME REFLEX POSITIONS ON THE FEET
These positions are approximate

Inside Right Foot
The same points are on the inside of the left foot

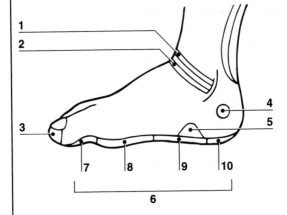

1 Lymph nodes in groin
2 Fallopian tube
3 Top of head
4 Uterus, prostate
5 Bladder
6 Spine
7 Cervical
8 Thoracic
9 Lumbar
10 Sacrum, coccyx

Outside Left Foot
The same points are on the outside of the right foot

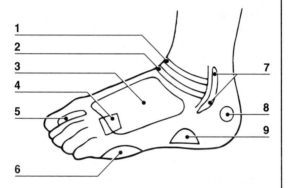

1 Lymph nodes in groin
2 Fallopian tube
3 Lymph glands on front
  of body
4 Breast
5 Lymphatic system
  drainage
6 Shoulder
7 Hip, sciatic nerve
8 Ovary, testicle

9 Hip, knee, leg

Treatment methods

When you go for treatment, there will be a preliminary talk with the practitioner. Then you will remove your shoes and socks and relax while the reflexologist begins to work on your feet (or hand if necessary), noting the problem areas. Reflexologists use their thumbs and fingers to apply gentle pressure. For each person the application and effect of the therapy is unique. Sensitive, trained hands can detect tiny deposits and imbalances in the feet and by working on these points, the reflexologist can release blockages and restore the free flow of energy to the whole body. Tensions are eased and circulation and elimination are improved. This gentle therapy encourages the body to heal itself at its own pace, often counteracting a lifetime of misuse. For the most part the treatment is very pleasing and

---

WHAT CONDITIONS IS IT USED FOR?

Reflexology is thought to be useful for the treatment of a variety of conditions including:

- Asthma
- Bowel disorders
- Headaches
- Hypertension
- Insomnia
- Menstrual problems
- Migraine
- Musculoskeletal pain
- Poor cardiovascular circulation
- Poor lymphatic circulation
- Respiratory disorders
- Stress-related conditions

soothing. There may be a little discomfort in some reflexes but it is fleeting, and is an indication of tension or imbalance in a corresponding part of the body. Treatment usually lasts for about an hour. A number of sessions will probably be necessary as the benefits of reflexology build up gently and gradually. The total number of sessions, and their frequency, will depend on your own body's requirements, and your reflexologist will discuss this with you. After treatment there may be a temporary reaction as the body readjusts or releases toxins; you may experience a feeling of well-being and relaxation; or perhaps be a little lethargic, "off color," or even tearful for a short time. This is transitory and is simply part of the healing process. Once your body is back in tune, you may choose to continue regular treatments to maintain your good health.

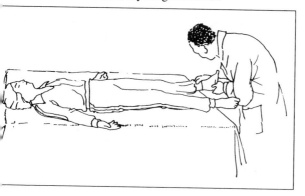

REICHIAN THERAPY

Definition
Movements designed to systematically release physical tension and repressed emotions, developed by psychiatrist Wilhelm Reich. (See also ORGONE THERAPY.)

History
Austrian-born Wilhelm Reich qualified as a doctor in 1922 and worked with Sigmund Freud in a psychoanalytic unit in Vienna. By 1939 when Reich moved to America he was already an accomplished author. He believed that the repression of emotions and sexual instincts could result in rigid patterns of behavior (character armor) and the tightening of certain muscles (body armor), both of which were caused by blockages to the body's energy, called bioenergy. Ill-health would result if blockages were allowed to remain untreated.

How does it work?
Reich suggested that bands of muscular tension (see box, *right*) prevent the flow of energy and consciousness through the body. By relaxing these chronic stresses, awareness would increase. Reich did not separate mind from body, and maintained that the release of muscular armoring would be accompanied by an emotional release and a change in mental attitude.

Treatment methods
Therapists try to help people identify how posture, breathing, and muscular tension reflect emotions. Techniques used are described on the next two pages.

REICH'S BANDS OF MUSCULAR ARMORING

7 Tension at the crown of the head.
6 Tension across the brow and eyes.
5 Tension in the throat, back of neck, and shoulders.
4 Tension in the chest and heart muscles.
3 Diaphragm tension (and poor breathing).
2 Tension in the gut and lower back.
1 Genital tension leading to sexual problems.

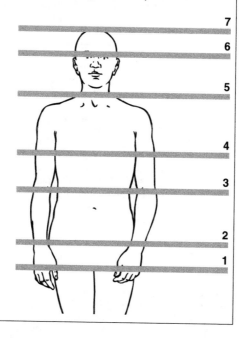

REICHIAN METHODS TO RELEASE MUSCULAR ARMORING

Active movements	Vigorous movements such as kicking and stamping are encouraged as a loosening up exercise.
Chest work	Blockages to breathing are removed as the therapist pushes down on the patient's chest who exhales or screams.
Convulsive reflex work	Therapists may work with the actions of coughing or yawning as convulsions are believed to break down armoring.
Deep breathing	The therapist sets a pattern of breathing which the subject follows. The patient may experience prickling or tingling sensations.
Deep massage	The therapist applies pressure to areas of muscle spasm.
Facial expressions	While maintaining breathing patterns and keeping eye contact with the therapist, the patient is encouraged to "make faces," mimicking certain emotions.
Stress positions	Positions are held which irritate the body leading to tremors or "clonisms."

REICHIAN METHODS FOR SPECIFIC BODY PARTS

Abdomen	Armoring is loosened in this area which includes the back and abdominal muscles and which is particularly tense if a person is defensive.
Chest	Breathing and laughing reflect armoring in this region. Special gestures may be used involving the arms and hands if emotions are being suppressed through the inhibition of breathing.
Diaphragm	A forward curvature of the spine suggests armoring in this region, which may be loosened by breathing exercises.
Eyes	Eye rolling and staring wide is used.
Mouth	Crying, shouting, or sucking are used.
Neck	Screaming and yelling may be used.
Pelvis	Kicking the feet or striking a couch with the pelvis may be used to loosen up this area of strong armoring.

RELAXATION THERAPY

Definition
A term used to describe a variety of techniques found in a wide range of therapies used to induce relaxation.

Types
Autogenic training, biofeedback, breathing therapy, flotation therapy, massage, reflexology, shiatsu and yoga, are just some of the therapies that involve varying relaxation techniques. All often have a common goal: to counter the effects of stress. The diagram (*right*) shows the body's initial response to stress, and information on the next page shows disorders related to stress, revealing the importance of relaxation therapy.

How stress affects the body

a Hair may stand on end.
b Pupils of the eyes dilate.
c Saliva output falls.
d The skin pales as blood vessels supplying it contract.
e The chest expands as breathing becomes faster and deeper to deliver more oxygen to muscles.
f The heart beats faster and harder; blood pressure rises.
g Glucose is released from storage in the liver to provide food for muscles.
h Digestion is slowed as the intestines' blood supply is partly diverted.
i In extreme fear, bladder or rectum may empty.
j Muscles tense, ready for flight or fight.
k If the skin is broken, blood coagulates more quickly.
l The body sweats, ready to cool itself if there is violent activity.

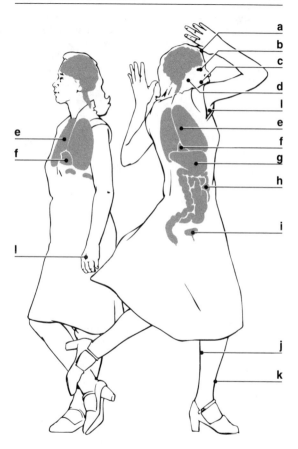

Excessive stress may contribute to the following disorders (and can also aggravate many pre-existing complaints):

Physical:
1 Headaches.
2 Exhaustion.
3 Excessive sweating.
4 Facial flushing.
5 Nasal catarrh.
6 Asthma attacks.
7 High blood pressure or fast pulse.
8 Heart disease or heart attacks.
9 Skin diseases.
10 Stomach problems such as indigestion and ulcers.
11 Vague pains in the back and limbs.
12 Diabetes.
13 Diarrhea.
14 Rheumatism and arthritis.

Psychological:
15 Depression may be mild or severe. A minority of severely depressed people may suffer from manic depression, extreme cycles of agitated, euphoric behavior alternating with deep depression.
16 Postnatal depression may last for days, weeks, months, or even years.
17 Schizophrenia is often brought on by stress within the family.
18 Anorexia nervosa is self-starvation usually indulged in by insecure or overpressured adolescents.
19 Prolonged aggressive behavior.
20 Overdependence on drink or drugs is frequently used to escape from stress.
21 Neuroses such as panic attacks and palpitations, phobias, hypochondria, hysteria, amnesia, and obsessive rituals may develop in a person anxious to escape from stressful reality.

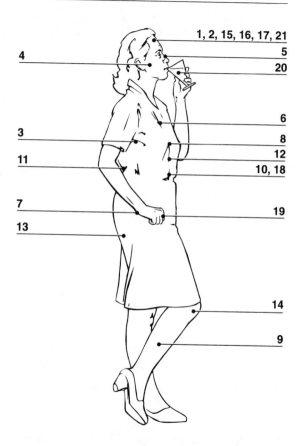

4

1, 2, 15, 16, 17, 21
5
20

3
11

6
8
12
10, 18

7
13

19

14
9

ROLFING

Definition

Also called "structural integration," this is a form of deep massage designed to correct posture.

History

Rolfing was developed in the USA in the 1930s by Ida Rolf who graduated in biological chemistry from Barnard College, New York, in 1920. It was not until the mid-sixties that Dr. Rolf's work was recognized and massage became popular.

WHAT CONDITIONS IS IT USED FOR?

Rolfing is a system of postural improvement not designed to treat specific disorders.

How does it work?

Rolfing therapists claim that when the posture is correctly aligned, individuals are supported by gravity and body systems are free to function properly. When posture is out of alignment the individual bends over with gravity, the body is unstable and muscles have to work hard to stop it toppling. Postural misalignment may occur for a variety of reasons, including injury and general patterns of sleeping, sitting, and walking. Rolfers believe that the mind and body are connected and that past traumatic experiences can also cause misalignment, as they result in increased muscle tension, leading to inflexibility and imbalance.

Treatment methods

The aim of rolfing is to structurally re-align the body so that ears are vertical above the shoulders, shoulders are

vertical over the hip joints, hip joints are vertical over
the knees, knees are vertical over the ankles. This is
achieved by manipulating the soft tissues—muscles,
ligaments, and fascia during which a therapist may use
fingers, knuckles, and elbows. There are usually ten
sessions (see box, *below*).

TEN ROLFING SESSIONS	
Session	**Body part on which the rolfer concentrates**
1	An introductory session designed to improve the patient's breathing
2	Feet and lower legs
3	Sides and small of the back
4	Inner part of the legs
5	Abdomen
6	Back of the legs and pelvis
7	Head and neck
8, 9, 10	Designed to integrate the shoulder and pelvic girdle with the spine.

Rolfing is often painful and people may experience
emotions such as sadness, fear, and anger.
For example, working on the jaws may release feelings
of sadness; the shoulders release feelings relating to
past burdens and stressful responsibilities; when the
back is being rolled, patients may experience past rage
and anger; while the hips are believed to be the location
of emotions connected with sexuality.
"Before" and "after" photographs reveal that some
people get slightly taller as a result of ten sessions of
treatment.

SHAMANIC HEALING

Definition

Healing carried out by a primitive and tribal doctor known as a shaman, from the Tunguso-Manchurian word *saman,* meaning "he who knows."

History

The shaman was the central figure in a primitive religious system that developed in pre-Bronze Age times in the far north of Asia. Even up to the 19th century, classical shamanism was still practiced in remote communities.

A modernized form of shamanism is found among the Khanty of Siberia, who still regard sickness as an indication of a lost or stolen soul.

The Mazatec Indians of Mexico include elements of Christianity alongside their shamanic deities. Female shamans take psilocybe mushrooms to induce an altered state of consciousness in which they can obtain healing advice from the spirit world.

Today the United Nations World Health Organization has a policy of encouraging traditional healers to continue using certain herbal and shamanic cures while training them in hygiene and midwifery.

How does it work?

In ancient societies the source of illness was believed to be supernatural so anyone attempting to cure such illnesses had to be both a physician and a priest. The shaman was someone familiar with the spirit world and able to enter it while in an ecstatic trance and frighten a demon to loosen its hold on a sick person.

It is not clear how shamanic healing works. It may be that the intensity of communal activity assists healing, or perhaps people get well because they truly believe in the power of the shaman.

It is now thought that the ritual drumming, dancing, shouting, and singing may induce the production of chemicals in the brain, such as endorphins, which are known to reduce pain.

An Eskimo shaman with the drum used to induce the trance state

Tulayev, shaman of the Karagas, Siberia, in 1927

WHO IS THE SHAMAN?

A true shaman is called by the spirits to his vocation before birth, inheriting the soul of a dead shaman. He is recognized at birth, usually by a physical sign, such as an extra tooth, and grows up aware of the suffering he will have to endure.

His initiation occurs during adolescence, when he may be tortured for days or even months. It was a common practice to make small cuts all over the body to discover any extra bones, another proof of shaman inheritance.

During the torture, he cries out in agony, faints, becomes hysterical, has visions, and generally resists his calling, which is said to cause the shaman sickness of mind from which he must cure himself. When he finally capitulates and accepts his vocation, he falls into a lengthy sleep, after which he awakens as the shaman.

Characteristics of a true shaman

1 Inherited vocation.
2 Physical and/or mental abnormality.
3 Goes into ecstacy at will by beating a drum made from the skin of the animal his soul rides during ecstasy.
4 Calls spirits to work for him and appeases local spirits, such as those of the polar bear and walrus.
5 Wears a ritual gown and headdress.
6 Sings, dances and performs a drama to bring about healing and appease the spirits.
7 Uses massage, Arctic herbalism and simple surgery.

TREATMENT METHODS

A variety of methods were used by the shaman, for example:

- In order to frighten a demon away, the shaman might dress up in animal skins and leap about making wild noises using sticks, a rattle, a drum, or simply shouting.
- He might attempt to extract pain by sucking it out from the patient's body through a hollow reed or tube of bone.
- Herbal remedies may be used to reduce fever or relieve pain.
- A protective amulet may be given to the patient to help guard against further spirit attacks. Such amulets were often teeth, claws, or horns of animals, bright stones, or cowrie shells.
- A fetish may be created for greater spiritual protection. This was an object into which the shaman planted a spirit. It was designed to guard its owner and was capable of harming others.
- The shaman may perform surgery or bone-setting. One type of surgery was trephining, in which holes were cut in the skull using flint to let out demons. Bone growth on fossil skulls indicates that some patients survived this operation.

SHIATSU

Definition

Shiatsu is Japanese for "finger pressure," and describes a therapy in which pressure is applied to specific points on the body along acupuncture meridians, using techniques that resemble a gentle form of ROLFING.

Types

Do-in is a form of self-stimulation shiatsu that does not require the presence of a practitioner.

History

Shiatsu developed from amna, an ancient Oriental massage system in which the hands and feet are rubbed and manipulated. Amna was often practiced by the blind and given for pleasure rather than as a therapy, with techniques being handed down between generations and used by family members to help each other.

WHAT CONDITIONS IS IT USED FOR?

Practitioners claim shiatsu is useful for a variety of conditions, including:

- Anxiety
- Arthritis
- Asthma
- Back pain
- Bowel trouble
- Bronchitis
- Catarrh
- Circulatory problems
- Depression
- Digestive disorders
- Fatigue
- Headaches
- Insomnia
- Migraine
- Painful menstruation
- Rheumatism
- Sciatica
- Some neurogenital conditions
- Stress and tension

Shiatsu emerged as an independent therapy at the turn of the century and was popularized by Tokujiro Namikoshi.

Today many practitioners provide treatments based on the Five Elements theory advocated by the late Master Shizuto Masunaga.

How does it work?

Shiatsu practitioners believe that disease is caused by a disturbance in the flow of energy around the body, known as Qi, chi, or ki (in Japanese). Stimulation to specific points on the body (known as acupoints, acupuncture points, pressure points, or tsubo), affects ki which flows around the body via meridians.

Rebalancing the body's life energy brings about relief from the pain caused by certain symptoms. Western philosophy views the process as stimulating the flow of both blood and lymphatic fluid which helps release toxins and tension from muscles. Shiatsu also encourages the brain to release endorphins, the body's pain-relieving hormones.

The importance of meridians

Meridians carry the vital life energy, ki. As the line of a meridian has a lowered electrical impedance (a property of nerves) it has been speculated that they are nerve pathways, although practitioners assert that ki energy does not flow through the nervous system.

There are twelve main meridians, each one controlling a specific organ, conventionally numbered with roman numerals. Just as all phenomena in Eastern medicine are categorized yin or yang, so too are the meridians. Yin meridians run upwards from the toes; yang meridians run downward from the head to the toes.

Meridian	Yin	Yang	Element
Heart	*		Fire
Small intestine		x	Fire
Bladder		x	Water
Kidney	*		Water
Pericardium	*		Fire
Triple burner		x	Fire
Gall bladder		x	Wood
Liver	*		Wood
Lungs	*		Metal
Large intestine		x	Metal
Stomach		x	Earth
Spleen	*		Earth

Two of the organs listed in Eastern medicine are not
recognized in Western medicine: the triple heater (or
triple burner, which controls endocrine glands) and the
pericardium (which controls circulation and is
important in sexual activity, sometimes known as the
heart constrictor) although this is the sac surrounding
the heart.

There are two meridians placed centrally on the body:
one down the front and one down the back. These are
the conception vessel (Yin) which begins near the anus
and flows centrally up the front of the body to the
mouth, and the governor vessel (Yang) which begins
near the anus and flows centrally up the back, over the
head to the mouth.

THE TWELVE MERIDIANS

Heart meridian

Small intestine meridian

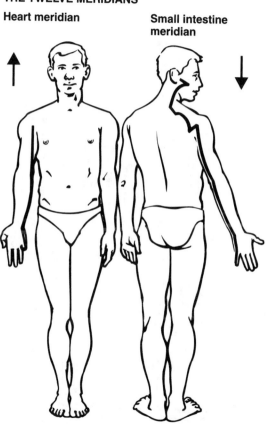

THE TWELVE MERIDIANS (continued)

Bladder meridian   Kidney meridian

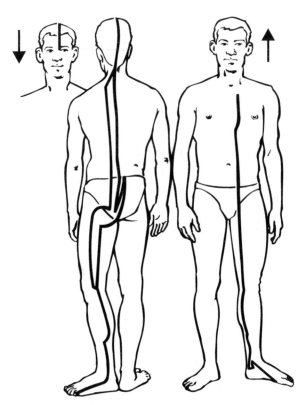

Circulation meridian   **Triple burner meridian**

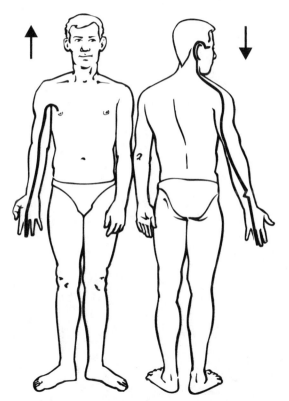

THE TWELVE MERIDIANS (continued)

Gall bladder meridian   Liver meridian

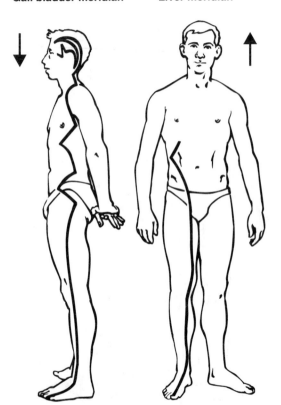

Lung meridian

Large intestine meridian

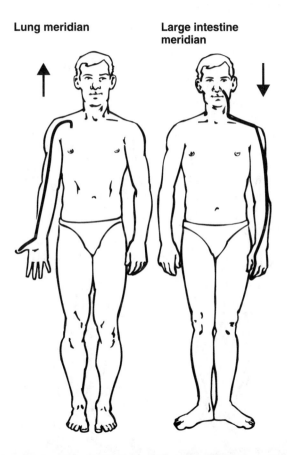

THE TWELVE MERIDIANS (continued)

Stomach meridian   Spleen meridian

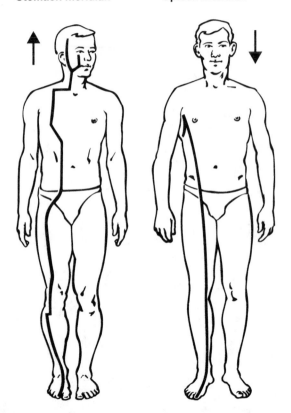

Conception vessel meridian

Governor vessel meridian

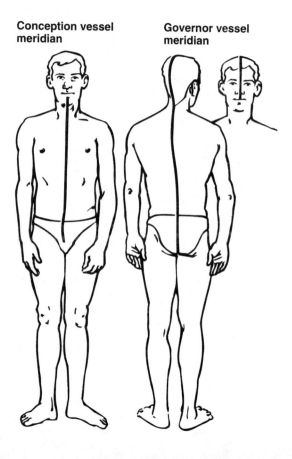

Body organs

Eastern medicine does not describe internal organs in the same way as Western anatomists. Instead of referring to them as physiological structures, the body's organs are divided into groups of six Fu (or Yang, positive) and six Zang (or Yin, negative) organs, according to their nature and function. Each of these represents one of the five elements and works with another, complementary organ. For example, the liver complements the gall bladder. The energy which connects organs flows throughout the body.

Treatment methods

After taking a case history during which a therapist may assess clients by observing their appearance and by listening to the sound of their voice, clients are asked to remain clothed on a treatment couch or on the floor.

The therapist feels the abdomen or hara, to determine how energy flows in the internal organs.

Accessing ki

Because interior and exterior aspects of the body are related, internal imbalances can be treated by working on the external part of the body. Along each of the meridians there are certain acupuncture points where ki may be accessed and manipulated. These points are known as tsubos in shiatsu. Acupuncture points along a meridian are numbered according to the direction of energy flow, and manipulation of different points is believed to result in changes in ki, the consequence of which is relief from symptoms of particular conditions. Different meridians have different numbers of points.

For example, the bladder meridian has 67 points; the heart meridian has nine.

Locating the tsubos, a therapist assesses the client to determine whether the flow of energy is depleted (kyo), blocked, or over-active (jitsu), and treats accordingly. There is no set order to the procedure, although some therapists may like to follow a regular routine, perhaps starting with the body, then moving to the head, arms, and legs. An example of some useful pressure points on the intestine meridians is provided on the next two pages.

FOUR TREATMENT TECHNIQUES

1 In order to increase the flow of blood and energy, the body is pressed at right angles

2 Energy blockages are broken up as the result of stretching and squeezing movements

3 Rocking is used to counteract agitation in the flow of energy, and

4 Pressure is applied to tsubos

Pressure along the meridians may be uncomfortable or even painful, although therapists disagree as to the amount of pain necessary to bring about change. Pain felt along a meridian indicates stagnation of ki to the corresponding organ. Some patients experience elation or depression after treatment. Others may experience a headache or flu-like symptoms, normal reactions to treatment that do not usually last more than a day or two.

EXAMPLE OF SHIATSU

The following examples demonstrate how selected points along the large intestine meridian and small intestine meridian might be used to treat certain disorders. The three columns above each illustration indicate the number of the acupressure point (tsubo) on the meridian (column 1), the Japanese name given to the point (column 2), and conditions for which this point might be useful (column 3).

SMALL INTESTINE MERIDIAN

3	Go Kei	Numbness and paralysis of fingers
11	Ten so	Shoulder pain, neuralgia
19	Chyo Ku	Ringing in the ears

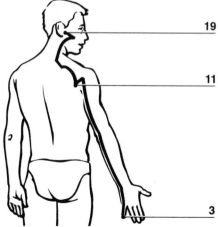

LARGE INTESTINE MERIDIAN

1	Sho yo	Diarrhea, fever
4	Go koku	Diarrhea, facial tension, general health, rash, toothache
10	Te San Ri	General well-being, pain and fatigue in the arms, sore legs
11	Kyoku Chi	Any arm problem
15	Ken Gu	Shoulder joint pains, frozen shoulder
20	Gei Ko	Facial tension, nasal obstruction, running nose

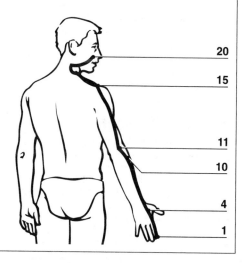

T'AI-CHI CH'UAN

Definition

An internal martial art in which exercises are used to stabilize the forces of yin and yang and improve overall well-being by easing the flow of life energy known as *Chi* (Japanese ki).

History

Often described as meditation in motion, t'ai-chi ch'uan is a complex physical discipline derived from a combination of Taoist, Buddhist and Confucian esoteric teachings. Exercise has been a traditional part of Chinese culture for thousands of years where it has long been accepted that the mind and body are intimately linked. Therapeutic exercises were developed from the observations of animal movements and sounds, believed to help promote an active but peaceful mind. Modern t'ai-chi ch'uan exercises were developed by an eleventh century Chinese thinker, Chang San-Feng.

WHAT CONDITIONS IS IT USED FOR?

T'ai-chi ch'uan is believed to be useful as a preventative therapy and can also be helpful in treating stress-related conditions such as anxiety and tension. In particular, it is believed to:

- Help combat illness (of both the mind and body)
- Help individuals maintain their health
- Help individuals realize their full potential
- Help individuals understand their inner nature
- Facilitate the development of willpower

SOME OF THE PHYSICAL BENEFITS OF T'AI-CHI CH'UAN

- Improves co-ordination
- Improves flexibility
- Improves stamina
- Improves balance
- Aids relaxation
- Promotes restful sleep
- Stimulates the circulation of blood
- Stimulates the circulation of lymph
- Stimulates the circulation of oxygen
- Deepens breathing
- Strengthens the heart
- Strengthens the lungs
- Strengthens the legs
- Massages the internal organs
- Tones the skin
- Improves aural, visual, and vocal efficiency
- Helps prevent illness

SOME NON-PHYSICAL BENEFITS OF T'AI-CHI CH'UAN

- Induces confidence
- Teaches self control
- Develops patience
- Helps calm and regulate the emotions
- Improves concentration
- Improves memory
- Increases mental alertness
- Facilitates the release of emotional tension
- Facilitates creativity
- Heightens perception
- Develops a sense of rhythm

Chang San-Feng was concerned with the martial
emphasis of army training in which he was required to
take part. He deserted and developed exercise
disciplines which were a longer form of traditional
kung-fu, and which were designed to assist spiritual
development.

Around the 14th century t'ai-chi ch'uan developed yet
further, into what is now practiced in thousands of
schools worldwide.

How does it work?

A series of flowing movements known as "forms" are
used, blending breathing, circular rhythmic movement,
and meditative concentration during which individuals
learn to identify self-constructed energy blocks.
Relaxed and fluid, the forms gently stir the circulation,
breath and chi, enabling their flow to nourish and
balance the body, mind, and spirit. Regular practice
increases mental clarity, endurance and flexibility; the
physical benefits include improved body tone and
elasticity, flexible and open joints, and a reduction of
stress-related symptoms such as high blood pressure.
Exercises used in the West are in fact only one-eighth
of the complete art of t'ai-chi ch'uan which, as well as
including disciplines for mental and physical control

PRINCIPLES UNDERLYING T'AI-CHI CH'UAN
- The human organism is designed to function as an integrated whole
- All life is movement and change within Unity
- Man is a microcosmic reflection of Macrocosmic Law
- Prevention is better than cure

and the storage of energies, includes t'ai-chi dance, sword and stick.

Treatment methods

There are 37 basic postures expanded to 108 or 128 to make a "long-form" or reduced to 12 or 24 for "short-form" movement, depending on the school of t'ai-chi followed. The forms have names such as "Grasp the Sparrow's Tail," and "Snake goes down into the Water." These are best performed in the open air where the forces of Chi can be drawn in and expressed through the body and the limbs.

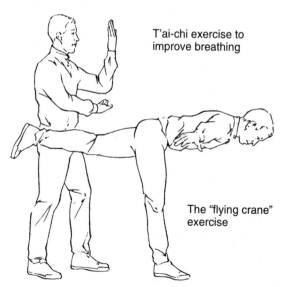

T'ai-chi exercise to improve breathing

The "flying crane" exercise

THERAPEUTIC TOUCH

Definition

Healers (rather than therapists) use their hands to bring
about healing, by placing them directly on a patient's
body or a small distance away from it. Contrary to the
laying on of hands, therapeutic touch therapists do not
necessarily believe they are channeling the power of a
God or spirit.

History

In 1777 Captain Cook, the explorer, landed in the
Pacific island of Tahiti. During his stay he complained
of severe rheumatic pain down one side of his body, hip
to toe. One day, while resting on board his ship, he was
visited by a dozen women, some from a family who
had befriended him. They said they had come to cure
him of the pain.

He wrote that he lay down on the deck and the women
crowded round him, each taking a part of him in their
big, strong hands and squeezing him from head to toe.
After some fifteen minutes he was glad to get away
from them, although he felt much relief from the pain.
The women repeated the squeezing before he retired to
bed and twice again the next day, after which the pain
had completely disappeared. These women asked for no

What conditions is it used for?

It appears that therapeutic touch works best for
psychosomatic illnesses but also for circulatory
illnesses, lymphatic disorders, and musculoskeletal
problems.

payment; they simply gave their "loving touch" freely. Today, using the hands to heal in this way is called therapeutic touch and is commonly used by nurses, especially in America where it was pioneered by Dr. Dolores Krieger, a professor of nursing in New York in 1974.

How does it work?

It is not clear how therapeutic touch works although healers believe that illness is caused by a deficit or imbalance in the energies in and around the human body and that they are somehow able to re-balance these energies to bring about healing.

Some people argue that healing may work as a result of the placebo effect.

TREATMENT METHODS

1 It is usually necessary to perform therapeutic touch in a quiet environment.
2 Persons going to do the touching need to clear their mind of irrelevant thoughts so that they can harness the psychic energy needed for their work. This is called "centering," which healers achieve by concentrating their minds, perhaps imagining a beautiful, calm scene.
3 Healers scan the patient's energy field by moving their hands all over the patient's body about 3 or 4 inches (7.5–10cm) from the surface. This is done in order to try and locate areas of sickness.
4 Healers place their hands on an area of sickness and allow their healing power to flow into the patient.

TRANSACTIONAL ANALYSIS

Definition
Concerned with the transactions between individuals, this form of therapy analyzes how we communicate and aims to help people realize and express their needs.

History
Transactional analysis developed from social psychiatry initiated by Eric Berne in San Francisco in the 1950s. Berne published his theory in *Games People Play*, in 1964, which became an international bestseller.

How does it work?
According to transactional analysis we all communicate using one of three "voices"(known as ego states)—a child, an adult, and a parent. Learning to recognize which voice it is we use when speaking, and what it signifies, can help use to realize what our needs are and to express them more clearly.

VOICES AND THEIR CHARACTERISTICS		
Voice	**Characteristics**	
CHILD	Adapts	Plays
	Demands	Thinks
	Feels	Wants
	Fights	
ADULT	Analyzes	Thinks
	Computes	
PARENT	Believes	Nurtures
	Controls	Protects
	Directs	

Treatment methods

For any situation, any one of the three ego states may be used. For example, we may respond to an adult question with an adult reply (**a**), or we may respond to the same question with a parental reply (**b**). The aim of transactional analysis is to learn how to focus on the "adult" voice when necessary. This is achieved by learning to recognize each different ego state and how we use them.

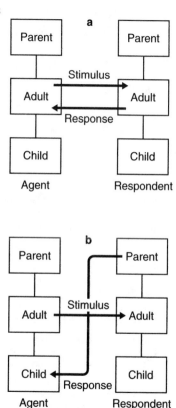

VISUALIZATION THERAPY

Definition
The use of mental images to improve overall health and
well being.

History
Witchdoctors and shamans have relied on the use of
mental images to cure disease for centuries. In the 17th
century treatments for the mind and body were
separated by new approaches to medicine.

The use of visualization to cure cancer was investigated
by Dr. Carl Simonton in Texas, who asked patients to
visualize health cells attacking cancer cells. Surgeon
Bernard Siegel has used visualization to reveal that
patients unconsciously know what's wrong with them
and therefore have the ability to heal themselves.

Types
Visualization is used as a treatment method in many
therapies including autogenic training, biofeedback,
hypnotherapy, psychosynthesis, psychotherapy, and
rebirthing.

WHAT CONDITIONS IS IT USED FOR?

Visualization therapy is used in the treatment of:
- Asthma
- Cancer
- Heart disorders
- Pain relief
- Phobias

It is said to be particularly helpful in the treatment of
children who have vivid imaginations.

How does it work?

It is common for most of us to form negative images of ourselves and situations, especially when we are feeling anxious or troubled. Constantly seeing yourself failing in some way, for example, reinforces your fears of failing and makes failure more likely. Therapists argue that by replacing negative self images with positive ones, we are more likely to achieve positive outcomes in our lives and spend less time dwelling on negative emotions and fears.

Treatment methods

Different therapies may use different visualization techniques but the overall purpose is the same: to deliberately imagine positive outcomes.

A patient visualizes the battle with virus invaders

YOGA

Definition
From the Sanskrit word for "union," or "oneness," yoga is a system of spiritual, mental, and physical training designed to improve overall health and well being.

History
The philosophies inherent in yoga were published in India beginning in 3000 B.C. Yoga was first practiced systematically by the mystic Patanjali, who compiled a series of sayings (sutras) in the fourth century B.C.

Equipment
None is required.

WHAT CONDITIONS IS IT USED FOR?

Yoga is used to improve overall well-being and may be useful in the treatment of:

- Asthma
- Back pain
- Bronchitis
- Colds
- Coughs
- Digestive disorders
- Hay fever
- Heart disorders
- Multiple sclerosis
- Pregnancy
- Sinusitis
- Stress

How does it work?
According to Hindu philosophy, the cosmos consists of seven ascending planes, each of which has a focus in the body (known as a chakra, see box, *right*) and is invigorated through yoga.

The seven chakras

1 Sahasrara (on the crown of the head, associated with the pineal gland)

2 Ajna (brow chakra, between the eyes)

3 Vishudda (throat chakra, also encompassing the cervical regina)

4 Anahata (heart chakra)

5 Manipuraka (solar plexus chakra, above the navel, in the lumbar region)

6 Swadhisthana (sacral chakra, below the navel, in the sacral region)

7 Muladhara (base chakra, near the coccyx)

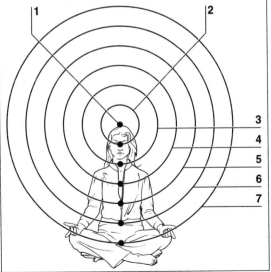

Practitioners also believe that breathing exercises
(pranayama) are an important part of yoga and that
correct breathing helps control emotions—such as
anger, grief, hatred—and certain bodily functions, such
as the heartrate.

The overall purpose of yoga is fourfold:
1 To increase suppleness so that joints become more
  flexible, lessening the chances of injury.
2 To increase strength and bone density and reduce the
  possible onset of osteoporosis.
3 To increase stamina so that you can keep going for
  longer, working the cardiovascular system and
  reducing the chances of heart disease.
4 To improve concentration.

Types
There are many types of yoga (see box, *below*), each
with a different focus.

EXAMPLES OF TYPES OF YOGA	
Type	**Main focus**
Bakti	Devotion
Hatha	Posture and exercises
Jnana	Intellect and understanding
Karma	Moral action
Raja	Mind control

Treatment methods

The philosophy underlying yoga is that the practice of
physical exercise combined with breath control helps
develop concentration and coordination, which in turn
develops mental and spiritual benefits and attributes.
Attending an organized class is the best way to learn
which poses (asanas) are most suitable for you, and
qualified teachers will be able to instruct you slowly
and meditatively to ensure safety.

Hatha yoga is the most popular form of yoga in the
West. It is not a series of exercises, but of poses known
as asanas; it is the stages toward assuming the postures
that really constitute the exercise, the final achievement
being the asana. Some are easy to assume; others
require much practice before the muscles and limbs are
supple enough. Each asana has a purpose, and very
often a name easily identified with the pose, such as the
bow, the lotus, etc.

On the next eight pages you will find glossaries of
relaxing poses, standing poses, sitting poses, and
advanced poses. The purpose of providing these
glossaries is to demonstrate the huge variety of asanas.
The illustrations are not intended as a self-help guide—
as they do not show how to attain the poses—and
anyone wishing to learn yoga is advised to attend a
class run by a qualified teacher.

An example of a yoga asana (The Bow) is given on the
next page.

THE BOW

Indian name	Dhanurasana
Benefits	● Extends the spine, helping to improve spinal flexibility ● Massages both the back muscles and internal organs
Perform with	The Cobra The Locust

This section shows 3 asanas: the bow, the half full bow and the full bow

1 Start position Lie on your front, face down on the floor.

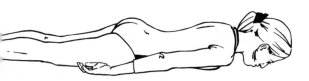

2 Bend your knees, reach back to grasp your ankles. Bring your heels to your buttocks, with your feet relaxed. Do not point your toes.

3 Inhale and arch your body upward, off the floor. Keep your arms straight as you lift your head, chest and thighs off the ground. Hold this posiiton, relax then repeat.

Rocking bow Once in the correct position you may like to rock gently back and forth. To rock backward, inhale; to rock forward, exhale.

Common faults
a Pointing the toes
b Bending the arms
c When stretching, pulling the heels to the buttocks
  instead of to the ceiling.
d Not lifting the chest and thighs off the floor.
● Twisting to one side.

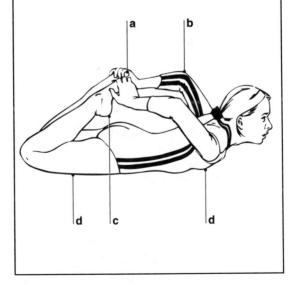

HALF FULL BOW

This an asana you may like to try before attempting the full bow.

1 Begin as for the bow, lying face down on the floor.

2 Resting on one arm for support, use the other to reach back and grasp one of your feet.

3 Gently raise your chest from the floor.

4 Raise your foot towards the ceiling, bringing your thigh off the floor.

5 Repeat the asana on the other side.

FULL BOW

This is an asana that you may try once you have
mastered the basic bow pose and your spine has begun
to become more flexible.

1 Begin as for the bow, lying face down on the floor.

2 Bend your knees, bringing your heels to your
buttocks. Turn your feet out. Instead of reaching back
to hold your ankles, reach back and hold your toes.

3 Gently pull your feet towards your head. As you bring your elbows forward, lift your thighs from the floor.

4 Arch upward in order to achieve the full bow, tilting your head backward and lifting your thighs as far from the floor as possible.

Once you have mastered the full bow position you
may like to try one of these variations:

a Try rocking back and forth gently.

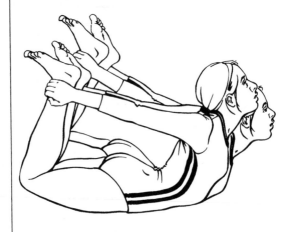

b Try bringing your feet to your head.

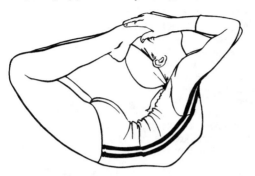

c Bring your feet tot the shoulders, the most advanced bow position.

Glossary of relaxing poses

1 Savasana: the corpse
2 Garbhasana: pose of a child
3 Puvamuktasana: the gas ejector
4 Dhanurasana: the bow
5 Bhujangasana: the cobra
6 Kurmasana: the tortoise
7 Salabhasana: the locust
8 Salabhasana (variation)
9 Halasana (Plow)
10 Salamba Saravangasana: shoulder stand
11 Anantasana: eternal pose
12 Uttihita Merudandasana: side raise
13 Uttihita Merudandasana (variation)

Glossary of standing poses

1 Tadasana: the mountain
2 Uttanasana: relaxation pose
3 Uttanasana (variation)
4 Parsvottanasana
5 Virabhadrasana: warrior
6 Virabhadrasana (variation)
7 Padangusthasana
8 Prasarita Padottanasana: leg stretch
9 Adho Mukha Svanasana: dog
10 Trikonasana: triangle
11 Parivrrta Trikonasana: reverse triangle
12 Nitambasana: side bend
13 Vrksasana: tree

7

8

9

10

11

12

13

Glossary of sitting poses
1 Dandasana: staff
2 Paschimottanasana: forward bend
3 Paripurna Navasana: boat
4 Baddha Konasana: cobbler
5 Virasana: hero
6 Pardvatasana
7 Bharadvajasana: twine
8 Padmasana: lotus
9 Ardha Matsyendrasana
10 Marichysana
11 Janu Sirsasana
12 Upavistha Konasana

Glossary of upside-down poses
13 Urdhva Dhanurasana: wheel (sometimes called Chakrasana)
14 Ustrasana: camel
15 Sirsana: head stand

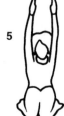

Glossary of advanced poses

1 Natarasana: lord of the dance
2 Ekapadahastasana
3 Ardha Vririjasana: half scorpion
4 Sarvangasana (variation)
5 Hasta Padasana: toe hold
6 Rajakapotasana: king of the pigeons
7 Viraparita Halasana
8 Kavasana: raven
9 Kukkutasana: cock
10 Uttiha Kurmasana: upright tortoise
11 Mayurasana: the Peacock
12 Lolasana: balance
13 Baddha Padmasana: bound lotus
14 Urdura Padmasana
15 Parbalasana
16 Ekapadahastasana
17 Janu Sirasana
18 Kapodasana: bird's head

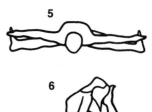

ZONE THERAPY

Definition
An early Western form of reflexology in which healing can be brought about by massaging certain zones in the foot.

History
Zone therapy was developed in 1913 by the American surgeon Dr. William Fitzgerald. He discovered that partial anesthesia of the ear, nose and throat could be achieved by applying pressure to certain parts of the foot. In a system he called "zone therapy," Fitzgerald argued that the body was divided into ten vertical zones and that applying pressure to one part of a zone could affect all other parts of that zone.

The horizontal body zones

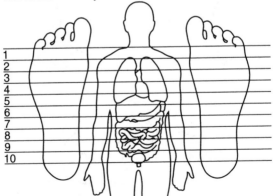

How does it work?
It is not clear how zone
therapy may have
worked although this is
likely to have been
similar to reflexology.
If, as reflexologists
claim, each part of the
body is connected via
nerves to several end-
points in the feet,
massage to nerve
endings in the feet may
affect their related
internal structures.

The vertical body
zones (*right*)

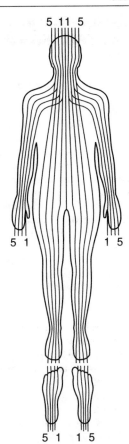

Glossary of medical-related terms

Abduction A movement outward from the center of the body or limb

Adduction A movement inward toward the center of the body

Anterior Toward or at the front

Atrophy Wasting away and/or emaciation, caused by aging, disease, infection, or injury

Benign Used to describe abnormal growth that will not spread to other tissues or organs and so is usually nonfatal; compare with MALIGNANT

Biopsy Surgical procedure in which a sample of tissue is removed for microscopic examination in a laboratory

Carcinogenic Cancer causing

Carcinoma Malignant growth of cancerous surface tissues

Cardiac Relating to the heart

Carpal tunnel Passage at the front of the wrist through which nerves and tendons extend from forearm to fingers

Caudal Toward the feet

Cerebral Relating to the brain

Congenital Condition of disease that is present at birth

Contracture Shortening of a muscle or tendon because of disease or injury and resulting in distortion or discomfort

Coronal Relating to the crown of the head

Coronary Relating to a crown, as in the coronary arteries whose branches spread above the heart

Cutaneous Relating to the skin

Diagnostic Used to describe a procedure or method for identifying disease or other cause of symptoms

Dilation Widening, either using a drug or mechanically

Distal Toward the extremities of the body

Eversion Turning outward

Extension Straightening of a limb or other body part

Flexion Bending or being bent, as of a joint

Frontal Toward or of the front of the body or body part; relating to the forehead

Inferior Below

Inversion Turning inside out

Lateral Toward or at the side

Malignant Used to describe cancerous growth that will spread to surrounding tissues and, if not totally removed, may be fatal; compare with BENIGN

Medial Toward the midline of the body

Metastasis The spread of an abnormal growth, especially cancer, from one part of the body to another

Palmar On the palm of the hand

Peripheral Toward the surface

Plantar On the sole of the foot

Posterior Toward or at the back

Pronation Turning to a face-down or palm-down position

Sagittal Relating to the median plane or a parallel plane of the body

Superior Above

Supination Turning to a face-up or palm-up position

Traction Method of treating broken bones by pulling apart and maintaining proper alignment

Transverse Crosswise, or at right angles to the front-back axis of the body

INDEX

Absent healing 10, 48–49
Abhyanga 129
Acupoint 10
Acupressure 10, 50–65
Acupuncture 11
Acupuncture points 11, 50, 51, 108–109
Agni 11
Alexander Technique 11, 66-73
Allopathic medicine 11
Anthroposophical medicine 11, 74–77
Anthroposophy 12
Amna 12, 456
Amulets, Ancient Egyptian 271–272
Amulets, fertility 264–267
Amulets, healing 270–275
Applied kinesiology 12, 330
Aromatherapy 12, 78–93, 353
Art therapies 12
Art therapy 12, 94–95
Asanas 13, 483
Astral body 13, 74
Astrological diagnosis 13
Astrology, medical 358–361
Aura 13, 96–105
Aura analysis 13, 96–105

Auricular therapy 14, 106–109
Auriculotherapy 14
Autogenic training 14, 110–115
Autosuggestion 14, 116–117
Aversion therapy 14, 146
Awareness through movement 15, 261
Ayurveda 15, 118
Ayurvedic medicine 15, 118–129

Bach™ Flower Essences 15, 130–141
Bach™ Flower Remedies 15, 130–141
Back-walking 349
Ba-gua 263
Balneology 16, 310
Basti 129
Bates method 16, 142–145
Baths 310–311
Behavior therapy 16, 146–147, 414
Bhutas 16, 121
Biochemics 17, 148–153
Bioenergetic therapy 17, 154–157
Bioenergy 17

Biofeedback 17, 158–163
Bions 384
Biorhythm cycles 164–167
Biorhythm diagnosis 17, 164–167
"Black boxes" 424
Blood-letting 335
Body armor 384, 442
Bone-setter 350
Breathing therapy 17, 168–169

Chakra therapy 18, 170–173
Chakras 18, 170–173
Charaka Samhita 18, 118
Character armor 384, 442
Charms 270
Chi 18
Chinese medicine 174–187
Chiropractic 18, 188–191
Christian healing beliefs 192–197
Christian Scientists 258
Clinical ecology 19, 198–201
Clinical theology 393
Co-counseling 415–417
Colonic hydrotherapy 19
Colonic irrigation 19, 202–203
Color therapy 19, 204–211
Combination remedies 19

Conception Vessel 19, 57, 65
Cosmic Orgone Energy 385
Couéism 20, 116–117
Counseling 415–417
Coventina's Well 196
Cranial osteopathy 20, 386, 390–391
Cranio-sacral therapy 20, 386, 390–391
Crystal therapy 20, 212–218
Cupping 20, 220–221
Cymatics 20, 222–225

Dance movement therapy 20, 226–229
Detoxification diets 232
Dhatus 127
Dietary therapies 21, 230–233
Distant healing 21
Do-in 21, 234–241
Dosha 21, 122–123
Dowsing 21, 420
Dowsing pendulum 421
Dream therapy 22, 242–243

ECT 22, 244
Effleurage 22, 355
Ego 22, 74
Electroconvulsive therapy 244
Electrotherapy 22, 244–245

Encircling 22, 246–249
Encounter group 250
Encounter therapy 23, 250–251, 417
Energy lines 23
Essential plant oils 23, 78–93
Etheric body 23, 74, 403
Eugenics 357
Eurythmy 23

Faith healing 23, 252–259, 252
Family therapy 415
Fasting 232
Feldenkrais method 23
Feng shui 24, 262–263
Fertility amulet 24, 264–267
Fertility rituals 267
Flotation tank 268
Flotation therapy 24, 268–269
Flower essences 24
Frictions 24, 355
Functional integration 261

Gate control theory 24
Gem essence therapy 25, 212, 218–219
Gestalting 393
Gestalt therapy 414
G-Jo 25
Governor vessel 25, 58, 65

Hacking 25, 355
Healing amulet 25, 270–275
Healing shrine 25, 276–281
Herbalism 26
Herbal medicine 282–293
Holy water amulets 197
Homeopathy 26, 294–305
Hydrotherapy 26, 306–313
Hypnosis 26, 314–319
Hypnosis, classical 315
Hypnotherapy 27, 314–319

Interdermal needles 27, 54
Ions 320
Ionizers 321
Ion therapy 27, 320–321
Iridology 27, 322–329
Jesus's healing miracles 254–257
Jitsu 27

Kappa 27, 122–123, 126
Kinesiology 27, 330–332
Ki 28, 466–467
Kilner screen 28
Kirlian photography 28
Kyo 28

Lacto-ovo-vegetarian diets 232
Laying on of hands 28, 332–333
Leeches 334–337

Leeching 28, 334–337
Life force energy 29
Lourdes shrine 276, 279–281

Macrobiotic diets 232
Macrobiotics 29, 338–339
Magnetic Field Therapy 30, 344–347
Magnetism and mesmerism 340–347
Magnets 344–347
Manipulative therapies 30, 348–351
Mantra 30, 365
Marma massage 31, 353
Mascot 270
Massage 31
Massage therapy 352–355
Mazdaznan 31, 356–357
Medical astrology 31, 358–361
Medical dowsing 420
Meditation 31, 362–365
Meditation, Buddhist 362
Meditation, transcendental 362
Megavitamin therapy 31, 232, 366–367
Meridians 32, 51, 57–65
Mesmerism 32
Mesmer's magnetic bath 341

Metamorphic technique 32, 368–369
Miasmas 33, 402
Miraculous healing 33
Mother tincture 33, 135
Moxa 33, 370–371
Moxibustion 33, 370–371
Music therapy 33, 372–375

Native American healing 34, 376–381
Naturopathy 34, 382–383
Netra Tarpan 129
Neurofeedback 34

Ojas 34, 120
Orgone 384
Orgone accumulator 384
Orgone energy 384
Orgone therapy 35, 384–385
Orthomolecular medicine 35, 366–367
Orthomolecular psychiatry 35
Oriental massage 35, 353
Osteopathy 36, 386–391
Our Lady of Lourdes Shrine 276, 279–281

Panchakarma 36, 129
Past lives therapy 36, 392–393
Pattern therapy 36, 394–395

Peer group bonding 393
Pétrissage 36, 355
Phytotherapy 36, 282–287
Pitta 37, 122–123, 125
Pizzichilli 129
Polarity therapy 37,
  396–399
Pranayama 37
Prenatal therapy 37,
  368–369
Press needles 37, 54
Pressure points 38
Primal scream 393, 401
Primal therapy 38, 393
  400–401, 417
Primitive healing amulets
  274–275
Primordial Orgone Energy
  385
Prismatic needles 38, 54, 56
Psionic medicine 38,
  402–405
Psychic ability 406
Psychic diagnosis 406
Psychic healing 39,
  406–407
Psychic surgery 39, 406,
  407
Psychoanalysis 412
Psychodrama 39, 408–409
Psychosynthesis 39,
  410–411
Psychotherapies 39,
  412–417

Pyramid healing 39,
  418–419

Qi 40, 51

Radiesthesia 40, 420–423
Radionics 40, 424–431
Re-birthing 40, 393, 413,
  432–433
Regression methods 393
Reflexology 40, 434–441
Reflex point 40
Reichian therapy 41, 393,
  442–445
Reincarnation 392
Reiki 41, 353
Relaxation therapy 41,
  446–449
Rhythmic system 41
Rolfing 41, 450–451

Samhita 41
Sclerology 41, 322
Self-hypnosis 116–117, 319
Seven-star needle 42, 54
Shamanic healing 42,
  452–455
Shen Tao 42
Shiatsu 42, 456–469
Shrine of Bishop St.
  Thomas Cantelupe
  277–279
Shirodhara 129

Spiritual healing 42, 252–259
Sports massage 43, 353
Structural integration 43, 450–451
Swedana 129
Swedish massage 43, 353
Swedish Movement Treatment 43

T'ai-chi ch'uan 43, 470–473
Talismans 270
TENS machine 44, 244–245
Thalassotherapy 44, 312
Therapeutic touch 44, 474–475
Theralism 44, 312, 313
Tissue salts 44, 148–153
Traction 350
Transactional analysis 45, 417, 476–477
Transcendental meditation 45
Transcutaneous Electrical Nerve Stimulation 244
Tridoshas 45
Triple burner 45, 57
Triple heater 45
Tsubo 45
Tuina 46, 353
Twelve healers, the 133

Unity Theory of Disease 403

Vata 46, 122–124
Vedas 46, 118
Vegan diets 233
Vegetarian diets 233
Virechana treatment 129
Visualization therapy 46, 478–479
Votives for healing 195

Well of Heads 197

Yang 46, 174–175, 186–187
Yin 46, 174–175, 186–187
Yin and Yang foods 339
Yoga 47, 480–501

Zone therapy 47, 435, 502–503